Memory Speaks

MEMORY SPEAKS

On Losing and Reclaiming Language and Self

Julie Sedivy

THE BELKNAP PRESS OF
HARVARD UNIVERSITY PRESS

Cambridge, Massachusetts
London, England
2021

First printing

Library of Congress Cataloging-in-Publication Data
Names: Sedivy, Julie, author.
Title: Memory speaks : on losing and reclaiming language and self/Julie
    Sedivy.
Description: Cambridge, Massachusetts : The Belknap Press of Harvard
    University Press, 2021. | Includes bibliographical references and index.
Identifiers: LCCN 2021007518 | ISBN 9780674980280 (cloth)
Subjects: LCSH: Language attrition. | Second language acquisition. |
    Language revival. | Language and languages—Political aspects. |
    Psycholinguistics.
Classification: LCC P40.5.L28 S435 2021 | DDC 401/.93—dc23
LC record available at https://lccn.loc.gov/2021007518

To Vera and Ladislav, and those who came before.

To Katharine and Benjamin, and those who will come after.

Contents

Memory Speaks

Nestled in my father's arms, I pose with my family in front of our home a few months before our departure from Czechoslovakia.

Chapter 1

Death

My father died as he had done most things throughout his life: without preparation and without consulting anyone. He simply went to bed one night and was found the next morning lying amid the sheets like his own stone monument.

It was hard for me not to take my father's abrupt exit as a rebuke. For years, he'd been begging me to visit him in the Czech Republic, where I'd been born and where he'd gone back to live in 1992. Each year, I delayed. I was in that part of my life when the marriage-grad-school-children-career-divorce current was sweeping me along with breath-sucking force, and a leisurely trip to the fatherland seemed as plausible as pausing the flow of time.

Now my dad was shrugging at me from beyond—"You see, you've run out of time."

His death underscored another, subtler loss: that of my native tongue. Czech was the only language I knew until the age of two, when my family began a migration westward, from what was then Czechoslovakia through Austria, then Italy, settling eventually in Montreal, Canada. Along the way, a clutter of languages introduced themselves into my life: German in preschool, Italian-speaking friends, the Francophone streets of East Montreal. Linguistic experience congealed, though, once my five siblings and I started school in

English. As with many immigrants, this marked the moment when English became, unofficially and over the grumbling of my parents—especially my father—our family language. What could my parents do? They were outnumbered. Czech began its slow retreat from our daily life.

I entered kindergarten knowing only a few words of English. Upon ascending to first grade, I was mortally offended when my teacher, taking inventory of the immigrant kids in her class on the first day of school, asked me, "What about you, Julie? Do you know a little English?" Indignant, I announced (in what I'm sure was still a thick Slavic accent), "I don't know a little English—I know a *lot* of English." A few years later, no teacher could distinguish my speech from that of my native-born peers. Today, people who know me are startled to learn that English was the fifth language I learned to speak, so thoroughly has it elbowed its predecessors aside.

Many would applaud the efficiency with which our family settled into English—it's what exemplary immigrants do. And to me at that time, the price of assimilation was invisible. Like most young people, I was far more intent on hurtling myself into my future than on tending my ancestral roots—and that future, it was clear, was an English-speaking one. In my world, Czech was a small language, spoken only on our tiny domestic island by people genetically related to me. English was the big, horizon-hungry language, the language of the teachers I adored or had to appease, the language of the TV shows my friends endlessly rehashed, of the books that held me in thrall and the books I thought I might one day write. It was the language of dreams and goals.

But there *was* a price. As my siblings and I distanced ourselves from the Czech language, a space widened between us and our parents—especially my father, whose English sat on him like a poorly tailored suit. It was as if my parents' life in their home country, and the values that defined that life, didn't translate credibly into another language; it was much easier to rebel against them in English. Even the English names for our parents encouraged dissent: The tender Czech words we'd used—*Maminka, Tatinek*—are impossible to pronounce with contempt, but they have no corresponding forms. In English, the sweet but childish *Mommy* and *Daddy* are soon abandoned for *Mom* and *Dad*—words that, we discovered, lend themselves perfectly well to adolescent snark.

I've wondered, recently, whether things might have been different for my father had his children remained rooted in their native tongue. Over time, we spoke together less and less. I remember watching him grow frustrated at his powerlessness to pass on to his children the legacies he most longed to leave: an ardent religiosity, the nurturing of family ties, pleasure in the music and traditions of his region (which, I'm now ashamed to say, we often mocked), and a tender respect for ancestors. All of these became diluted by the steady flow of our new experiences narrated in English, laced with Anglophone aspiration and individualism. As we entered adulthood and dispersed all over North America into our self-reliant lives, my father gave up. He moved back home.

For the next two decades, I lived my adult life, fully absorbed into the English-speaking universe, even adding American citizenship to my Canadian one. My dad was the only person with whom I regularly spoke Czech—if phone calls every few months could be described as "regularly," and if my clumsy sentences patched together with abundant English could be called "speaking Czech." My Czech heritage began to feel more and more like a vestigial organ.

But loss inevitably clarifies that which is gone. When my father died, and with him, my connection to Czech, it was as if the viola section in the orchestra had fallen silent—not carrying the melody, it had gone unnoticed, but its absence announced how much depth and texture it had supplied, how its rhythms had lent coherence to the music. In grieving my father, I became aware of how much I also mourned the silencing of Czech in my life. There was a part of me, I realized, that only Czech could speak to, a way of being that was hard to settle into, even with my own siblings and mother when we spoke in English. I suddenly felt unmoored, not only from my childhood, but from the entire culture that had shaped me.

I have been thinking about that loss ever since, becoming intimate with its outline and its various shadings. And I have been thinking about *language* my whole life, often all day and every day since I first wandered into a linguistics class as a fresh university student. In my subsequent work as a researcher in psycholinguistics, a field that is preoccupied with the psychological aspects of language, I have puzzled through the minute details of how we learn and use language. But little about my studies prepared me for the inexplicable void I felt in connection with a language I rarely spoke anymore.

This book is my attempt to make sense of that loss, to honor it and give it a home within the framework of my academic knowledge of language. A semblance of coherence began to emerge once I peered through a number of different windows, considering not just my own experiences but those of others. I've tried to relate these experiences to the work of researchers who study language and migration in its many facets, including the ways in which languages ebb and flow within an individual's mind, and the ways in which they are buffeted about in the world by the winds of societal change.

Languages are living things, and as with all things that are alive, the possibility of death is a constant companion. In this book, I will explore why a language can wither in a person's mind once it has taken root, what this decline looks like, and how the waning of language can take on a magnitude that spreads beyond personal pain to collective crisis. My own experience of language loss has prompted me to think more deeply about people who are staring down a true linguistic void—those whose native language is now endangered, and who are struggling not only to keep their mother tongue from slipping away from them in their day-to-day lives but also to prevent their language from being extinguished altogether. My linguistic studies had made me aware of the great risks facing many of the world's smaller languages. But it was the loss of Czech from my own small life that allowed me to *feel,* in the spongy parts of my bones, the irreplaceability of a mother tongue. Theirs is a loss I could easily spend the rest of my life thinking and writing about, and still be unable to reach out and touch.

At the heart of language loss is a cruel paradox: the attrition of a language is often driven by dreams of a better life—a life of prosperity, security, and acceptance. Of the thousands of languages that are still alive today, a mere few lay claim to the lion's share of status and privilege within their societies. Speakers of less powerful languages respond to these inequalities by ceding space in their lives and minds to the dominant language around them, in effect bartering who they are for a chance at a good life.

Like many people whose lives have been apportioned between languages and cultures, I have the sense that I am really an amalgam of selves in intermittent conversation (and occasional argumentation) with each other. As languages and cultures mix with each other, and as people more and more often split their lifetimes between more than one language community, this sense of duality has become the natural state for many. In the coming pages, I will explore how and why language so often defines the boundary between dual selves, and why we may feel as if we are different people in each of our languages.

In the end, can multiple languages co-exist peacefully, either in a person's mind or within society at large? Because so few languages have come to dominate so much of the linguistic landscape of the world, the survival of many smaller languages rests on multilingualism—but languages inevitably compete with each other, and along with multilingualism comes the potential for conflict. I will reflect on some of the challenges that arise when languages try to share space within a person's mind or within a society, and I will question whether it's possible to see conflict as a source of benefits as well as a source of dangers.

As I've grappled with the erosion of my mother tongue, it has become clear to me that what once felt like a great linguistic emptiness in my life was not irrevocable. By taking a few steps in the right direction, it was in fact possible to step out of the void and onto solid ground—Czech remains, after all, the official language of an independent nation of ten million people. Once my life settled somewhat, I was able to spend time in the land of my birth, not as a tourist, but as a short-term resident in the house where my father grew up. I was able to feel once more the warm embrace of my language, which, as it turns out, had been patiently waiting for me to come home. But not everyone has the option of stepping out of their linguistic void onto solid ground. Toward the end of the book, I will delve into the possibilities for linguistic revival that exist for some individuals whose childhood was anchored in a language since neglected, as well as the daunting obstacles that face communities whose languages have traveled worryingly far along the road to extinction.

My experience of regaining some of the language I used to speak with my father has been life-altering. It has deepened and calmed my sense of who I am, forging a peace treaty between the various, fragmented parts of myself. And it has cast a new light on the old question of how to make a home in a place that is foreign to your ancestors. For me, living as I do in Canada, that question is decidedly fraught, as I now make my home on lands that have, for thousands of years before me, been claimed by peoples who have borne the brunt of cultural dislocation and whose languages are among the most endangered in the world. It is not a question I will be able to answer definitively by the time I get to the end of this book—but it is one whose answer, I now believe, begins with the understanding that for all of us, language is not just a means of sharing knowledge; it is also a temple, a refuge, a sacred mountaintop, and a home.

My first visit to Prague, in 1994 as a young graduate student, was spent in the company of linguists after we attended an academic conference. (By then, my father was living several hours away in Moravia—but feeling pressed by the demands of a young family left at home and the weight of academic deadlines, I stupidly decided against taking a few extra days to visit him there.) One of these linguists, an eminent scholar by the name of Barbara Partee, served as our tour guide; she had spent considerable time in Prague during and after Czechoslovakia's Velvet Revolution, and was delighted to show off her favorite spots in the city. She'd learned an impressive amount of Czech, which she spoke with visible effort and a thick American accent. (I had never heard Czech spoken with an American accent before, but it sounded exactly as I might have imagined.) When I spoke to shopkeepers and waiters in Czech, it was with the same embarrassment I might feel if forced to wear a dress in public that had been sitting in the back of my closet for decades. My language was drab and outdated, hanging on me with crooked hems and ill-fitting seams. I kept apologizing for how much Czech I had forgotten. At one point, as Barbara and I struggled to patch together some sort of conversation in Czech, she exclaimed in wonder, "You've forgotten more Czech than I'll ever learn!" How difficult it is to learn a language, and how easy it is to forget one.

I belong to the demographic group whose members are among the most likely to forget their native languages: the immigrants of Generation 1.5, a term that refers to those who came to their adopted country as children and began learning the language of their new home before puberty.

There is no age at which a language, even a native tongue, is so firmly cemented into the brain that it can't be dislodged or altered by a new one. Like a household that welcomes a new child, a single mind can't admit a new language without some impact on other languages already residing there. Languages can co-exist, but they tussle, as do siblings, over mental resources and attention. When a bilingual person tries to articulate a thought in one language, words and grammatical structures from the other language often clamor in the background, jostling for attention. And if attention is allotted disproportionately to the new language, the older one suffers the consequences.

But a child who is removed from her linguistic berth in her early years and moved to another is all the more susceptible to losing the native language. Researchers who study language attrition among immigrants have consistently found that the depth of loss of a native language is related to the age of immigration and learning of the new language—the younger the child, the more profound the loss in adulthood. In contrast, those who emigrate much later and adopt a new language as teenagers or adults may eventually struggle when speaking their native language—using it becomes slow and effortful, its words become slippery, and, when the native language falters, chunks of the new language may be spliced in to replace phrases of the native language that elude recall. But adult immigrants rarely see their native language *fall apart*—the structure and grammar of their first language doesn't usually disintegrate to the point where they hardly appear to have ever learned the language at all.

A child who is relocated at a young age may end up with a moth-eaten version of her native language, losing mastery of forms she had previously used correctly. Just how tattered the language may become can be seen in a detailed paper by Maria Polinsky, who writes about the Russian spoken by adults who moved to the United States from Russia between the ages of three and eleven.[1] Reading this paper made me wince. Because Czech is so similar to Russian in its grammar, and because her study subjects were analogues of myself, I felt that I was reading, grammatical detail by grammatical detail, an account of my own language loss. Slavic languages have the sort of grammars that a friend of mine, who was learning Czech as an adult, once described as "character-building." For example, not only do verbs take different endings depending on their tense and on who is performing the action (a feature common among languages like French and Spanish), but nouns are even more notorious shapeshifters, submitting to what's known as a *case system,* a method of announcing the noun's grammatical function by its form. The Czech word for "dog" can be uttered in any one of a number of forms (for example—*pes, psa, psovi, psem, psův*), depending on whether the dog is performing an action or is on the receiving end of one, whether you are calling it to get its attention, whether you are doing something *for* the dog, or *with* the dog, whether you are referring to something it owns, and so on. Not only that, but the pattern for the various cases depends on which one of several categories of nouns a word happens to fall into—so the word for "dog" would have very different case templates than, say, the word for "woman" or "town." Oh, and adjectives, numbers, or anything else that precedes a noun (for example, each word of the phrase *those three angry dogs*) also change shape based on their case. Not surprisingly, when children have only a couple of years of practice with the language before being uprooted from it, they have trouble holding on to all these variations. Polinsky found that the intricate system in Russian, which has six distinct cases (Czech has seven), was often flattened by her Americanized immigrants into a much cruder system of two cases. Similar distortions occurred in many other corners of the grammar. The errors all looked mortifyingly familiar to me.

Grammatical features such as case are not just stylistic flourishes or embellishments; they are the bedrock upon which the language is built, and they are used almost flawlessly by native-speaking children before they enter kindergarten (hence, I assume I once did as well). The sparks of self-recognition I felt upon reading Polinsky's paper made me realize that, from the perspective of those Prague shopkeepers who heard my version of Czech in 1994, I wasn't just wearing the equivalent of outdated, poorly fitting clothing. The very body that wore the clothing must have seemed deformed, missing digits and possibly entire limbs.

In my own large family, I can trace the correlation between age and attrition over the succession of my siblings: Czech has been most resilient among the oldest siblings and weakest among the youngest (with the exception of the very youngest of us, who has spent a considerable portion of his young adult life living in our ancestral country). This is a mirror image of the "age of acquisition" effects described by language researchers—the younger a child is when she begins to learn a second language, the more proficient she is likely to be in that language as an adult.

It's not clear why children are so much more likely to yield their first language to a newcomer. It may be that the same plasticity of the brain that allows children to learn new languages more successfully than adults also makes any languages the child already possesses that much more vulnerable to being overwritten. It may be that knowledge of the first language is not stable until adolescence or later; like a young plant whose root system is still shallow, it may not be able to survive a drought of language contact. Children who are very young may have only a partial mastery of their native language before turning their energies to the new one. Or it may be that children, whose identities are still amorphous, feel less allegiance to their old languages and old ways of being and are more eager to assimilate and blend in with their peers.

Whatever is responsible for language attrition—and it may well be all of the above, to varying extents—not everyone experiences the same degree of language loss. Surprisingly, there doesn't seem to be a clear, linear relationship between attrition and the amount of time a person spends using their first language or the length of time they have lived in the new country. There are cases of people who have had little opportunity to speak their language for decades, but who can summon an impressive fluency in it, while others in similar situations stumble through a conversation with great difficulty, constantly stopping to search for words.

Several factors seem to guard against the erosion of a first language through disuse. One of these is having a natural gift for language learning. Language aptitude isn't thought to be especially important for the mastery of a *first* language, perhaps because almost all children are equipped with a robust enough talent for learning their native language, or perhaps simply because, over the course of a typical childhood, they eventually get so much practice with the language that they learn to speak it well regardless of how quickly or slowly they acquire it. But talent for language seems more important in situations where native-like attainment is elusive. Researchers have identified a cluster of skills that are not related to general intelligence but that help people learn new languages, especially if they begin learning them in adulthood. These skills include a sensitivity to speech sounds and an ability to match them to written symbols, an ability to grasp the grammatical pieces of a sentence and to notice grammatical patterns in a language, and the ability to quickly learn and retain new words. It appears that these same abilities also stave off attrition among immigrants who are most vulnerable to first language loss—those who, like me, were immersed in their second language before the age of puberty.[2] Perhaps language aptitude is similar to being genetically blessed with a high level of cardiovascular fitness—everyone benefits from working out, but a lucky few seem to perform maddeningly well with very little training or after a winter of neglecting their exercise regimen.

Immigrant children are also less likely to lose their first language later on if they have learned to read it, though it's not entirely clear why this is the case.[3] It may be that being able to read gives these immigrants continued access to their language in the absence of conversational partners. Reading may also help the child's native language grow a deeper and broader root system, by feeding them more complex sentence structures and less common words. Linguists who study the differences between text and speech have found that text contains language forms that are rarely found in speech, and that children learning their first language have a better command of these forms if they read or are read to.[4] A child who reads in her first language may have a more mature mastery of it, which would protect against its loss. And, to a child who is making those in-the-moment choices about how much mental space to give each of her languages, reading may make the family language and culture more valuable and less readily ceded to the majority language that permeates everything else in her environment.

When I think back to my book-obsessed childhood, I try to imagine how different my relationship with the Czech language might have been if I'd had access to library shelves stuffed with books in Czech, if I'd had Czech versions of the nerdy, gutsy role models I found in my English books—the Nancy Drews, the Harriets who spied, and the Annes who lived in green-gabled houses. In the days before global e-commerce, our family's collection of Czech books was limited to a handful of volumes that my parents were able to bring from home or that were sent by relatives from overseas. I loved the two or three children's books among them, but my voracious appetite for reading had to be satisfied by books in English. This only entrenched the sense I had of English as a large, roaming language, a language for exploration—whereas Czech was a small and cozy language, a language to retreat to, like the warmth of your grandmother's kitchen.

I suspect that access to Czech literature as a child would have profoundly affected me. The families described in the English books I read were fascinating, but they did not seem much like my own family, and the characters in the books were like interesting versions of someone I might become someday, if I became a slightly different person than I was. I didn't really discover Czech literature until I was a young adult, spurred by a creative writing instructor who remarked that my writing reminded him somewhat of Milan Kundera's—an author I had never heard of. When I began to read Czech authors—Kundera, Bohumil Hrabal, Karel Čapek, all of whom I could read only in English translations—I had an odd sense of coming back to something familiar. Here was a way of seeing the world that felt, well, more like *me*. People in these books related to each other in ways that seemed absurd through North American eyes and ears but that were somehow perfectly normal if I flipped on a more Slavic lens. I felt a sense of relief, akin to the draining of a loneliness I didn't know I had. If I'd had reading experiences like these in childhood or adolescence, would it have been easier for me to embrace my Czech heritage? Would I have been more curious about my parents' experiences and the historical events that shaped them? Would I have stopped asking why they couldn't be more like my friends' parents? And would I have been eager to maintain my Czech language, in order to tap into this vein of literature that felt like home? It's not hard to imagine that being able to read books in Czech as a child would have increased the language's value to me.

What is an ancestral language worth? All speakers of minority languages, whether they realize it or not, carry within themselves a tally of their language's value, a sense of the price they would be willing to pay to keep it. In my own family, there was much talk, especially from my father, about the beauty of the Czech tongue, and much prodding to try to use it within the family and considerable complaining when it was not. Outside of our family, the English- and French-speaking communities where we lived were at worst indifferent toward Czech; there was not the fear or stigma that is attached to some immigrant languages. Still, the price of maintaining our language across generations was apparently too high. Czech *had* value— just not as much value as English did, so we were lured toward this new language and sacrificed a part of who we were to attain it.

How easy it is to forget a language, even under benevolent conditions. But when a language is tainted with painful memories, it becomes even more fragile. My grandfather once told a story of traveling through Europe and trying to find a language in common with a man he had just met. The other man tried French—no luck. My grandfather proposed German, but the other man could not speak it. Eventually they realized they both knew Russian. But my grandfather, who had once been proficient in Russian, and who had spent five years of his life in a Soviet labor camp, suddenly found himself unable to remember enough Russian to converse.

For my grandfather, Russian was a second or possibly third language, not the language he spoke with his mother and father, or the language that was at the core of his identity. But what happens if one's own mother tongue is linked to hideous memories, as was true for many Jewish people who lived in Germany after their country succumbed to Nazism?

A glimpse of the consequences can be seen in the research of Monika Schmid, who assessed language erosion among thirty-five German-speaking Jewish people who emigrated to English-speaking countries between 1933 and 1939. Over this period, Jewish people in Germany, who had almost completely assimilated into the German majority and spoke German as their mother tongue, were told in the harshest ways possible that they were not entitled to view themselves as Germans. Would those who survived sever themselves from their native identity and language? Schmid speculated that the degree of trauma they suffered at the hands of their fellow German speakers might affect how willing they were to shed the German language. The gradual escalation of Nazi-led atrocities over time provided her with a naturally occurring historical experiment: those who left later rather than earlier would have been subjected to the worst levels of aggression and the most violent forms of denial of their German identities—and would have had the most reason to distance themselves from the German language.

Schmid divided her group of émigrés into three phases: In the first phase, from 1933 to August of 1935, the persecution of Jews began by blocking the opportunities of professionals and denying them the right to participate in public life. Jewish shops and businesses were boycotted, and Jewish doctors, lawyers, and judges lost their licenses. Those who left during this period did so mainly because they found themselves unable to continue in their chosen line of work. The majority of Jews in Germany felt the stress of heightened hostility from their fellow citizens but hoped that normal life would eventually return. The second phase began in September of 1935, when the passage of the Nuremberg racial laws made it a crime for "non-Aryans"—that is, Jews, Blacks, and Romani—to marry or have sex with people of so-called Aryan descent, with prison terms for those found in violation. Jews were stripped of their German citizenship regardless of how long their families had lived in the country and were forbidden to fly the German flag (which by then bore a swastika). The strict segregation of Jews and non-Jews caused Jewish businesses to collapse, and many Jewish families became impoverished. In the third phase, beginning in late 1938, the Nazi government deported Jews who were Polish citizens—including those who were German-born—out of Germany to Poland, which tried to bar their entry, leaving thousands stranded at the border with no food or shelter. Some who tried to re-enter Germany were shot. Jewish children were not allowed to attend public schools, and Jewish cultural activities and publications were banned. *Kristallnacht,* an event during which paramilitary groups smashed and ransacked thousands of Jewish businesses, homes, and synagogues, marked a definitive turning point. Thirty thousand Jewish men were arrested and sent to concentration camps, and all Jews now felt that their lives were in immediate danger; those who managed to flee did so in a state of abject fear and desperation.

Monika Schmid analyzed recorded interviews with Jewish people whose emigration from Germany spanned all three phases, conducting a rigorous assessment of their vocabularies and grammatical features. These interviews were all conducted in German about sixty years after the participants had left Germany for English-speaking countries.

Like most people who shift away from their native language in adulthood, those who had emigrated during the first two phases showed fairly subtle signs of language loss. Phase 1 emigrants had a slightly thinner conversational vocabulary than continuous speakers of German, but otherwise spoke like natives. Phase 2 emigrants showed even less complexity of vocabulary and structure, but still did not make mistakes that marked them as nonnative speakers. Among those who emigrated after *Kristallnacht,* however, many no longer sounded like people who had been born into the German language; a number of them spoke with accents, and they used language structures that would be considered ungrammatical by native German speakers. For many of these speakers, the German language became so tainted that they actively tried to eject the language from their memory. One former Jewish resident of Düsseldorf stated that "when the war broke out, I vowed I would not speak, write, nor read German ever again."[5] And one post-*Kristallnacht* émigré described how traumatic it was to hear the German language: After the war, she accepted a job in Germany, believing that she could work and live in that country again. But upon arriving at the border and actually hearing German being spoken, she was overcome by panic and ended up avoiding contact with German speakers as much as she could during her two-year posting in Berlin. When interviewed several decades later, she asserted that America was her country and that English was her language—a personal reality reflected by the disarray of her spoken German.

Jews were not the only people whose desire to speak their native tongue was extinguished by the Nazis. Schmid also writes of Holocaust survivors of Romani origin, who were identified as "gypsies" to be deported to camps partly on the basis of their ability to speak Romani. Many of the survivors, once settled into new countries after the war, assimilated completely to the languages of their new homes, having no wish to speak the mother tongue that had marked them for extermination.

It's impossible for me to read these accounts of mother tongues silenced by trauma without thinking of the language crimes of my own adopted country, Canada. The report of the Truth and Reconciliation Commission, which was charged with documenting the history of the residential school system for Indigenous children, is drenched with accounts of the denigration of Indigenous languages, driven by explicit policies of linguistic extermination. Children were told their languages were uncivilized, and if they spoke them, they risked harsh penalties. Like the Romani, their native languages singled these children out as worthy of punishment. But unlike those who were able to escape the Holocaust, there was nowhere for them to go, no unsullied adoptive language that could eventually become home. They were caught between their native languages, which were vilified as primitive and dirty, and the language of those who tore them from their families, and, in some cases, beat them or raped them. Under such circumstances, why would you ever want to speak at all?

In truth, language is almost never abandoned altogether, regardless of how linguistically homeless or stateless a person might feel. Someone who is monolingual does not lose their language, barring a brain injury or a stroke that wipes out entire populations of neurons. People do not simply forget how to speak—just as no one has ever come across a society that has given up language entirely. When a language dies (but its former speakers survive), always, always, it has been ceded to another language or forcibly replaced by it. It's impossible to understand this process without grasping how a person might forget or stop using their native language in favor of another.

Two languages living inside one person's head are very different from two languages residing in different brains. A bilingual mind is like a household that contains more than one person. Intimate living arrangements between two people have a way of changing their interpersonal dynamics and perhaps even their personalities, and in the same way, cohabiting languages are bound to change each other. As with any couple who lives together, divisions of labor emerge and personal domains are defined: I'll keep track of the finances while you take care of the children's medical appointments; I'm a good cook and you have an eye for interior decorating. Some couples have a roughly equal division of tasks and responsibilities, and the skills and flexibility to step in for each other on a regular basis. Others are more rigid, their responsibilities more sharply defined. In some couples, one person may dominate the other, putting stark boundaries around what the partner is permitted to do and where she is allowed to go: you can take care of the domestic chores, but I will deal with all aspects of the outside world.

Languages that share a brain are like this too. Perhaps more books are read in one language than the other. One language might be used more in the workplace. You may want to slip into one language at home with your family and use another when out with friends. You may be able to write poetry in only one of your languages, feeling inept in the other, which you may nonetheless expertly and creatively deploy for spinning tales at the pub. You may be able to worship in only one of your languages, the other feeling somehow too profane. Defending yourself in court or giving a radio interview may be comfortable in only one of your languages.

This isn't to say that each language within a bilingual person inevitably has a narrower range than the sole occupant of a monolingual mind. Just as a couple can be composed of two people who have each cultivated more skills than the average single person, a person whose two languages stretch over many domains may have more virtuosic control of each tongue than the average monolingual person has over their one language. But rigid divisions of labor can hem in and impose limits on one or both languages. Much like a person who, upon the death of a partner, is confronted by all the things he doesn't know how to do, a bilingual person accustomed to relying on one language to perform certain functions may discover that the other language is no longer up to the task. And if one language wholly dominates the other, so that the lesser-used language is squeezed into smaller and smaller corners and is given voice less and less often, the bilingual person may start to skew monolingual.

Minority languages so often find themselves pushed into ever-shrinking spaces. They are typically barred from public life, absent from signs on the street or in businesses, relegated to hidden domestic spaces. Sometimes marginalization has the force of law, as with the language laws in Franco's Spain that made it illegal to publish in Basque or Catalan or use these languages in public. Occasionally, individuals in positions of power take it upon themselves to sweep minority languages from the spaces they control: for example, a 2018 *Los Angeles Times* article described how a manager of a coffee shop offered free coffee to customers who reported staff using a language other than English.[6] And on many, many occasions, I myself have witnessed parents and children speaking to each other in their family language, only to find themselves within earshot of someone who remarks, "Why don't they speak English?" What all these people and laws are saying is that Spanish (or Arabic or Urdu or Mandarin or Czech) belongs in the kitchen and not out in public.

When I was growing up, I never saw Czech on store signs, let alone in government documents. It was only very rarely that I glimpsed a Czech newspaper or magazine, generally one that was sent to us from "over there," not one that was produced and read by my fellow Canadians. I didn't ever hear Czech spoken on the streets or in shopping malls. Like many immigrants, the habitat of my mother tongue was more or less restricted to my own household, and I was startled if I ever came across a person I didn't know who spoke it.

Thomas Laqueur, a historian and writer who grew up in a German-speaking household in West Virginia, describes the moment in his childhood when he realized that German was not merely a family code, but a language that could be spoken by people outside of his household. One day, as he and his brother fought over a popsicle outside a convenience store, screaming at each other in German, a woman approached them and, in German, offered to give them money so they could each have their own popsicle. The young Thomas ran home in great excitement to announce the news that he had just met another member of their "linguistic species."[7]

Though I had always known that our family language had deep roots in a place far away, it still came as a shock to discover how it felt to be surrounded by Czech speakers for the first time in my life, on that brief conference trip back to my homeland in 1994. As we pulled into the train station in Prague, a Czech voice came over the loudspeaker announcing departure times and platforms. I had never heard any voice vested with official authority speaking in Czech; it felt as if one of my brothers or uncles had, as a prank, grabbed the microphone and started speaking in our own family code. I expected the announcer to be pulled away at any moment by someone with real authority.

Of course, in my mind I was well aware that train announcements in Prague would be made in Czech. But standing on that railway platform, what I *felt,* in the goosebumps that prickled my skin, was: *My god, there's a whole nation full of people who speak this language.*

Now, from my adult roost, I can look back and see the ways I failed to nurture the language within me and the ways in which I contributed to its shrinking from my life. There was a time when I would still speak Czech to my siblings in the schoolyard. Upon hearing this unfamiliar language wafting between us, my classmates would hold their bodies more stiffly and carefully, as if suddenly discovering that we were more different from them than they had realized. So, as soon as we could, my siblings and I spoke the language of the schoolyard with each other. It then seemed natural to bring it home. Everyone smiled upon hearing our growing mastery of English.

I have a clear memory of coaxing my younger sister to take her first steps—she was about a year old, golden-haired, grinning, and I was six. I recall putting myself at some distance from her, beckoning to her, and saying, in English, "Come on, little girl. Come on! Come on little girl. You can do it!" Why did I speak to her in English and not Czech, here, in the private sphere of our home? I can only guess at the feelings of my child-self. But the clarity of this memory, down to the specific words I used and how they sounded in my mind, makes me think that it was significant to me in that particular moment that I was speaking English. Perhaps I felt proud that I was bringing my sister a gift from the big, important world into our small Czech nest. Perhaps I felt exhilarated that I could adapt my English to this new task. Perhaps I was already dreaming of how I would take my golden baby sister by the hand and show her all the wonderful things I was discovering outside of the walls of our home, preparing her for the bewildering and wonderful Anglophone world Out There.

I am guessing that my parents, if they overheard this exchange, might have smiled benignly.

Here are the things that no one tells a six-year-old immigrant child speaking to her baby sister in English: Be careful. If you continue down this path, your ancestral tongue will one day become more effortful for you to speak than this new language is now. The world will not smile at you when you speak it, and you may find you stop speaking it entirely. This language is a thin thread of connection between you and the entire nation that will shape you into adulthood whether you are aware of it or not, and whether you want it to or not. If you let this thread fray, there will be things about yourself you may never understand. You will become a linguistic orphan, a person without a mother tongue.

No one told me these things then, or in the moments when, as an older child, I began speaking to my parents in English because I was too tired to speak Czech, because the vocabulary I learned from English books and teachers was better suited to the ideas I was trying to express than the smaller collection of Czech words I possessed, because I'd learned to love the sound of my voice in English.

And years later, when I began having my own children and felt the inklings of a desire to pass on my heritage language, I was already adrift. I had moved to upstate New York, far away from my parents and relatives who spoke Czech. It was the early 1990s, before Czech books could be bought over the internet, before Czech podcasts or TV shows streamed into your home from across the ocean. Perhaps if I'd been born a generation later, my linguistic legacy might have been somewhat different. During my formative younger years, Czechoslovakia truly was a remote, impenetrable place. For reasons of technology and politics, little passed through its borders, either in or out. Telephone calls overseas were so expensive, there was no possibility of leisurely conversations with relatives back home. Letters were opened, read, and censored. There was no question of being able to go back for visits, even if we could have afforded it. The Communist government did not consider my family's departure legal, so we would have been subject to prison sentences upon arrival. I grew up doubting I would ever return to that country in my lifetime.

Nowadays, I witness how some young people who straddle countries and cultures are able to travel with their families to their ancestral country every year or two, and how they can pull up magazines, blogs, movies, and YouTube videos on their screens in the privacy of their bedrooms and conduct secret flirtations with someone across the world who shares their language. I imagine what it might have felt like to know, not as an abstraction, but as a fact of daily life, that there is a whole nation of people who speak your language.

Such close contact was unimaginable during my childhood, and by the time my children were born, my ability to speak Czech was crumbling. My husband spoke only English. How could I possibly generate enough verbiage on my own for my children to decently acquire the language? The Czech words I could produce were riddled with errors and dredged up with great effort. And even if I did, on my solitary linguistic island in Rochester, New York, converse with my kids in Czech, I knew exactly what would happen as soon as they started going to school or playing with the neighborhood kids: they would do what I had done, and switch right over to English. If

I, fully immersed in Czech spoken masterfully by my parents in my early years, had been unable to fully retain it, how could they possibly maintain a language passed down by just one speaker?

Had I known and understood the implications of neglecting my mother tongue, I suspect I still could not have avoided making the same choices. In almost every situation, speaking Czech was like swimming against a stiff current, and the rewards for thrashing against it felt insufficient as I struggled to make my place in the world. Life for an immigrant is exhausting enough.

But this doesn't mean the loss of my language wasn't terrible and deep. Or that I don't grieve. That I don't wish things had been different and the current less insistent.

I am hardly alone in my language grief. When I first wrote about the loss of a heritage language and its painful consequences, I received a flurry of emails from strangers, including the following message sent to me by a fellow immigrant to Montreal:

> My parents said we would be Canadians, not Hungarian refugees, and we spoke nothing but English, and a little French. We arrived in 1957. In 1993, my wife and I traveled to Budapest to visit, my first return. I was overwhelmed by the experience and at one point, broke down and cried. I had trouble defining what brought on this flood of emotion. After all, I had been only six years old when we left. Although I had thought of myself as Canadian, there clearly was an entombed part of me that was opened on the return to my birth city.

Losing your native tongue severs you not only from your own early life but from the context of your life. You lose access to the books, films, stories, and songs that articulate the values and norms you've absorbed without knowing they live in your cells. You lose the embrace of an entire community or nation for whom your family's odd quirks are not quirks at all. Your sense of who you are has blank spaces in it.

But the private feelings I share with this Hungarian-born man are dwarfed by the collective loss felt by entire communities of Indigenous peoples who have found themselves unmoored from their ancestral cultures and languages. It is a disconnection that can have devastating consequences for members of these communities. A 2007 study led by Darcy Hallett found that in British Columbian communities where fewer than half of the members could hold a conversation in their Indigenous language, young people committed suicide six times more often than in communities where the majority spoke the language.[8] In the midwestern United States, psychologist Teresa LaFromboise and her colleagues found that Native adolescents who took part in activities related to their traditional language and traditions did better at school and had fewer behavior problems than kids who were less connected to their traditional cultures—in fact, cultural connectedness buffered them against adolescent problems even more than having a warm and nurturing mother.[9]

It is one thing to become personally estranged from a language that continues to thrive somewhere on the planet—the possibility of reconnection is always there, and at no time greater than the present moment in history. It is quite another to be wrenched away, along with all your people, from a language that is in danger of disappearing entirely, or whose last native speaker has already died. That is a form of irrevocable loss that I can only contemplate from a distance.

Around the world the last native speakers of languages are dying in great numbers. It's ironic that in our current epoch of the Anthropocene, we humans are even better at extinguishing languages—which exist only as products of human minds and human societies—than we are at obliterating other species of animals. In 1992, linguist Michael Krauss noted that about 10 percent of mammals and 5 percent of birds were considered to be endangered.[10] Sobering statistics to be sure, but, as he pointed out, they don't compare with the threats faced by languages. Linguists generally agree that at least half of the world's languages are in danger of becoming extinct over the next few generations. Krauss was even more pessimistic, estimating that of the world's more than 6,000 languages, a mere 600 or so could be considered secure, and that 90 percent of the languages currently in existence could die off within a century.[11] "Should we mourn the loss of Eyak or Ubykh any less," he asks, "than the loss of the panda or California condor?"[12]

As someone who spent almost half a century studying and documenting native Alaskan tongues, Michael Krauss did mourn the death of languages, no doubt with great depth of feeling. He witnessed the last flickering years of Eyak, a language that had been whittled down to a half-dozen speakers by the time he began to study it in the 1960s. In 2006, when his own health began to falter, he noted that the last native speaker of Eyak, sixteen years his senior, worried about his health more often than the reverse. It was Krauss's hope that Eyak would, at the very least, outlive him.[13] It was not to be; Marie Smith Jones, the last native speaker of Eyak, died in 2008, eleven years before his own death in 2019.

Among the preserved remains of the Eyak language is a poem, "Lament for Eyak," written by Anna Nelson Harry, another of Eyak's last speakers, and translated by Krauss. The poem is a river of grief:

> My poor aunt.
> I couldn't believe you were going to
>   die.
> How would I hear you?
> I wish this,
> to go back to you there.
> You are no more.
> My child speaks to me that way.
> I just break out in tears and lament.

All alone here I'll go around.
Like Ravens I'll live alone.
My aunts are dying off on me and
    alone I'll be living.
Why, I wonder, are these things
    happening to me?
My uncles also have all died out on
    me and I can't forget them.
After my uncles all
    died off,
my aunts are dying off next.
I'm all alone.
With some children I survive,
on this earth.
Only I keep bursting into tears.
I think about where my
    aunts are.
She is my aunt and my last aunt is
    gone.

Where will I go next?
Wherever will I go next?
They are already all extinct.
They have been wiped out.
Maybe me, I wonder, maybe Our
    Father wants it this way for me,
that I should live alone.
I only pray for it and my spirits
    recover.
Around here,
that's why this land,
a place to pray,
I walk around.

I try to go there.
Alone,
alone around here I walk around on
    the beach at low tide.
I just break into tears.

I sit down on a rock.
Only the Eyaks,
the Eyaks,
they are all dying off.
Just a few at Eyak
    there.
They survived from Eyak,
but they too are becoming extinct.
Useless to go back there.
My uncles too have all died out on
    me.
After my uncles all died out my
    aunts next
    fell,
to die.

Yes,
why is it I alone,
just I alone have survived?
I survive.[14]

I had read this lament many years ago as a young PhD student, along with Krauss's 1992 paper, titled "The World's Languages in Crisis," which galvanized the academic linguistic community to invest more deeply in documenting and preserving the world's endangered languages. At the time, the plight of the world's languages resonated for me intellectually. But it wasn't until years later, after my father's death, that I found myself really contemplating the experiences of the speakers of these languages. If I felt existentially shaken by the loss of my own contact with Czech, I wondered, how would it feel to know that the loss was permanent and irrevocable; how would it feel if Czech no longer existed, not just in my own life, but *anywhere* in the universe?

Why are we seeing such a mass extinction of languages? It seems no accident that languages are quickly disappearing at the same time as so many plants and animals. In fact, the fates of biological species and languages appear to be deeply connected. Both are increasingly threatened by the way of life of modern humans. And both seem to depend on the properties of the land that contains them. For reasons that are not well understood, languages have proliferated most readily in the same climate zones that teem with animal and plant life—in coastal zones, wet environments, and places where the seasons don't swing between dramatic changes in temperature or precipitation. The most linguistically diverse place on the entire planet (and among the most biologically diverse) is Papua New Guinea, with more than 800 languages currently spoken there. This means that, on average, there is a separate language there for every 10,000 people. At that density, the United States would be home to more than 32,000 languages, and the United Kingdom and France would each have more than 6,500.

Mark Pagel, a biologist who studies evolutionary processes, suggests that a profusion of both languages and wildlife is possible when many distinct habitats are packed into a small geographic area.[15] For animals, diverse habitats have the effect of limiting competition among species; each species evolves highly specialized traits for its particular habitat, and because many of these adaptations don't transfer well to other habitats, species become sorted into separate niches rather than competing within the same pool of resources. Less competition means that there is less risk that some species will be pushed out or annihilated by a few dominant ones. In the same way, if people are able to feed themselves without having to travel great distances, they're more likely to develop a specialized culture within their habitat and not have to interact a great deal with other groups, thereby reducing the need for a shared language. Paradoxically, *isolation* from competitors—either biological or cultural—is one of the drivers of diversity on a larger scale.

Modern society shreds isolation to pieces. It levels many small, distinct, self-contained habitats into larger, more uniform habitats, with grave consequences for many of the species and languages that they harbor. Like invasive species such as zebra mussels, European starlings, and the dreaded kudzu vine, a small number of languages can come to dominate these habitats and push out many of the languages that were formerly spoken there. The world's 6,000 or so languages are far from equally dispersed around the globe: Just 5 percent of languages are concentrated within 94 percent of the world's population, leaving the remaining 95 percent of languages to be spoken by a mere 6 percent of all humans. Just eight languages (Mandarin, Spanish, English, Bengali, Hindi, Portuguese, Russian, and Japanese) claim more than 100 million speakers each; these are the linguistic versions of kudzu.[16] English is the viniest, most invasive of all languages—in countries where it is the dominant language, it had already managed to obliterate 90 percent of its competitors by 1992 and is a serious threat to those remaining.[17]

It's not surprising that a biologist like Mark Pagel sees languages through a Darwinian lens, comparing languages to species. But lately, linguists have also been borrowing biology's notions of competition and evolution as a way to understand language diversity and language death. Metaphors, though, are never a perfect fit for the abstractions they're meant to clothe—in this case, it's precisely in the misalignment of the seams where we can find insight into why languages are so vulnerable in our times, even more so than species.

If languages are in even greater danger of extinction than animal species, it's because speakers of languages don't actually have to die in order for their languages to go extinct—they just have to stop speaking them to their children. Linguists agree that one of the surest signs of impending extinction is when a language is no longer being learned by children. Such languages are considered to lack "reproductive capacity"—like endangered species that simply can't produce enough offspring to ensure their survival.

At times, diminished reproductive capacity has come about through a forced sterilization of languages, through explicit policies meant to eradicate them and absorb their speakers into a dominant culture. Prohibiting people from speaking their language to their children in their own homes is hardly practical. But children can be made to live outside of the family home and separated from their ancestral language and culture. In North America and Australia, Indigenous children were forcibly taken by the state from their homes and families, to be housed and educated in residential schools. In many of these institutions, language eradication was the official goal: children were punished for speaking their native languages, visits from family members were discouraged, and letters and conversations between parents and children had to take place in English.

Even when children remain at home, however, their experiences at school can loosen their attachment to their native language. Certain languages can be banned from school grounds and children punished for speaking them. Ngũgĩ wa Thiong'o, a Kenyan academic who writes primarily in Gikuyu, describes the repressive rules at a Kenyan school in the 1950s, meant to promote the use of English and discourage children from speaking Gikuyu. Anyone caught speaking this or any other African language at school would be made to wear a token of shame around his neck. The only way to remove the humiliating object was to catch another child speaking Gikuyu— by trickery if necessary—and pass the necklace on to the new offender. Whoever was caught wearing the token at the end of the day was singled out and punished. Thiong'o describes in vivid detail how one boy, who had been the end-of-day offender on numerous occasions, was flogged in front of the other children until his shorts split and blood splattered onto the adults who were whipping him. To the young author, the lesson regarding Gikuyu was clear: "There was nothing this language could teach me, at least nothing that could make me become educated and modern. Gore to the students who spoke Gikuyu; glory to those who showed a mastery of English."[18] As a child who entered school speaking a language that was different from the language of instruction, I can attest to the fact that it takes much less than this to make a student reluctant to speak her language, not just at school, but at home as well.

Preventing children from learning or using their family languages is a brutally effective way to disrupt them. Language learning is a child's game; the childhood brain absorbs it more readily and completely than the adult brain. A language taken up later in life is almost always destined to be spoken with an accent and littered with grammatical errors. Keeping a child from using her language throughout much of her childhood makes it likely that, even if she is re-immersed in it as an adult, she will always feel somewhat of an outsider to it; she will be marked by her errors, and it will be that language whose words slide out of her grasp when she is tired at the end of a long day. In the end, she will be less likely to speak it to her own children.

There are other ways in which a dominant group can make swaths of a shared territory uninhabitable for other languages, whether intentionally or not. Governments can ban the use of a minority language in public and shut down any publications in that language (as has been the case for Kurdish in Turkey, or Basque and Catalan under the dictator Francisco Franco); the aim is to reduce it to a private, domestic language that never gets close to the levers of power. Less malevolently, a society may simply place one (or more) of its languages on the official language pedestal, legislating that all legal transactions, court hearings, and so on be conducted in that language. This means that those who know the official language—but not others—will never have to face any communication barriers, except in the most private crevices of society. While official language designation may not be motivated by an intent to eradicate other languages, it has much the same effect as applying fertilizer to kudzu.

In truth, dominant languages often manage to crowd out other languages even without legal fortification or official regulations. Unlike other biological organisms, which can't decide to add a postscript to their DNA or swap one chunk of genetic code for another, human beings can and do decide of their own volition whether to learn a new language, and which language to use in what circumstance. We can choose to morph into members of other linguistic species. The gains offered by learning a dominant language are usually so apparent that outright punishment for using another is rarely necessary. In the end, language loss is often the result of countless in-the-moment choices made by children and young people to speak a language other than their ancestral language—language death can be the result of children like me.

For Salikoko Mufwene, who studies the evolution of languages, a better-fitting metaphor is to think of languages not as akin to animal species, but as similar to viruses.[19] Languages can't live on their own as independent organisms—like viruses, they are parasitic on human hosts, and their survival and spread depends on their hosts' behaviors and patterns of interactions. This means that to understand why some languages fan out and consume others, we need to understand the people who carry them. Like epidemiologists who try to predict the spread of diseases, we need to know how and where people live and work, who they speak with and who they avoid, who they live with, and where their children go to school. If neighborhoods are sharply segregated bubbles, where residents interact very little with people outside of their physical communities, a viral language will be unable to jump these gaps in human interaction. But if the various communities within a society are porous, their boundaries fluid, with people dipping in and out of communities and flitting among a variety of social circles, the opportunities for infection will be abundant.

As it happens, the way that people are distributed throughout space and the ways in which they interact with each other are even more critical for language than they are for viruses. Language is exceptionally hard to transmit. A language is not like a coronavirus, which can hover in the air after a host has coughed and then colonize the airways of an innocent who walks by. It's not even like the HIV virus, which requires intimate contact, but perhaps just once, and with only one infected host. To "catch" a language, you need repeated and sustained contact with its hosts, and usually not with just one but with many. So much contact with language is required that researchers fret about the linguistic health of children who are not exposed to enough of it. In a well-known study, Betty Hart and Todd Risley warned that "impoverished" language contact—consisting of a mere 10 million words over a child's first four years, in comparison to the average 45 million words—could result in deficient language skills among certain children.[20]

In fact, the language virus is so hard to transmit that mere exposure, even frequent exposure, will not do the trick. A person can't become an Arabic speaker, for example, simply by bathing in a sea of Arabic speech—as I often do, living in a city with many recent immigrants from the Middle East and having close relationships with people who speak Arabic among themselves when we gather socially. In order to learn the language, you have to make a deliberate effort to speak Arabic, and Arabic speakers have to be willing to speak it back to you. This doesn't happen in my case; the Arabic speakers I know have enough knowledge of English to spare me the trouble.

Here, too, the limits of metaphor reveal something essential about language death. A language can't flourish without its host's complicity. A virus may thrive and spread despite the host's best efforts to drive it out of its bloodstream or avoid passing it on to others. But a language needs a host who takes active steps to promote its well-being. If a language tries to take root within a host who is passively indifferent to it, it is doomed. Maintaining a language takes time and energy. Hence, the language must have something to offer the host, benefits that justify the costs.

It's useful to look at corners of the world where some of the world's most invasive languages *haven't* pushed out other languages. Mufwene points out that in Africa, unlike in North America and Australia, the European languages of colonizers haven't been as much of a threat to smaller local languages. He argues that this is because the goals of the colonizers were very different on the various continents, resulting in different linguistic ecosystems. In the Americas, the colonizers' goal was to establish remote replicas of their countries of origin, an aim that was flagrantly advertised by slapping old place names onto locales that, at the time, resembled their namesakes only in the dreams and aspirations of the namers—hence the profusion of names such as New England, New France, New Amsterdam (a name eventually dislodged by New York), New Orleans, and so on. These "new" places were set up to receive a steady flow of the conquerors' populations and to be infused throughout with the conquerors' languages and cultures, a task made much easier by the extinction of 90 percent of the native population of the Americas. Those natives who did survive, particularly in North America, were expected to melt into the new culture. Reinforced by eighteenth- and nineteenth-century beliefs that nationhood rested on the bedrock of a unified language, the new governments embraced forceful policies of assimilation, such as sending all native children to residential schools. More importantly for Mufwene, the colonizers installed an economy that managed to penetrate all levels of society. The natives' means of subsistence were eradicated—in some cases, as with the Plains tribes who depended on the buffalo for survival, their chief resources were literally driven to extinction. No local economies remained as alternatives to the dominant colonial economy. In order to participate in the economy in any meaningful way, one had to interact with speakers of English (or French) who themselves had no intention of learning the Indigenous languages. The message that was constantly dangled before the natives was: all this could be yours, if only you become just like us. Opportunity beckoned, but there was little in the way of an alternative choice.

The situation in Africa was quite different. The goal of the colonizers was to exploit and extract resources from the African countries for the benefit of their home nations, but there was no intent to repopulate these countries with Europeans or to amend the cultural soil to make it hospitable for transplanted Europeans. And while Europeans held the levers of power, and disproportionately claimed the fruits of the economy for themselves, they were not involved in all aspects of economic life, and they interacted little with locals outside of their administrative roles. For the most part, Europeans did not operate farms, sell their wares at the market, own taxi companies, or open restaurants. For many Africans going about their daily life, knowing a European language has not been necessary. More than that, it has not been particularly useful. Unless they aspired to a white-collar job, available to only a tiny portion of Africans, there was not much point. In this ecosystem, European languages have been less contagious than we might expect, despite their elevation to official language status. For example, although French is the sole official language of Mali, Niger, and Burkina Faso, less than a quarter of the population of these countries speaks French, and it is almost always spoken as a second language rather than as a native tongue. Mufwene argues that European languages have remained somewhat closeted as languages of the elite in Africa—they are learned in school and are spoken in office buildings, lecture halls, and government offices, but they are not the languages you would speak in the streets, let alone at home in your family village, where they are considered foreign.

Mufwene argues that, more than European languages such as English or French, it is the larger African languages that serve as a *lingua franca* for speakers of different tribal languages—and that it is these languages, rather than the big global "killer" languages, that are most threatening to the local languages and to language diversity in Africa. Whether this will continue in the future remains to be seen. A 2018 report issued by the *Organisation Internationale de la Francophonie* claims that the use of French in Africa has been growing, with about 40 percent of the total African population currently speaking French, and predicts that if trends continue, almost 80 percent of the population will speak French in fifty years.[21]

Comparing languages to viruses may help to describe the mechanisms by which languages are lost in the currents of change, but it also makes it harder to evoke grief over their loss—much easier to mourn the majestic Bengal tiger than a virus whose own host failed to nurture it. And therein, perhaps, lies the most revealing gap of all between the metaphor and reality of language loss.

It is true that it is individuals who—often as youngsters—make the countless in-the-moment decisions to speak one language rather than another. These decisions can eventually starve their native languages out of them. In each of those moments, a more dominant language may have seemed the most useful. But to state it this way, in words glazed with utilitarianism, doesn't capture the depths of sorrow they or their children may come to feel at the death of their language. I have not once read a lament for an extinct virus that runs like a river of grief.

Like the death of a species, the death of a language is the accumulation of many individual losses that add up to a devastating, irrevocable sum. Except in cases where a language dies because all of its speakers have been slaughtered or washed away in a flood, it is gradually forgotten in the same way that an individual gradually forgets a language he used to speak with ease. It withdraws from collective memory in much the same way an atrophied language withdraws from the mind of a single person.

A person who uses a language only for limited functions becomes unable to wield the language properly in certain contexts. Written language, for example, uses a richer vocabulary and more varied and complex structures than spoken language, so someone who does not read or write in a language that they speak has a shallower lexicon and less control over elaborate syntax rarely used in speech. A person who is not exposed to the poetic or ceremonial forms of their language does not have a sense of its stylistic agilities. Someone who speaks only with intimate family members does not know how to speak to a person in a formal setting or address someone of a different social status. This can result in gaffes like the one committed by my younger sister, who once used the informal *ty* form when speaking with a Czech bishop—to the utter mortification of my father, who rushed after him to apologize for his daughter's unspeakable rudeness. A public blunder like this is a cruel reminder of outsider status, regardless of your country or language of birth.

In the same way, when a language recedes from many of the spaces it used to occupy, the language itself inevitably shrinks. Like a body weakened by inactivity, a language atrophies first in the muscles that are least often flexed. And a language that is confined to the kitchen is able to exercise very few of its original functions.

As documented by linguists like Monika Schmid and Maria Polinsky, attrition is first seen in the variety of words at a person's disposal—the most common ones remain, the more unusual ones fade. Gradually, a person comes to use fewer syntactic structures, and those that remain are the most common, simplest ones. And eventually, especially among child speakers whose command of the language has not yet had a chance to grow strong, grammatical distinctions are flattened out and formerly precise uses of words and forms meld together into greater vagueness.

Over time, the shrinking of individual speakers' language is reflected in the collective language of the community, as more and more of the language's speakers are marginal speakers who are able to use it only in limited domains. The entire language suffers a reduction of scale and complexity. Squeezed into small spaces, it literally becomes a small language, until, less and less able to serve the needs of its speakers, only remnants—if anything at all—remain in the memories of its speakers.

Linguists have begun to carefully document this process of flattening and simplification in dying languages. In one such case study, Katherine Matsumoto describes a community of Shoshone speakers on the Duck Valley Reservation, which straddles the boundary between Nevada and Idaho.[22]

Although there are about 2,000 speakers of Shoshone, the language is rarely spoken in public, especially since it's considered rude to speak Shoshone in the presence of anyone who does not speak the language. Most people of working age in Duck Valley do not speak Shoshone, so it is rarely used in conducting business or providing services. It is hardly ever heard at Tribal Council meetings. Matsumoto reports that, by and large, Shoshone speakers in this community reserve their use of the language for joking around with their friends (elders apparently claim that Shoshone is much funnier than English) or for talking about work in the fields or about the activities of people they know.

Like many Indigenous communities in North America, mastery of the language is stratified by age. Those born before 1950 remember speaking Shoshone at home and first encountered English when they were forced to attend residential schools along with other Native children, none of whom knew any English either. Children often used their mother tongues at school, even though they risked punishment in doing so. But those born as few as ten to twenty years later reported that *none* of the students spoke Native languages at their school, even when they had learned these languages at home. The students all spoke English by that time and preferred to use English when speaking with schoolmates.

The rapid ascendance of English over Shoshone is visible in the fraying structure of the Indigenous language. In many respects, the

Shoshone spoken by its oldest speakers is more complex than English. As in Czech, Shoshone words change their shape to reflect different cases, distinguishing between grammatical subjects and objects (although Shoshone only distinguishes between two cases, rather than the seven that are sadistically required by Czech). Rather than simply noting whether nouns or pronouns are singular versus plural, Shoshone introduces a three-way distinction, with separate forms used to indicate that there are two of something. And it has an elaborate system of referring to objects in space. Where English makes do with a meagre collection of four pronouns that resort to a binary distinction to signal that objects are either relatively near or relatively far (*this / that, these / those*), Shoshone makes a five-way distinction. When referring to something, you need to indicate whether it is in the immediate vicinity, close by, in the mid-distance, far but within sight, or so remote as to be invisible. Multiply this by the two-way case system and the three-way marking of singular, dual, or plural, and you get a total of thirty different forms against English's paltry four.

Among younger speakers, the intricate patterns of the language have begun to unravel. Speakers have become inconsistent in their use of these grammatical distinctions or have dropped some of them altogether. For example, some speakers are merging the five spatial variants into two or three, or even failing to make any spatial distinctions at all.

Rapid changes and simplification have been noted for other endangered languages around the world. Speakers of Breton (spoken in the Brittany region of present-day France) have recently abandoned a range of forms used in more formal styles and converged upon a single informal "monostyle."[23] In Australia, when linguist Annette Schmidt documented the dying language of Dyirbal, she found that the language's grammatical norms had splintered; whereas older speakers followed systematic grammatical patterns, the version of Dyirbal spoken by younger people was wildly unstable.[24] Younger speakers had organized the language into *some* sort of system—though much simpler than the traditional language—but the system of one speaker rarely meshed with that of another, with the language devolving into a collection of individual dialects.

Simplification of the language's structures has also been observed for, among others, East Sutherland Gaelic (Scotland), Central Pomo (northern California), and Mani (Sierra Leone).[25] Much is still unknown about the trajectory of language death—is it similar for every endangered language? Is structural change an inevitable harbinger of a language's impending death throes? Can the changes ever be reversed? But like the simplified and unstable grammar of a speaker whose mother tongue has atrophied, these changes are symptoms of language loss.

What exactly is lost when a language dies? To many people—particularly those who speak one of the "big" languages of the world, I imagine—it may seem like cause for celebration rather than mourning when a small group of people gives up an insular language to join the global family of English (or Spanish or Russian or French) speakers. Surely, linguistic unity and the ability to communicate with anyone nationwide or worldwide can only foster greater harmony among people, a state longed for by the peaceable inventors of "universal" languages like Esperanto. Why speak of the *death* of a language at all? Isn't the worldwide shift to fewer and fewer languages really less like death and more like the global dispersal of digital technology, flush toilets, and pop music, all eagerly adopted by people around the world for their obvious benefit?

To a linguist, the widespread loss of languages is an intellectual emergency. The world's languages contain a dazzling range of devices and patterns. To lose 90 percent of them would be to lose a sense of what language *is*. A language may rely on as few as eleven speech sounds to carry the load of everything that needs to be said, or it may disperse the burden among as many as 164.[26] The rules dictating how sounds may be combined are as variable as cuisines—for example, in Mandarin, a unit of meaning must be squeezed into a single syllable, whereas English allows meanings to sprawl out over multiple syllables, as in the words *cardigan* or *petunia,* which form indivisible chunks of meaning; Japanese prefers its consonants to be elegantly interspersed between adjacent vowels, like a traditional dinner-party seating plan in which each man is placed next to a woman, whereas Czech encourages its consonants to fraternize together in dense clumps, even in entirely vowel-less words like *prst* and *skrz*. In many languages, you conjugate verbs by attaching a suffix to its tail to indicate its subject as first-, second-, or third person; in Stoney Nakoda, this marker may be tagged to the verb's nose or injected straight into the verb itself between its first and second syllables— it depends on the verb, and you just have to know the specific requirement of each one. And languages differ in the information they consider important enough to enshrine in the grammar of the language: Mandarin doesn't require its speakers to explicitly mark whether an event took place in the past, present, or future, trusting that this can be discerned from the context; Turkish speakers must not only mark tense, but are also obliged to include a grammatical tag to indicate whether they actually witnessed the event they're describing or heard about it secondhand.

It's often the small, isolated languages spoken in remote corners of the world that stretch our conception of what a language can look like—much like the organisms found in remote and extreme environments such as ocean depths, hydrothermal vents, frozen sea water, or acid baths expand our sense of the shape that life can take. These small languages typically evolved in societies that are strikingly different from those that gave rise to the better-known languages of the world, and they have neither descended from the common ancestors of the world's dominant languages nor absorbed much of their material through contact. To study some of these languages is to experience a kind of linguistic vertigo, with nothing solidly familiar underfoot.

Some languages have developed patterns that appear to defy learnability. For example, in his book *What Language Is,* John McWhorter contrasts the streamlined regularity of Persian, whose system of verbs can be captured in simple and orderly tables, with the wild irregularity of Ket, an endangered language of Siberia. In Ket, pronoun tags are typically attached to verbs to identify the subject. Rather than opting for a neat one-to-one correspondence between prefix and pronoun, there are two whole sets of tags, with one set attaching to one class of verbs, and the second set attaching to another class—you have to memorize which class of verbs takes which set of pronoun prefixes, as there is no identifiable rule for this. To make matters more complicated, many (but far from all) verbs take *two* pronoun tags that mean the same thing. For example, *digdabatsaq* means "I go to the river," with both the *d* and *ba* meaning "I," much as if we'd said in English "I go to I the river." But there's more. You need to know that the verb's meaning can change depending on whether you double the pronoun. Specifically, *digdabatsaq* means "I go to the river and come back a bit later." But *digdaddaq* (which involves the double use of the same pronoun prefix *d*) means something different: "I go to the river and stay for the season." The same word with just one pronoun tag—*digdaksak*—means "I go to the river and stay some days or weeks." McWhorter tries to put himself in the skin of a child trying to figure out how to disassemble these complex words into their component meanings: "Even said slowly and in the singsong cadence of Mommy-talk, this is like playing Stravinsky for your baby instead of Mozart." How babies born into Ket ever learn the language is a mystery but, unable to riot or protest, learn it they do—or, at least, they have learned it for many generations until now.[27]

In other languages, there might be a puzzling *lack* of complexity, an avoidance of devices that have been thought to be key building blocks of human language. Linguist Dan Everett created a stir among academic linguists when he claimed that Pirahã, a language spoken by an isolated Indigenous group in the Amazon, showed little evidence of recursion in its structure.[28] Recursion is the property of Russian doll–style nesting of phrases within larger phrases of the same type—for example, nesting a noun phrase like *the boy* inside a larger noun phrase like *the boy's father,* or embedding a clause such as *he left yesterday* within another clause to yield *she told us he left yesterday.* This ability to compress complex meanings into small spaces in a language has been argued to be part of an innate linguistic capacity of humans. But according to Everett, the Pirahã avoid this strategy. Instead of saying *John's brother's house,* they would say something like: *Brother's house. John has a brother. It is the same one.* Or, instead of saying *The tiger got the boy and the girl,* they would say: *The tiger got the boy. The girl also.* If recursion is such a powerful expressive device, and if the capacity to use it is an integral part of the human brain, then why would Pirahã speakers not make use of it? It seems like the equivalent of not availing oneself of the wheel.

Just as a diversity of cuisines stimulates and heightens our appreciation of food, the diversity of languages holds endless delights for the linguaphile—perhaps you too are one of these people whose neurons zip and zing in pleasure when untangling the confounding patterns of an unfamiliar grammar and who love the sensation of being in a public space ringing with the sounds of various languages. But the argument for linguistic diversity goes well beyond the aesthetic. Language is melded into our humanity. Though other animals clearly communicate with each other, our species seems to be alone in being able to press complex thoughts into symbolic forms and pass them back and forth to each other. We are unique in the extent to which all aspects of our lives revolve around our linguistic exchanges. (Just imagine a day empty of all language, spoken or written!) The boundaries of human language—which become unknowable if the vast majority of human languages ever spoken are lost—give shape to the notion of what it means to be human.

What's heartbreaking is that so many of the world's languages are dying off right at the very dawn of a scientific understanding of language. Although language is entirely the product of the human mind, and each human infant comes into the world ready to learn whatever version of language it encounters at birth (no matter how Stravinsky-like this language may be), this doesn't mean we're endowed with an innate intellectual understanding of how language works. An analytical grasp of language is no more automatic than a detailed understanding of the mechanics of vision, for example. It has taken scholars many centuries and much clever theorizing and experimentation to gain a sense of how and why it is that we experience colors, shapes, and motion in the ways we do, even though humans have been experiencing colors, shapes, and motion since long before we were human.

It is only recently—beginning with an explosive growth spurt in the field in the 1960s—that linguists have come to appreciate the extent to which languages are like solar systems, proteins, or spider webs; they are elegantly structured objects that obey their own internal logics, that absorb randomness and variation in intricate and patterned ways. But their natural laws come from something *in us*—something in our own brains and in the stresses and strictures that bear down upon human beings as we struggle to trade thoughts with each other. Like mathematicians who have built an abstract conceptual system to capture the physical realities of the world around us, linguists have begun to erect the theoretical machinery needed to describe the structures of human language. And they have noticed that certain patterns occur again and again in the world's languages, like repeating musical motifs. Do these more common structures reflect an eagerness of the human mind to structure information in certain ways? Are infants born with a bias to learn some kinds of patterns more easily than others? Are certain linguistic structures ruled out by the limitations of what can reasonably be kept aloft in working memory? There are hints that a language's structure may be linked to the kind of society that contains it. For example, some scholars have argued that complicated sentence structures, in which numerous clauses are nested within each other, have burgeoned mainly in languages that have a writing system; written sentences need not be committed to memory or executed within the flow of running speech, allowing them to burst through constraints imposed by speech.[29] Other linguists have suggested that the extravagant complexity and irregularity found in languages like Ket may be best nurtured within small and insular communities, in which people learn the language from birth or not at all; languages that admit many speakers who learn it past their linguistic prime may not be able to afford the extravagance.[30]

Very recent, too, are some of the technologies that allow scientists to dive into the murky pools of our minds, where language lies beyond the reach of conscious introspection. Some researchers devise tests that measure reaction times down to slivers of seconds, relying on tiny wedges of time to pry apart competing theories about how we retrieve words from memory or how we map out the structure of a sentence we're about to utter. Eye movements can be tracked continuously with infrared cameras as people hear or read language, and this allows us to see how they resolve the ambiguities that language is marbled with—how hearers decide when to open up the scope of possible interpretations or clamp down on one best version, all after hearing only fractions of what the speaker will eventually say. And brain imaging offers the equivalent of being able to peer into the orchestra pit and see which of the brain's instruments are active when we speak or comprehend: Do the same basic instruments come to life regardless of the language we speak? Or do some sections stay fairly idle for some languages while others are pushed to virtuosic levels? If different languages rely on different neural circuits, how might this affect other, nonlinguistic tasks taken on by the speakers of different languages? There is some evidence, for example, that perfect musical pitch is more common among people who speak tonal languages, in which changes in pitch are used to distinguish between the meanings of different words that have identical strings of consonants and vowels.[31]

But so far, all of these advances have been limited to the study of a tiny portion of the world's languages. For example, linguists Florian Jaeger and Elisabeth Norcliffe pointed out in 2009 that the sum total of our knowledge about the mechanics of speaking comes from a mere 0.6 percent of the world's languages, most of which are closely related to each other and share many similarities.[32] The knowledge base has not broadened much since then.

Here we are, then, at a point where we have sharpened some new tools, strengthened our theories, and refined our questions about language. And now we are racing to answer them before the languages disappear. For a linguist, it's a bit like having just figured out how to do genetic sequencing on the eve of a catastrophe that is about to wipe out the majority of organisms on earth.

At regular intervals, I come across news articles about how linguists are "saving" one dying language or another. Almost always, what these saviors are really doing is simply recording the language and describing as many of its features as possible before its last native speakers die off. Their labors result in tangible products: dictionaries, grammars, and archives of recorded stories, songs, and snippets of oral history. These products do have value. They stave off some of the scientific consequences of language loss—reading about the unusual conjugation patterns of Stoney Nakoda, for example, adds to our understanding of human language even if no speakers of the language remain. And to be sure, these materials can also be vital pedagogical tools for a community eager to preserve and transmit its language, just as French and German dictionaries and grammars have been consulted by countless (mostly adult) learners of these languages.

But these products are not the *language,* and on their own, they can't save a language from extinction any better than film footage and detailed anatomical drawings can save the white rhino. To survive, the language needs to reproduce itself, virus-like, from speaker to speaker to speaker to speaker. It's true that ample documentation can help a community bring back some version of the language after its official extinction—as is in fact happening now with Eyak, based on Michael Krauss's half-century of work among its last native speakers.[33] But a language raised from the page will inevitably be different from what was spoken for generations by those who were raised in it, and new speakers will need to fill in the many holes that are left.

The prospect of linguists being able to preserve everything that even a handful of speakers know about their endangered languages is less than hopeless. A living language embodies knowledge and skills that its speakers are not even aware of possessing, only fragments of which can be captured in the pages of a traditional dictionary or grammar text. In fact, there are still undocumented corners of *English,* the most written-about language in human history. You might think that by now linguists should know everything there is to know about English. But each month, journals publish yet more articles pointing to new facts about English that need to be accommodated by existing theories, or debating the appropriate contexts of use for this or that word or phrase.

To illustrate with just one example: in a recent twenty-eight-page article, Eric Acton dissects what he calls the "social life" of the English article *the,* noting that "speakers must wield *the* with care, for the use of this unassuming function word, commonest of all English expressions, can in fact send potent social signals. Reference to one's own spouse as 'the wife,' for example, paints a different picture of the speaker's marriage than does a reference to 'my wife.'"[34] Piling up example after example, Acton tries to pin down the nuanced habits of this little word—or rather, because that's far too large a topic for a single paper, he limits himself to a discussion of its subtle signals when used specifically with a plural noun that describes a group of people, such as *the baby boomers.* The presence of *the* often has a distancing effect (as it does with the reference to "the wife"), placing the speaker or writer firmly outside of the group in question. Thus, when the

Swiss-born photographer Robert Frank titled his book of photographs *The Americans,* he triggered the following reaction from a reviewer: "What was most upsetting about Mr. Frank's take . . . was first of all, his title. It is as though the people in his pages were an alien species and he a more evolved anthropologist."[35]

In combing through transcripts of proceedings of the US House of Representatives, Acton finds that speakers are more likely to use the article in phrases such as "the Democrats" or "the Republicans" when they are outside of the party in question and less likely when they are a member of it. But even in reference to the other party, the article is typically dropped when cooperation between the two groups—rather than the distance between them—is being highlighted. ("These are problems that Republicans are anxious to work with Democrats on.")[36] And outsider status is not a requirement for using *the*—Acton finds some examples where it is clearly used by members of the group being described. (For instance: "The Democrats are united on the need for a new direction in Iraq," uttered by Democrat John Larson.) Acton concludes that what is essential to the use of *the* with plural group nouns is a sense that the group is a monolithic entity rather than a collection of distinct individuals, and that this monolithic sense often has a distancing effect, but can sometimes be used to emphasize solidarity within one's own group.

You won't find any of this in a basic grammar of English. (I certainly didn't in the few grammars I consulted at my local library.) Nor will you find many of the other peculiar habits of the most common word in English. But if you're a native speaker of English, you'll immediately register when a nonnative speaker includes or omits *the* in ways that sound off, even if you find yourself unable to explain what the proper "rule" is. I often imagine the impression future people would have of English if it were to go extinct and one could only reconstruct the language based on the textbooks used by students who are new to the language. No doubt it would seem far more rudimentary than the actual English language that flows from our mouths, with all the subtleties and shadings we instinctively put in but rarely think about, let alone set down in textbooks.

Nuanced linguistic investigations like Eric Acton's are luxuries that are afforded only to languages that are already well described. When linguists document an endangered language from scratch, they typically start with a list of content words—nouns, verbs, then perhaps adjectives and adverbs. This is sensible. It's far easier to point to a plant and ask, "What do you call this?" than it is to demand of a speaker, "Does your language form sentences in the passive voice and if so, how is the passive structured and what are the situations in which you would use it?" (Just try asking a fellow English speaker *that* question and see how far you get.) Moreover, a great deal of cultural knowledge is woven into vocabulary, making it a valuable resource to preserve. Linguists Daniel Nettle and Suzanne Romaine point out that many Indigenous languages are "verbal botanies," cutting fine distinctions among species of plants found in the local environment, many of which have no English (or Latin) names.[37] To cite just one example, the Australian language Wangkajunga splits blue-tongued lizards into three linguistic categories, hinting at distinct zoological classifications.[38]

Environmental knowledge can also be packed into words that mark time, in the labels for specific months or days in lunar calendars. In the Pacific Islands, where Indigenous peoples have sustained themselves through fishing, these names are often linked to the behavior of fish: the Kiribati name for the night after the new moon means "to swarm"; in Trukese, the night of the full moon translates as "night of laying eggs."[39] The calendar folds into itself instructions about when to cast nets into the ocean. Words like these rest upon generations of deep expertise and provide outsiders with clues for how to understand the natural environments that these languages inhabit, an understanding that becomes completely lost if the language dies without leaving any of its traces in records or archives. (Of course, the person doing the documentation must be interested in preserving this knowledge; an early dictionary of the Alaskan language Eyak by the Russian explorer Nikolai Petrovich Rezanov contained little in the way of local flora / fauna or native cultural terms—but it was laden with the names of items such as muskets, canons, anvils, and even vodka, the Eyak term for which translates roughly as "utterly rotted water."[40])

A language's lexicon can also provide some insights into how its speakers think and what they value. In English, a person who is short of intelligence or common sense is "dumb"; in the Jaru language of Australia, a fool would be described as "having no ears."[41] In one language, intelligence makes you articulate; in the other, it allows you to listen and learn.

The importance of extended families is imprinted into the kinship terms of many languages. In English, family terms like *brother, aunt, sister-in-law* contain information about gender, generation, and whether the relationship is by blood or marriage. But there are dramatically different systems for naming relatives. Many languages (such as Bengali, Korean, Hungarian, and Stoney Nakoda) also fix the relative age of family members, so there would be a different word for an older brother than for a younger brother. In Hawai'ian, the word for *mother* also embraces aunts, and cousins are linguistically identical to siblings. On the other hand, while English speakers are satisfied with the single word *cousin,* Sudanese children have to learn separate names for their father's brother's children as opposed to their father's sister's children, and different names again for their mother's brother's children and their mother's sister's children. Other languages show an intriguing lopsidedness, having, for example, certain distinctions made on the mother's side of the family but not on the father's side.

Lists of words can provide some clues about the interior lives of various peoples and perhaps even how they interpret their own bodily sensations. Christopher Dowrick, a physician and mental health scholar, writes that certain common words—such as *depression*—don't have easy equivalents in many other languages: "It's not just that specific words like *depression* do not exist in certain languages. It is more that different cultures and languages are constructed in such different ways that there may be no room for a concept like depression, rendering it virtually meaningless."[42] When Margaret Lock interviewed Japanese women for her 1993 book on menopause, *Encounters with Aging,* she was struck by the fact that these women never used a word that corresponded to the English term *hot flash.* "That's a big signal to an anthropologist," she noted. "This is not a symptom that is bothering most of the people. Otherwise, they would have a clear, resounding word that unequivocally describes it."[43] And indeed, when she spoke to doctors about the menopausal symptoms their patients reported, night sweats and feeling flushed with heat barely made the list, even though these are some of the most common complaints of women in the West.

Admittedly, it's not always clear what to infer from dictionary mismatches across languages. Surely, the fact that English has no word that aligns exactly with the German word *Schadenfreude* doesn't mean that English speakers never revel in the misfortune of others. And although the Russian word *žalet'* may be unknown to many who don't speak that language, I doubt there are many people in the world who don't have a visceral grasp of its meaning: to lovingly pity someone. Still, there is something intriguing about the fact that some languages—but not others—have erected specific words to capture these emotions, even if we don't quite know why this is. It hints at subtly different ways in which a culture fixes its beam of attention on the human experience. At the very least, documenting these languages reminds us that there are many different ways of understanding the world and our place in it.

As valuable as such compilations may be, however, it's no easy task to describe a language in a way that truly captures how a language breathes and moves while it is still alive. A Czech grammar may be able to explain that one should use the pronoun *ty* to address close friends and family members and *vy* to address strangers, superiors, and colleagues (unless invited to use *ty*). But these simple rules aren't enough to help you navigate the complicated social mazes in which these pronouns wander, out there in the real Czech world. What insights about family relationships should you glean when you witness a child calling her grandfather *ty,* but the child's aunt, the same man's daughter-in-law, addresses him with the formal *vy*? And how to parse the social structures in a village where customers address the owner of the grocery store—who happens to be of Vietnamese descent— using the informal *ty,* when doing so with almost any other shop owner would be irredeemably rude?

So much of what we know about our language goes beyond the words and structures of what we think of as the language itself. A grammar usually describes a language as if it were an object that can be dissociated from its speakers, like an image of a dress laid out on a bed ready for someone to put on. But native speakers also know what their language looks like when it's *worn*—how the language drapes and flows, how melody can alter the different meanings of a phrase, how a particular word needs to be welded to a certain gesture or incline of the head, how the significance of a phrase deepens if there is a pause *here* rather than *there,* how *this* person but not *that* person is allowed to utter a certain word to a certain someone. It's so rare to see such information in an official description of the language that I am startled when I do. In his *Grammar of the Yiddish Language,* Dovid Katz provides an unusually sensory account of how to use a marker in Yiddish called an *adjective diminutive,* a tag that is attached to an adjective and which can evidently be used to soften the force of a blunt statement or insult. According to Katz, an adjective bearing this tag "is pronounced slowly in falsetto. It is often accompanied by a gentle forward and downward thrust of the head and the opened palm of one hand, with optional horizontal vibration of the same hand and its fingers, and a slight smile."[44]

And so here is the rub: so much of a language can't be captured if it's severed from the real interactions that its speakers have with each other, immersed in the particularities of their culture in that specific time and place. The truth is that language doesn't so much *contain* culture as intertwine with it, and this intertwining confounds even the simple task of nailing down the meanings of its words.

When I run the Czech word *litost* through Google Translate, I am told that its English equivalent is *regret*. But here is what the writer Milan Kundera has to say about it:

> *Litost* is a Czech word with no exact translation into any other language. It designates a feeling as infinite as an open accordion, a feeling that is the synthesis of many others: grief, sympathy, remorse, and an indefinable longing. The first syllable, which is long and stressed, sounds like the wail of an abandoned dog.
>
> Under certain circumstances, however, it can have a very narrow meaning, a meaning as definite, precise, and sharp as a well-honed cutting edge. I have never found an equivalent in other languages for this meaning either, though I do not see how anyone can understand the human soul without it.

One can only understand *litost,* suggests Kundera, by taking an emotional bath in the situations that might give rise to this specific feeling:

> Let me give an example. One day a student went swimming with his girlfriend. She was a top-notch athlete; he could barely keep afloat. He had trouble holding his breath underwater, and was forced to thrash his way forward, jerking his head back and forth above the surface. The girl was crazy about him and tactfully kept to his speed. But as their swim was coming to an end, she felt the need to give her sporting instincts free rein, and sprinted to the other shore. The student tried to pick up his tempo too, but swallowed many mouthfuls of water. He felt humiliated, exposed for the weakling he was; he felt the

resentment, the special sorrow which can only be called *lítost*.
He recalled his sickly childhood—no physical exercise, no
friends, nothing but Mama's ever-watchful eye—and sank into
utter, all-encompassing despair.

LET ME GIVE you my own example of *lítost*.

One consequence of being raised in a family language, isolated
from Czech culture at large, is that I never learned to swear in Czech.
My parents were complete and utter teetotalers when it came to
cursing—the closest I ever got to know an officially bad word was
when my mother would occasionally blurt out "Kurník šuplík!"
which I guess is the equivalent of exclaiming "Fudgsicles!" And I
simply did not meet enough Czech speakers in the intimate settings
that are required to learn how to properly swear.

In my social universe, there was only one source of prestige to
knowing a foreign language: being able to supply friends with novel
or exotic curse words. Alas, my friends' demands went unmet. It was
in their reaction that I first began to suspect that there was something a bit off about not knowing the forbidden words of your mother
tongue. It's like not knowing your mother's first name: people will
start doubting that you *have* a mother. Some of my friends took it as
hard evidence that I was lying about knowing any Czech at all, while
others simply lost interest in my language or me. (My younger sister,
far more resourceful than I, dealt with this schoolyard dynamic by
declaring the word *zmrzlina* to be the filthiest word in the entire
Czech language. Although that word *is* obscenely hard for English
speakers to pronounce, its meaning in Czech couldn't be more benign: ice cream. Years later, I learned of a punk rock band named
Zmrzlina in the San Francisco area, where my sister had lived for
several years, and I wondered whether the incessant pleas for Czech
swear words had followed her into adulthood.)

As I grew older, it seemed more and more outrageous to me that
I didn't know the most vivid and powerful words of my own lan-

guage. I became slightly obsessed with swear words in Quebec French, which mostly revolve around religious objects. I watched in fascination when a friend dropped the word *tabernacle* in the presence of her grandmother, an event that provoked a swelling vein in the grandmother's forehead and an abrupt termination of my visit. I resented having no access to words that could achieve such dramatic results within my own family.

When I visited my family's village in my forties, I admitted to my cousin there that I regretted having no cursing skills in Czech. She snorted and declined to tutor me, suggesting that I could find all those words on the internet. Which of course I did, along with their literal translations. But none of those resources helped me to understand the various ways in which those words might be pronounced to express surprise versus annoyance versus rage, or which words were truly the *worst* words, the ones that would make your grandmother blanch and guarantee your permanent exile from polite society.

At some point during my visit, I found myself at a bus stop surrounded by pubescent boys. In the tussling, shoving exchanges among themselves, they began throwing around some of those words I had seen on the internet. And I felt completely lost. I had no way of interpreting this swearing. What did it mean that they permitted themselves to use these words in my presence? Were these particular words mild enough to be uttered in front of an adult stranger? Or had they pegged me for a foreigner, too stupid to understand the depth of their transgressions? Was I supposed to react with indignation or disgust, and was I fueling their contempt of me by remaining so passive? I knew what the words they were saying *meant,* but I had no idea what it meant that they were saying them to each other in front of me.

I realized too that even if I could find someone willing to tutor me in the subtleties of swearing, it was too late for me. I had been deprived in my early years; I'd had no interactions that would sear into me the shock of those words. Even if I gained an intellectual understanding of the social situation that was playing out at the bus stop in that moment, even if I understood that I should be outraged at the boys' disrespect, I would probably never experience that outrage in my body, either as a surging pulse or a throbbing vein.

I had never before felt like such a *tourist* to my mother tongue. I felt *lítost* seeping into my pores and working its way to my bones.

There is plenty of *lítost* to go around. It's there in that email message sent to me by the Hungarian-born man whose parents tried to raise him as nothing but a Canadian. *Lítost* is what my father must have felt when he asked us to write a letter to his mother for her birthday and was told that we didn't know how. *Lítost* is probably also a familiar emotion to many linguists who have documented a language in its death throes.

Can the meaning of *lítost* be stretched to also encompass the feelings of those who know they are the last people standing between their language and endless silence? I doubt it. Perhaps in some language somewhere there is a word for this. English certainly does not have one.

Eyak's last native speaker, Marie Smith Jones, knew this. In 2005, journalist Elizabeth Kolbert traveled to Alaska to speak to her, with the aim of writing an article about the dying language for the *New Yorker* magazine. When Kolbert asked her how it felt to be its last speaker, Smith Jones replied: "How would you feel if your baby died? If someone asked you, 'What was it like to see it lying in the cradle?' So think about that before you ask that kind of question."[45]

There is no turning back the clock to a world in which small groups of people live self-sufficient lives, with limited contact with others and minimal pressure on their languages. But many advocates argue that language loss need not be inevitable, even in today's connected world. Hope for language salvation lies not in isolation now, but in multilingualism. No doubt more and more people will need to speak the world's big languages out of sheer necessity. But unlike a white rhinoceros or giant tortoise that can only claim membership in one species, humans can belong to two or more languages at the same time. For example, it is possible for members of linguistic minorities to speak the dominant language of their society *and* their own smaller ancestral language.

In their book *Vanishing Voices,* Daniel Nettle and Suzanne Romaine argue that multilingualism was a natural human condition that existed even in precolonial Papua New Guinea, that hotbed of linguistic diversity.[46] Although local groups were largely self-sufficient in meeting their daily needs and acquiring the staples of living, they did trade with each other, often interacting across language barriers at festivals or ceremonial occasions where goods would be exchanged. They created alliances with each other and looked to neighboring groups for spouses. The flow of interaction was especially high among the smallest language groups, where one group was constantly abutting others. In the lowland village of Gapun, which is situated in a dense linguistic area, men over forty years of age typically understood about five different languages. Speaking foreign languages was apparently not only routine but prestigious, and boys would be sent out to neighboring groups to learn their languages, with the aim of acquiring valuable skills as mediators and orators—much like the elite of nineteenth-century Europe sent their children abroad to acquire facility in foreign languages, hoping to expand their influence and opportunities.

Nettle and Romaine describe this scenario as one of "linguistic egalitarianism"; each group stayed grounded in its local language, which helped define the boundaries of that group as a cohesive community, but members of different communities spoke other languages in order to be able to interact with each other. Because people were so attached to their local groups, their knowledge of other, useful languages did not supplant the desire to speak their own community language.

But language dynamics in our modern world have moved far beyond a traditional egalitarianism in which members of each group learn the languages of several other groups in order to lubricate the interactions between them. The world's 6,000 to 7,000 languages are crammed into only 200 countries, many of which are organized around a single official or dominant language. This sets up the potential for enormous asymmetries in power between languages, asymmetries that are only magnified by the emergence of large international languages. A growing number of people around the world feel they need to learn English to participate in the global economy, but residents of English-speaking countries rarely feel the need to reciprocate by learning the languages of other countries.

Perhaps the biggest threat to the diversity of languages is not the sheer usefulness of linguistic behemoths like English but the danger of growing to have feelings for them. Very early in my own life, English became far more than an expedient language. It was the language that animated my friends, teachers, and many of my role models. It was the heartbeat of the books I loved and the TV shows that drew me in, and it was inseparable from my dreams of who I wanted to become. It wasn't enough to learn to *speak* English—I felt the need to merge with it, to become indistinguishable from those who'd been raised in the language from birth.

It is in ecosystems like these that a weaker mother tongue faces its most ferocious competition. The majority language encroaches on the terrain of the heart, demanding love and not mere competence. It begins to fill the voracious human need for social attachment, identification, and a sense of loyalty to a culture larger than yourself.

This is increasingly the ecosystem of many of the world's smallest, most endangered languages. Through opportunity or necessity, their speakers claim membership in multiple communities. A young man raised in the Stoney Nakoda language may leave his reserve for university, develop close relationships with people who identify as Canadians, and come to see himself as bicultural as a result. A proud speaker of Catalan may feel herself to *also* be Spanish; she may fall in love with and have children with someone who speaks only Spanish. Is there a point at which enough speakers of Stoney Nakoda or Catalan come to feel that these languages are no longer essential to who they are, or are simply not worth the price one must pay to maintain them and pass them on to the next generation?

Is it possible for two or more languages to co-exist in the human mind without one coming to dominate the others? Can a person be loyal—in her heart, and not just her mind—to more than one language? What kind of linguistic ecosystem is needed to maintain equilibrium between competing languages? And are such ecosystems possible in our world today?

The survival of thousands of the world's languages may come down to this: whether we are spacious enough in our minds, hearts, and communities to claim more than one language as our own and love them simultaneously.

My mother, siblings, and I *(second from right)* sit at the airport in Vienna, patiently waiting to board our flight to Montreal, Canada.

Chapter 2

Dreams

Success speaks English. This is the water I've swum in ever since our family arrived in North America.

Often, this assertion has gone unstated, siphoning its authority from the absences and silences around me—the absence of Czech heroes and heroines in the history books and biographies I read as a child, the dead silence of the Czech language in all aspects of public life.

Or, it has been insinuated. By the concern the school principal expresses at my lack of English the day my mother takes me to be registered for school. By my teacher's praise at my emerging fluency in English. By the embarrassment of my parents at their own accents and grammatical quirks. By their wordless acquiescence to the alien pronunciation of our surname; English speakers typically place stress on its second syllable (Suh-DEE-vee), making it not only not our name, but not a *possible* Czech name (all Czech words mark stress on the first syllable—SEH-dih-vee).

Success speaks English. At times, this assertion has been openly, forcefully stated. It has been the blueprint for my future and my siblings' futures: a good job requires education, which requires mastery of English. Without a strong command of English, opportunities and prosperity are limited—this was painfully evident from the ceiling that hovered over my parents' prospects.

Success speaks English. Every now and then, this assertion has had the force of an existential claim about language and culture, and not merely a description of historical and geographic happenstance. At its most extreme, it equates English with cultural values that foster success: it's not just that one has to speak English in English-speaking countries in order to be successful, it's that the drive to succeed is *intrinsically* bound up with English-speaking culture. Such an argument was made in 2004 by the late Samuel P. Huntington in his book *Who Are We?* He worried that waves of immigration from Latin American countries would lead to a cultural rift in American society, with the Latinate hunk of the population gaining enough mass to uphold its own norms. Large numbers of Spanish-speaking immigrants, he warned, would inevitably swerve away from American values of individualism, ambition, and work. His belief in the monogamous marriage between American culture and the English language is carved into the following lines of his book, provocative enough to have earned widespread quoting: "There is no Americano dream. There is only the American dream created by an Anglo-American society. Mexican-Americans will share in that dream and in that society only if they dream in English."[1]

Huntington's claim feels deeply familiar to me, even though I've heard very few people willing to state it so baldly. It feels familiar because there is no doubt that I've absorbed it into my psychic bloodstream. For as long as I can remember, all my plans, ambitions, and goals were dreamed up in English. It never occurred to me that they could be dreamed in any other language.

I hear echoes—or perhaps the consequences—of Huntington's claim in the autobiography *Hunger of Memory,* written by Richard Rodriguez, a son of working-class Mexicans who immigrated to the United States. Rodriguez's tale is a searing, aching tale of the chasm between his two languages. For him, Spanish was the tender language of family closeness. He also describes it as a language of "extreme public alienation." Like me, he grew up steeped in awareness that the language spoken at home was not one that was spoken out in public. This knowledge suffused his home language with the glow of intimacy. He recounts how, when his parents spoke to him in Spanish, "those sounds said: *I am addressing you in words I never use with* los gringos. *I recognize you as someone special, close, like no one outside. You belong with us. In the family.*"[2] But Rodriguez's early language memories are tinged with something darker than simple nostalgia: "Plainly, it is not healthy to hear such sounds so often. It is not healthy to distinguish public words from private sounds so easily. I remained cloistered by sounds, timid and shy in public, too dependent on voices at home."[3] When language divides the space between family and the rest of the world, he suggests, it is dangerous to become too attached to one's mother tongue. It places limits on one's dreams.

Rodriguez ultimately became a controversial opponent of bilingual education, arguing that children from linguistic minorities are socially disadvantaged when their parents or teachers fail to nudge them into English as early as possible in their schooling. He declares that what he most needed to learn in school was that he "had the right—and the obligation—to speak the public language of *los gringos.*"[4] As a Mexican-American child who spoke Spanish at home, he felt at first that he was entitled to speak only his private language, that participation in the larger Anglo-American world was closed off to him. His teachers, who clearly did not feel this way, were so concerned about his progress in English that they visited his parents and suggested it would be in their children's interest if the family spoke only English at home. His parents acquiesced. This was the end of the family's intimate language. On one occasion soon after, the young Richard stumbled into a room where his parents were speaking in Spanish to each other; upon his entry, they switched to English. In that instant, he felt the shock of estrangement: "Those gringo sounds they uttered startled me. Pushed me away. In that moment of trivial misunderstanding and profound insight, I felt my throat twisted by unsounded grief. I turned quickly and left the room. But I had nowhere to escape to with Spanish. (The spell was broken.) My brother and sister were speaking English in another part of the house."[5]

As the children's mastery of English outran their parents' ability to speak it, communication between the generations sputtered rather than flowed. The parents would ask the children to speak slowly, to repeat themselves, and still, they often misunderstood. Fewer and fewer words passed between parents and children—a situation that plunged his mother into anxiety and his father into a resigned, silent withdrawal. But his father was not shy, notes Rodriguez, something he only realized by observing him speaking in Spanish with his relatives. When he spoke in Spanish, "he was quickly effusive. Especially when talking to other men, his voice would spark, flicker, flare alive with sounds. In Spanish, he expressed ideas and feelings he rarely revealed in English. With firm Spanish sounds, he conveyed confidence and authority English would never allow him."[6]

For Rodriguez, the loss of the family language along with its cocooning intimacy was an unavoidable price to pay, albeit a painful one, for engagement with the English-speaking world. He insists that his teachers were right to pry him away from the security of Spanish, that his success at school—and ultimately in life—might have been compromised had he been allowed to spend more time in the comfort of his family language. Nonetheless, he also describes how, in coming to speak English with ease, he felt almost as if he had betrayed his family, as if he were responsible for shattering a family bond.

There it is, the perennial immigrant equation: the sacrifice of the private language for admission to the public sphere; the betrayal of the family traded for acceptance by society.

For Lily Wong Fillmore, a linguist whose research has focused on second language learning, this equation demands that immigrant families pay too heavy a price. In a paper she published in 1991, she cautioned against the well-intentioned practice of submerging immigrant and Native American children into English at too young an age.[7] Summarizing the results of detailed interviews with about one thousand minority-language families in the United States, she noted that children who attended preschool programs in English quickly lost the ability to speak their heritage language. Early immersion in English, she argued, interfered with the development of the more fragile minority language, rather than the other way around. And the effects of this immersion rippled throughout the family: when pre-schoolers were enrolled in English programs, their families were almost five times as likely to turn away from their home languages in favor of English—despite the fact that a great majority of these parents could barely speak English. Early schooling in English, argued Wong Fillmore, was accelerating the assimilation of immigrant children into the dominant language, with a swift shedding of their heritage language. While such an outcome might seem desirable, she warned that the loss of a fully bilingual generation in immigrant families, a generation that could serve as a bridge between its older and younger members, could have dire consequences for family dynamics.

As in Richard Rodriguez's home, an abrupt turn away from the family language creates a rupture in communication between children and parents. Generations become incomprehensible to each other. Wong Fillmore relates the experiences of a Korean family in which the children had been taken into protective custody when school staff discovered bruises on their bodies. The children in this family had stopped speaking Korean at home, even though the parents could speak very little English. A crisis erupted when their grandfather came to visit from Korea. Because the grandfather could not speak English at all, the children were ordered to speak Korean to him. They did the best they could, but, as is so often the case with those who stop using their native tongue before it has fully set, they struggled with nuances. In particular, they no longer controlled the intricate honorific markings in the Korean language, a system that enfolds politeness and respect into its grammar. Certain grammatical forms *must* be used, even in casual speech, when speaking with someone who is of a higher social rank or even a person just slightly older than oneself. These honorific markers are braided into many components of each sentence: they affect the forms of pronouns, nouns, and verbs; certain honorific suffixes may need to be attached to subjects or objects of a sentence; other honorific markers may be required at the end of the sentence. When the children attempted to speak Korean, it was clear that this intricate system had begun to crumble, just as my own control over Czech's byzantine case system eroded through disuse. But to the Korean grandfather, the children's grammatical errors were not just symptoms of language neglect; they were evidence of profound disrespect and incompetent child-rearing. As Wong Fillmore concludes, "He did what the situation called for: He scolded his son—the children's father—for not having trained his children properly. The father did what the situation required of him: He punished the children—with a stick—for their rudeness and disrespect."[8]

When early mastery of English leads to a fraying of the relationship between parents and children, children may succeed in the school curriculum, but their success comes at the cost of the "home curriculum," as Wong Fillmore calls it. When children and parents live together but don't feel at home in a common language, parents can't impart life lessons, offer consolation, or even understand the details of their children's problems and struggles. When parents speak a stilted tongue, their children have trouble seeing them as competent adults worthy of respect and authority, or even as individuals with complex thoughts and feelings. How can parents be their children's parents when a barrier of language has been erected?

Many immigrants, including my own mother and father, make the decision to move to a new home not for themselves but out of dreams for a better future for their children. But in reaching for that future, they sometimes strike a devil's bargain (perhaps without foreseeing the consequences) in which they lose their children in exchange for that dream. Some parents, faced with extreme circumstances, are left with few alternatives but to put their children on a boat to sail away from them forever. Families who are able to stay together still face another form of real and permanent separation: to capture their dream, parents set their children adrift on a sea of English, as Jamie Ford so poignantly captures in this passage from his novel *Hotel on the Corner of Bitter and Sweet*:

> Young Henry Lee stopped talking to his parents when he was twelve years old. Not because of some silly childhood tantrum, but because they asked him to. That was how it felt anyway. They asked—no, told—him to stop speaking their native Chinese. It was 1942, and they were desperate for him to learn English.
>
> "No more. Only speak your American." The words came out in Chinglish.
>
> "I don't understand" Henry said in English.
>
> "Hah?" his father asked.
>
> Since Henry couldn't ask in Cantonese and his parents barely understood English, he dropped the matter, grabbed his lunch and book bag and headed down the stairs and out into the salty fishy air of Seattle's Chinatown.[9]

As a child, I shared Rodriguez's awareness of the schism between public and private languages, but I, for my part, needed no additional nudging to claim English for myself. From the moment I could form words in it, I felt I had as much right to this public language as anyone else. Perhaps by virtue of my earlier exposure to four other languages, I held the arrogant belief that *all* languages were mine to speak.

Nor did I immediately feel the loss of the family language, so eager was I to swim in the open water of Anglophone aspiration. It was my parents, and especially my father, who tried to resist our linguistic assimilation, unlike the parents of Richard Rodriguez and Henry Lee, who aided and abetted their language loss. But the current of

English proved too strong to swim against. In fact, language loss among most immigrants seems to be an almost unstoppable force, with only slight variations in the lifespans of heritage languages within immigrant families.

Samuel P. Huntington argued that this is not the case for present-day America. Unlike previous generations of immigrants, he claimed, the influx of Latin American immigrants currently arriving in the United States resists dissolving into the mainstream—they are more likely to live in enclaves, less likely to marry outsiders, and they hold on more tightly to their language. As a result, he worried, the cultural and linguistic unity of America is in danger, and along with it, the ambition and drive that has propelled the country forward.

Anxieties over the loss of America's linguistic identity are not always proportional to the realities, to put it mildly. As far back as 1751, Benjamin Franklin fretted that German immigrants in Pennsylvania "will shortly be so numerous as to Germanize us instead of us Anglifying them, and will never adopt our Language or Customs, any more than they can acquire our complexions."[10] Clearly, Americans of German origin who arrived in Franklin's time have thoroughly blended into the American background—language, customs, complexions, and all.

But it's reasonable to ask whether recent changes in immigration patterns in the United States might leave a lasting linguistic legacy. Since the passage of the Immigration and Nationality Act of 1965, which removed many restrictions on immigration, the percentage of foreign-born people in the United States has swelled; it rose from 5 percent in 1965 to 14 percent in 2015.[11] And it has completely redrawn the ethnic profile of the country, with people of Asian and especially of Latin American origin claiming a much larger share of the population than before. The number of Spanish speakers living in the United States now exceeds the entire population of Canada.

Whenever Huntington's fears are answered with hard numbers, however, it appears that Anglification continues to thrive, even in the face of these demographic shifts. Study after study reveals the formidable forces of linguistic assimilation. In a 2007 report prepared for a subcommittee of the US House of Representatives, Rubén Rumbaut summarized the most convincing evidence of continued absorption into English, drawing on data from the US census as well as from two studies that surveyed thousands of young people from immigrant families living in Southern California or South Florida, areas that are home to some of the thickest concentrations of Spanish-speaking immigrants.[12]

It is certainly true that more people living in the United States report speaking a language other than English at home (possibly in addition to English) than they did in the past—census data show that between 1980 and 2010, this figure rose from 11 percent of the population to 20 percent.[13] So there is indeed evidence for a sizeable and growing minority who are not monolingual English speakers. And it is indeed the case that Spanish speakers vastly outnumber speakers of other non-English languages—of the 59 million who spoke a foreign language at home in 2010, almost 37 million spoke Spanish, with the remaining 22 million scattered among all the other languages (Chinese—a category that actually encompasses several distinct languages—came second at fewer than 3 million). Spanish speakers cluster in certain areas along the Mexican border and in large cities such as Chicago, Miami, and New York. Thus, while the majority of US counties are overwhelmingly monolingual, with the vast majority of the population speaking *only* English at home, some areas are awash in bilingual speakers. In Miami, El Paso, and Elizabeth, New Jersey (across the Hudson River from New York City), more than two-thirds of the population is bilingual.

In these areas, children from Spanish-speaking families do not feel the stark separation of private and public languages that I or Richard Rodriguez grew up with. In cities like Los Angeles or Miami, for example, Spanish is certainly not confined to the home. It spills out into the streets, where it overlaps and mixes with English. It is heard on television, seen on store signs, and it is the language of choice in many business settings—and not just in small shops, but in banks and office towers, spoken by some of the community's most successful members. It is precisely these displays of Spanish as a public language that provoke the anxieties of monolingual English speakers, who feel at a rare disadvantage compared to bilingual residents. At regular intervals, news articles appear, asserting that English is now superfluous in places such as Miami, and that linguistic alienation is driving scores of Anglos out of the city.[14] As far back as 1983, Thomas B. Morgan wrote an article for *Esquire* magazine titled "The Latinization of America." In an issue devoted to "tales of America in crisis," he asked his readers, "What does it mean when you walk the streets of your own country and don't understand a word of the language?"—a question that is loaded with assumptions about who owns the country and the languages these rightful owners cannot speak.[15]

One might think that in areas where their native tongue is so heavily concentrated, immigrants would cling to their languages for generations. But Rumbaut's 2007 report found astonishingly little evidence for this. An immigrant language wanes and fades within a couple of generations, even in areas where many people speak it. Being born on American soil virtually guarantees linguistic allegiance to English; overall, only 9 percent of US-born people of immigrant ancestry speak a language other than English at home. And while the rate of language loss is somewhat slower among Spanish-speaking immigrants, particularly from Mexico, even Spanish as a heritage language flickers out and dies by the third generation. Rumbaut found that living in an intensely bilingual environment—those enclaves that Huntington worried about—did not prevent this. Even among immigrants living in San Diego and Los Angeles, two cities with some of the highest concentrations of Spanish speakers within the United States, Spanish did not persist. He found that, on average, Mexican immigrants no longer speak Spanish at home within two generations and are no longer competent in Spanish within about three. (Immigrants from the Philippines showed the fastest rate of language loss, shedding competence in their ancestral language of Tagalog in about a generation and a half.) Rumbaut concludes:

> To put it another way, the probability is 97% that the great-grandchildren of Mexican immigrants will not speak Spanish. With only three out of 100 persons of Mexican origin speaking Spanish after the third generation, the language is clearly on life support if not entirely dead. If the vast majority of Mexicans in Southern California cannot retain fluency in Spanish or a preference for its household use beyond the third generation, then its survival prospects elsewhere in the United States are probably equally dim. Contrary to Huntington's assertions, even the nation's largest Spanish speaking enclave, within a border region that historically belonged to Mexico, Spanish for all intents and purposes appears to be well on the way to a quiet natural death by the third generation of U.S. residence.[16]

It is interesting that Huntington was worried about Spanish-speaking immigrants *retaining* their heritage language rather than failing to learn English, as if one implied the other. On the latter score, Rumbaut found absolutely no reason to believe that new immigrants are deficient in English beyond the first generation. Among those who, like me, arrived in their adopted country before the age of six, a robust 97 percent preferred to speak English rather than the language of their birthplace. By the third generation, only 1 percent of Latin American immigrants preferred speaking Spanish to English.

In the end, there was little reason for Richard Rodriguez's teachers or parents to worry about his reluctance to speak English at school. Admittedly, all children are different, and the young Richard may have been unusually reticent. But it's doubtful that he would have avoided speaking English for very long, regardless of his home language. Once in school, immigrant children usually shift language preferences very quickly, pivoting away from their home language in favor of English. And it doesn't take long for them to perform better in English than in Spanish.[17]

Nonetheless, the challenges that immigrant children face in school are very real. Even though they quickly embrace the majority language, it still takes children from immigrant homes between four and six years to catch up to their monolingual English peers, and subtle differences may linger for even longer.[18] Early struggles in school could plausibly cripple a child's zeal for learning, erecting permanent barriers to achievement. But abandoning the family language is a poor prescription for an immigrant child's success in English. While the English skills of immigrant children do indeed depend on the richness of that language in their daily lives, several studies have shown that the English spoken by their *parents* often has little, if any, impact on the children's English proficiency, mainly because the quality of the parents' English is not very good.[19] To learn, children need to spend time with English that is more varied and complex than their own. Most immigrant families would be better off speaking their heritage language at home and enrolling their children in an after-school drama club or some other activity that is saturated with a richly textured English. Richard Rodriguez, as a self-described bookworm who devoured stacks of library books in his room, was guaranteed to learn more English than his parents could ever supply at home through their diligent but limping speech.

In short, it is the immigrant's language that is most likely to be drowned out by the mainstream language. Muting a heritage language at home may do little to nourish a child's competence in the majority language, but it very clearly starves the former. In 2013, a team of language researchers published a report, endorsed by the American Academy of Pediatrics, urging parents to *continue* using their native language at home, advice that is precisely the opposite of that given to the parents of Richard Rodriguez by his well-meaning teachers. To retain a heritage language, a child needs all the exposure he can possibly get to overcome its disadvantage in broader life. Children who grow up in households where conversation is shared equally between a minority and majority tongue are still more articulate in the majority language. Some researchers suggest that parents who truly want their children to master their heritage language need to show stalwart commitment to the enterprise: both parents, along with any siblings, must speak the language at home, books and media in that language should be abundantly available, and the parents may even need to become part-time language teachers to support their children's literacy in the language.[20] A tall order for any immigrant family, let alone those who are overwhelmed, as mine was, by the daily demands of survival and adaptation.

It's hard to avoid the heartbreaking conclusion that the Rodriguez family's abrupt shift into English at the cost of family intimacy was a needless sacrifice on the altar of success. Or of national unity, for that matter. When we see statistics showing a high concentration of Spanish speakers in certain areas, this does not reflect a stubborn resistance to English on the part of immigrants. Rather, the stable presence of the Spanish language is due to the regular inflow of new Spanish-speaking immigrants into these regions. If the demographic shifts we've seen in recent decades make it easier for Spanish-speaking immigrants to preserve their family language—along with the English they rapidly ingest—then it appears to do so only slightly, extending the life of a family language by no more than a generation or so. It seems that Mexican immigrants (along with all others) have well absorbed the lesson that "there is no Americano dream."

Heritage languages show no greater resilience in other Western nations. In France, where 90 percent of immigrants speak a language other than French, a complete linguistic turnabout is seen in the second generation: among immigrant children born on French soil, less than half grow up to speak a language other than French, and if they do, the heritage language is squeezed into very small spaces, restricted to conversations with parents or other older relatives. Even in the private space of home, French prevails; more than 80 percent of second-generation immigrants speak French at home with their partners, and a tiny proportion—5 percent—prefer speaking their heritage language to French.[21]

In Canada, multilingualism and multiculturalism are legally sanctioned, and immigration rates are about double those in the United States, but there, too, heritage language loss is almost universal within three generations. In fact, it is often compressed into two or fewer—immigrant kids who arrive in Canada before the age of ten are just as likely as their native-born peers to abandon their heritage language in favor of either English or French. A 2015 research study concluded that, without the institutional reinforcements that would allow a heritage language to be widely used in public spaces, its prognosis is grim; languages that are confined to private spheres cannot possibly survive beyond a generation or two.[22]

One way to understand why heritage languages do not linger very long within immigrant families is to read Richard Rodriguez's poignant memoir, in which the Americano dream is one that intertwines aspiration with loss. Here is another: ask an economist to predict the language patterns of immigrants, and you will hear the word *incentives* faster than you can get the question out. To a practitioner of what has been nicknamed "the dismal science," much of human behavior can be explained, predicted, or manipulated through a lucid accounting of costs and benefits, grounded in the assumption that humans are mostly rational creatures who try to make the best of the choices available to them. Dismally or not, the economists Barry Chiswick and Paul Miller have combed through data from many countries to answer this question: Is it worth it for immigrants to learn the dominant language of their country? They concluded that it is, even if you look solely at the monetary benefit (which is only one very crude measure of incentives). In the United States, the earnings of immigrants who are fluent in English are estimated to be about 15 percent higher than those of immigrants who have not mastered English. Across other countries—including Australia, Canada, Germany, Israel, Spain, and the United Kingdom—the increase in earnings associated with proficiency in the dominant language runs between 5 and 30 percent, with the smallest advantage being in Spain and the largest in Canada. In the dry, unadorned language of economists, Chiswick and Miller note:

> Is investment in destination language proficiency profitable for immigrants? Considering only the labor market impacts, a 15 percent increase in earnings per year from going from "not proficient" to "proficient" would imply a 30 percent rate of return on the investment if it involved a half of a year of full-time language training, a 15 percent rate of return if it required a full year, and a 7.5 percent rate of return if it required two full years. Even if it required two full years, this is a high rate of return on the investment. Yet, this computation does not take into account the consumption, social and civic benefits, or the lowering of the costs of other investments in human capital. Thus, it appears that the investment in destination language proficiency is a profitable investment for immigrants and for society.[23]

In other words, success speaks English—or whichever language is spoken by the majority in the new country.

Naturally, few immigrants are able to drop everything, sacrifice a paycheck, and show up, day in and day out, at language classes for two years or even six months, regardless of the favorable return on investment. Costs and opportunities must be factored in as well. To inject greater realism into their predictions about how proficient immigrants are likely to become, Chiswick and Miller developed a model in which the likelihood of becoming fluent in the dominant language is determined by three general variables: First, the amount of exposure to the dominant language that is easily available to the immigrant; second, a variable they called *efficiency,* which describes the ease of "converting" a person's exposure to the language into actual gains in proficiency—children, for example, have much higher efficiency than adults, soaking up the new language with greater ease; and third, the degree of incentive to learn the language.

They found that this simple model made a number of correct predictions. For example, they found that immigrants who lived in enclaves, which were tightly packed with their fellow countryfolk, tended to be, not surprisingly, less proficient in the language of their adopted country than those who circulated among neighbors who spoke only the dominant language. This is as expected, based on their model: exposure to the dominant language would be lower in the segregated immigrant neighborhoods, as would the incentive to learn the language—jobs might be available within the community even for those who spoke the dominant language poorly or not at all, thereby reducing the need to learn that language in order to survive.

Education and age of migration, both of which affect the efficiency variable—that is, how readily people can slurp up linguistic knowledge from the language available in their environment—are very obviously related to the ability to speak the destination language, as confirmed in the data collected by Chiswick and Miller. But another dimension that affects efficiency is how similar or different the destination language is from the immigrant's native tongue. It usually takes longer to learn a language that is very different from one's mother tongue; an immigrant whose native language is Norwegian typically finds it easier to learn English than an immigrant who speaks Polish, who in turn will find it easier than an immigrant who speaks Korean. Chiswick and Miller found that the greater the distance between the native language and the destination language, the lower the proficiency attained by first-generation immigrants. They also found that those who intended to stay in the new country for a prolonged period became more proficient than those who expected to return home after a shorter stay, presumably because they expected to reap a greater long-term return on their language learning investment, which again emphasizes the role incentives play in language learning.

A framework like this offers a neat structure for thinking about the dramatic shift in language that takes place between the first and second generations. Adult immigrants who aren't already proficient in the destination language often have to take up menial jobs where they don't have the opportunity to exercise their language skills and where they may not even interact with many people. I'm reminded of my father's first job driving a delivery truck for a bakery, or his later solitary job installing doors and windows into people's homes. My mother, who tended to the home and six children, had just as little exposure to English as he did. But we children were entirely submerged in English once we started attending school. Moreover, our efficient young brains could easily convert this wealth of exposure into language skills. As for incentives, what clearer message of English's return on investment could there possibly be than the view we had of the yawning gap between our parents' daily struggles to put food on the table and the opportunities and financial rewards reaped by our English-speaking teachers and our English-speaking friends' parents?

Richard Rodriguez also had a clear view of this language gap. He writes about the fatigue from physical labor that seeped into his father's body and made its home there, and how his mother was fired from the job she'd worked so hard to get—as a typist in a department of the California state government—when she made a mortifying error in typing up a letter to a Washington cabinet officer; while taking dictation, she heard the term "urban guerillas," but typed "gorillas." Like me and most of my siblings, Richard became a zealous student. As he went through school, he admits, he didn't want to simply *emulate* his fluent, educated teachers—he wanted to *be* them.

Immigrant children are aware, far more than children who are born into the majority group, of language and of the various doors it closes or opens, and this awareness can fire an intense ambition to master the language of success. These children have ample opportunity to see firsthand that when language skills open up educational opportunities for immigrants, the rewards can be especially abundant. In a 2004 study, Hoyt Bleakley and Aimee Chin analyzed the relationship between English language proficiency, education, and the earnings of immigrants who had arrived in the United States between birth and 17 years of age. They predicted that those who were youngest when they immigrated would have absorbed more English than older arrivals, and that their earnings would reflect this. Indeed, they found that immigrants who arrived in the United States after the age of ten suffered a drop in English proficiency for every additional year of age upon arrival, providing yet more evidence for the hurdles that are strewn in the paths of those who try to learn a new language after puberty. These older arrivals also had much lower earnings: participants who described themselves as speaking English "poorly" earned 33 percent less than those who described themselves as speaking "well" and 67 percent less than those who spoke "very well." In this last group, it was clear that language had been the key that opened doors to higher education and subsequent wealth; almost all of the difference in earnings could be attributed to the level of education that was attained by the immigrants, with those arriving earlier in their lives soaring to greater educational heights than those who arrived as adolescents.[24] Data like these suggest that it is not a lack of incentives—much less ambition or desire—that impedes first-generation immigrants from mastering the dominant language and tasting its attendant fruits of success and prosperity; rather, it is the costs that biology has inflicted upon them.

Rodriguez, who completed his undergraduate degree at Stanford and his master's degree at Columbia, and then pursued a doctorate in English Literature, has little patience for those who fail to understand the urgency of English acquisition for immigrants. He rails against advocates of bilingual education, who, in his view, want to remind immigrant children of their difference and who take for granted their own comfortable place in that same society. Dipping his pen into blistering sarcasm, he writes: "Those middle-class ethnics who scorn assimilation seem to me filled with decadent self-pity, obsessed by the burden of public life. Dangerously, they romanticize separateness and they trivialize the dilemma of the socially disadvantaged."[25]

But Nancy Dorian, a linguist who has written extensively about endangered languages and language loss, is somewhat less contemptuous of "those middle-class ethnics." She admits that those who express a desire to connect with (and preserve) their ancestral tongue often belong to the third generation of immigrants, whose experiences are very different from that of the first or second generation. The second generation—particularly those who grew up under circumstances similar to Rodriguez's in the latter part of the twentieth century—saw and felt, at close range, the stigma that stained their mother tongue. They were busy scrabbling for a better life they believed could only be achieved by abandoning this tainted language and becoming indistinguishable from the rest of society. Members of the third generation have historically been the first to be secure in their social position; not feeling the hot breath of poverty and marginalization on the backs of their necks, they yearn for the heritage they have lost. It is true that they don't feel the same pressures their parents did to assimilate. But it is also true that, bereft of their parents' and grandparents' language, they have lost something that is worth mourning. This mourning "is so widespread and recurrent a response to ancestral language loss as to be something of a cliché among immigrant-descended groups," writes Dorian.[26]

I question Rodriguez's conclusion about the extent to which retaining his Spanish language might have hindered his success in life. But I do share his memories of an urgent, ever-pulsing drive toward

English. As a result, my own children fit the third-generation cliché as much as Rodriguez and I exemplify the stereotype of the second generation. My children have no memories of anything but a middle-class life and professional parents. They were spared bearing witness to their parents' mind-numbing exhaustion or their frantic calculations at the grocery store cash register. As adults, they have expressed regret at not knowing Czech. When we visit the Czech Republic together, their Slavic heritage is as inaccessible to them as it is to any Anglo kid whose ancestors arrived in North America many generations ago. They experience no resonance to the language, no sense of recognition of any of that country's songs or stories, no odd feeling of being home.

At these times, I feel as culturally disconnected from my children as I do from my parents.

Winds of change have been howling, ever harder since the time I stepped off an airplane as a bewildered four-year-old into my new North American life. Increasingly, the forces of globalization are reshaping the narrative of immigration that has dominated much of the twentieth century, in which newcomers trade their languages and identities for the gleaming opportunities that await them in their new home. The incentives described by economists are real, but they are depicted in broad brushstrokes that smudge the details of the realities facing many recent newcomers. These days, the immigrant equation no longer looks like a fixed, immutable law of nature, and immigrants' relationships with their ancestral languages are more complicated and more varied than they used to be.

According to Huntington, the story is changing because mass migration is allowing immigrants—particularly those from Latin America—to import their own culture and language rather than adapting to Anglo-American ways and melting into the mainstream. But the true story is far more subtle and complex than this. If the immigrant equation has begun to unravel, it's not just a result of the recent surges of migration or the greater ease of maintaining contact with the ancestral home and culture. It is also because, more and more, the implicit contract between newcomer and adoptive home is being shredded.

In the 1970s, my father, with his halting English and limited formal education, was able to provide a measure of stability for his children, attaining a steady foothold on the socioeconomic ladder. Our family could eventually afford to buy a modest house in a quiet neighborhood, and, through a combination of scrimping and scholarship, we were even able to attend private high schools where we co-mingled (though not always happily) with more affluent peers. But the economies of Western nations have changed dramatically since then, particularly in the United States. The bulging middle class was once ample enough and open enough to welcome newcomers who arrived with a wide range of linguistic and job-related skills, but as the manufacturing sector has either shrunk or moved elsewhere, many countries are moving in the direction of an hourglass-shaped economy; there's a growing chasm between labor-intensive, low-paying jobs that demand little in the way of education, and knowledge-intensive, well-paying jobs that require many years of formal schooling.[27] (This trend toward increased job polarization, in which the economy is becoming concentrated into either very high-level or very low-level jobs, has been noted particularly for the United States, but it is also evident in Europe, as are striking regional and local inequalities.[28]) Immigrant families who are absorbed into the lowest tiers of the economy risk becoming trapped there, regardless of how well or how quickly they assimilate. In fact, their children do assimilate, but given that they are often forced to settle in neighborhoods that are dangerous, unstable, and saddled with inferior schools, what they assimilate into is not an upwardly mobile middle class, but a slice of society that has been disenfranchised and demoralized for generations.

At the same time, some immigrants glide directly into the upper tiers of the economy—more than ever, the universities, hospitals, and high-tech companies of many nations are staffed by highly educated foreigners who speak the local language with a marked accent. (In European countries where English is the main language used in universities or certain companies, they may not speak the local language much at all.) Their children have immediate access to a profusion of opportunities, and they may not see their parents' language as an impediment that needs to be shed as quickly as possible.

In an economy where learning the majority language is no guarantee of success, and where social mobility depends less on how quickly immigrants adapt than on what their starting point was when they arrived, the incentives to assimilate are not evenly distributed. In fact, sociologists Min Zhou and Carl Bankston have argued that under certain circumstances, immigrants are best served by *resisting* assimilation—that is, by retaining their heritage languages and maintaining tight networks of fellow ethnics.[29] This can apply at both ends of the socioeconomic spectrum. For those who are shut out of most decent jobs—and all the more so if their legal status is tenuous— ethnic networks can be a lifeline, providing work as well as financial and social support when needed. Moreover, nurturing a distinct ethnic identity can help immigrant kids resist the allure of an alienated youth culture that often surrounds them. Thus, what Huntington saw as an unwillingness by Mexican immigrants to adapt to American norms may in fact be a rational survival strategy for people who confront a withholding economy; it is precisely their children who are most likely to experience downward social mobility and face "generations of exclusion" from mainstream society.[30]

In contrast, children of high-achieving immigrants who are recruited into plum jobs may circulate within a social universe where members of their ethnic group have higher incomes and better educations than the average native-born citizen. This is particularly true of Chinese-Americans or Indian-Americans, whose parents are especially likely to arrive in the United States as highly educated professionals, on work visas that are arranged for them by their employers.

Zhou and Bankston note that second-generation immigrants from Asia are especially likely to look for role models among their own ethnic group—and with good reason. For them, success often speaks Mandarin or Cantonese or Urdu, in addition to English.

In Huntington's world view, the degree to which immigrants do well depends to a large extent on whether their heritage culture is compatible with the mainstream culture of their adoptive home. It might be tempting to reach for this as an explanation for why certain ethnic groups fare so well or so poorly within a single country. But this view fails to acknowledge the role of the host country in driving such disparities, or the cultural malleability of immigrants who must forge a life in whatever circumstances are available to them. Increasingly, there is no single mainstream into which immigrants are funneled—rather, there are multiple streams that branch off, and many immigrants are carried along on one or another of these streams depending largely on where they entered into the flow.

Researchers have noted how immigrants from the same ethnic group often have very different outcomes depending on where they settle. For example, Maurice Crul found striking differences among first- and second-generation Turkish immigrants who settled in Stockholm compared with those who arrived in Berlin. In Stockholm, these newcomers enjoyed a clear upward trend in social mobility, making strong gains in income and education between the first and second generations, whereas the situation for their counterparts in Berlin stagnated or worsened.[31] Crul attributes the disparity largely to differences in the educational opportunities that were available to the two groups: in Berlin, most of the immigrant children were streamed into vocational education while most of those who arrived in Sweden followed an academic track that prepared them for higher education. Sweden offered better in-school support, which meant that their success in school was less reliant on their parents' limited ability to help them with their homework. Moreover, in Stockholm, unlike in Berlin, preschools were free and widely available, which meant not only that the immigrant children were able to attend them, but also that their mothers were far more likely to attend school themselves or hold down jobs.

As noted by Min Zhou and Carl Bankston, the old assimilation-in-exchange-for-success narrative has historically allowed many old-stock Americans to overcome their unease with newcomers. In large part, the story was an accurate description of the immigrant trajectory throughout much of the twentieth century: immigrants did indeed assimilate, and they did indeed, for the most part, succeed. But the story also fed the vision of America as a special land of opportunity—anyone could succeed as long as they laid down their cultural impediments and embraced American norms and ideals. It is a vision that has outrun the realities of migration. And if this narrative no longer describes today's realities, then it is perhaps time for host countries to question whether or not they can truly call themselves lands of opportunity.

As useful as it can be, looking at language solely through an economic prism can obscure the fact that immigrant children are avid traders in another currency, less easily quantified than annual earnings, that lends English its magnetic force. In the corners of the schoolyard, outside of the protective sphere of parents and teachers, they must face the childhood rites of social inclusion and exclusion. The social spoils never go to children whose English halts, trips, and stumbles off the tongue, or comes out with a malodorous accent.

We like to think that children are guileless innocents when it comes to social hierarchies, that they learn prejudice from their unenlightened parents and other adults. My social media feeds regularly feature adorable videos of children who are blind to social differences—such as the one of a White five-year-old who insisted on getting the same haircut as his Black friend of the same age, so that people wouldn't be able to tell them apart. But general claims of such innocence are misleading: although children do learn much from their adult role models about how to treat others, it's also true that from a very young age they show an instinct for sorting people into social categories. Perhaps this should come as no surprise, given that we humans are a hypersocial species, in which the success of an individual cannot be separated from the success of their group. A child who remains blind to social divisions that are deemed important by the adult world or who fails to gain acceptance by a group (with any luck, a group that is thriving) may be destined for a life of limits. It seems that children arrive in the world ready to navigate the social mazes of being human—psychologists are finding that while children may not be born with a fixed set of social biases, they do show, from a very young age, an eagerness to learn how their society is structured and stratified. They are drawn to people like themselves. They readily learn which characteristics—language, race, gender, or class—their society has elevated to social relevance. And they display a shocking readiness to absorb beliefs about various groups from others.

When it comes to race, for example, even tiny babies are not colorblind. Researchers observed that at just three months of age, both African and Caucasian babies preferred to look at faces from their own racial group. That is, Ethiopian babies gazed longer at African faces and Caucasian Israeli babies preferred Caucasian faces—but African Israeli babies, who were members of a racial minority, were equally interested in both types of faces, suggesting that even at this age, tiny humans' feel for racial differences hinges on their experience of them, and they recognize the importance of paying close attention to faces of the majority group.[32] Some of the consequences of doling out their attention in unequal ways are apparent; even three-month-old babies have trouble telling people apart if they are of a different race, showing an eerily adultlike propensity to visually merge "others" into an indistinguishable mass.[33]

At about a year of age, around the time the first recognizable words drop from their mouths, this perceptual awareness of differences begins to congeal into personal choice. Phyllis Katz, a developmental psychologist who studies attitudes toward race and gender, reports that one-year-old infants usually prefer a doll with the same racial characteristics as themselves, rejecting another that appears to be of a different race. By the time they are three years old, if they are shown photographs of people they've never met, they're more likely to choose those of their own race as candidates for friendship (though again, this preference tends to be weaker or absent for children who belong to a racial minority). And at the same age, many children express negative attitudes and stereotypes of other races. Katz describes showing one three-year-old White girl pictures of a White child and a Black child in various scenarios and probing her interpretation of them. Upon viewing a picture in which garbage was strewn all over the floor, the little girl asserted that it was the Black child who had thrown the garbage and would be reprimanded by the teacher, and, in another picture, that the Black child would lose at a game of checkers. When asked why, the girl stated simply, "Because she is Black." (Her mother, a self-described liberal, was aghast).[34] Katz notes that, by the age of five, about half of the children she studied voiced negative attitudes toward people of other races. Another study, based in Canada, reported anti-Black biases in *85 percent* of the White children who took part in the research, also at the innocent, guileless age of five.[35] So much for those adorable videos.

As much as children pay attention to race, they seem to pay even more attention to language. Katherine Kinzler and her colleagues found that, by five or six months of age, babies gazed longer at a person who spoke to them in their native language than at one who spoke in a foreign language. This bias even extended to *accent;* babies showed greater interest in a person who spoke their own language with a native-like accent than someone who spoke it with a foreign accent. At ten months of age, infants were more likely to choose a toy offered by a speaker of their own language rather than a toy offered by a foreign-language speaker; again, this bias extended to favor someone who spoke with a native-like accent over someone who spoke with a foreign accent. And at the age of five, when American kindergarteners were asked to choose prospective friends based on photos and voice recordings of other children, the young research participants picked the children who spoke English with a native-like accent over those who spoke a foreign language or even an English flavored with a foreign accent.[36] In fact, children's language biases trumped their race-based biases: English-speaking American five-year-olds favored a child of a different race but who spoke native-like English over a child of the same race who spoke foreign-accented English.[37]

For many young children, language carves up social categories even more decisively than does race—in fact, small children seem to view language, even more than race, as part of the *essence* of a person, as something that defines them in an immutable, permanent manner. One study found that five-year-olds believed that an adopted child would grow up to speak the language of the birth parents and not the adoptive parents.[38] In another, children deemed language to be more unchangeable than race.[39] These young participants saw a photo of a child and heard a voice recording that supposedly belonged to that child. They then had to choose which of two adult faces accompanied by voice recordings represented the grown-up version of that child. The adults were depicted as either being of a different race or speaking a different language than the child—forcing the participants, for example, to decide whether a White boy who spoke English would grow up to be a Black English-speaking man or a White French-speaking man. The participants, who were mostly White American five- and six-year-olds, found it easier to believe that a person would grow up to be of a different race than that he or she would grow up to speak a different language. By the age of nine or ten, children's responses more closely resembled those of adults: the fictional children in the study were deemed more likely to change language as adults than to change race. (Not surprisingly, children's own experiences with language and race can hasten a more realistic understanding of these social categories. For example, when Black five- and six-year-olds were tested, they realized, as did the older White children, that race is a more stable personal trait than language. And, in a separate study, a group of bilingual five- and six-year-olds understood that a person was more likely to grow up to speak a different language as an adult than to grow up to be of a different race—but only if the test used the same two languages the children themselves spoke.[40])

Some scholars have suggested that language is such a potent cue to group membership because for much of humanity's history it actually *was* one of the most reliable ways to tell if someone belonged to your group or not. Before the rise of farming or industry, people tended to live in small groups, with many more languages occupying a small region than we see today. Unless people travelled very far from their home communities, they might never in their life encounter someone with a different skin color or markedly different facial features than themselves. But they would certainly encounter people from other groups who spoke different languages. And, given how hard it is for adults or even teenagers to learn a second language and sound like a native speaker, it would be easy to identify someone who had learned your language but had not been raised in the community from childhood. Language was a reliable badge of the gradations of belonging.

There are many examples throughout history of language being used to target victims of genocide. The biblical story of the battle between Gilead and Ephraim, as recounted in the Book of Judges (and set down in written form about 550 BCE), provides a vivid account of the fatal consequences of speaking the wrong dialect of Hebrew:

> The Gileadites captured the fords of the Jordan opposite Ephraim. And it happened when *any of* the fugitives of Ephraim said, "Let me cross over," the men of Gilead would say to him,

"Are you an Ephraimite?" If he said, "No," then they would say to him, "Say now, 'Shibboleth.'" But he said, "Sibboleth," for he could not pronounce it correctly. Then they seized him and slew him at the fords of the Jordan. Thus there fell at that time 42,000 of Ephraim.[41]

There may be sound evolutionary reasons, then, for humans to be born with a wariness of those who speak differently. The behaviors that researchers see in their laboratories, as they study how children form social categories, may be echoes of very old ways of distinguishing between "us" and "them."

But mostly, when I read about these lab studies, it strikes me that they are like miniature models of schoolyard politics. Perhaps Richard Rodriguez's reticence at school came not just from believing that English didn't belong to him, but also from detecting that it was socially hazardous to speak it with an accent. He relates how proud he was to announce to his startled family that a teacher had praised him for losing all trace of a Spanish accent—certainly, I would have been proud to receive similar praise as a child. Perhaps one of the reasons my siblings and I brought English into our home so quickly was so that we could master it among ourselves, away from the judgmental ears of our peers at school. And it was readily apparent to us that simply knowing another language marked us as different from the other children. Even before we began to speak English at home with each other, we learned to avoid speaking Czech with each other at school. I remember learning this lesson from my older brother when, at the end of a school day, I caught sight of him among his friends and ran to him, greeting him in Czech. His friends demanded to know what language I was speaking, and my brother's response to me came in the frostiest English possible. Deeply wounded, I walked home alone, even though I had never before navigated the route on my own.

This story too has its correlates in the laboratory: In one version of the friend-choice study, monolingual children were more likely to pick a monolingual friend over a bilingual friend, avoiding those who spoke an unshared language even when they shared a common one. This was true regardless of whether the participants lived in the mostly monolingual community of Fayetteville, Arkansas, or the bilingual city of Montreal, where my own family lived, and where meeting people who speak more than one language is a daily occurrence.[42]

Children who are born into the dominant language anchor themselves firmly to their language, believing that language is a part of themselves that cannot change. This makes it all the more striking to see how readily minority-language children loosen their bonds to the language spoken at home and how they work to alter their own speech. Immigrant parents who speak to their children in English usually have a noticeable accent, as did my parents and those of Richard Rodriguez. Yet, even if that is the earliest form of language a child hears, she will not grow up to speak English with a foreign accent. From a very young age, she discerns the normative patterns of language in her culture and leans toward them and away from the sounds she hears at home. When psychologists in the United States tested the social preferences of five- to seven-year-old children raised in Korean-speaking households, they found that the children preferred peers who spoke English with an American accent over those who spoke English with a Korean accent, despite the homey familiarity of the Korean-tinged English.[43] Little wonder, then, that an immigrant child's own speech soon begins to resemble the speech of her most-valued peers.

More than my teachers, who reacted to our native language with polite neutrality, it was my peers who taught me to hide my knowledge of Czech. These early lessons shaped my sense of who I was, where I belonged, and which children were friendship material when it came time for me to choose my own companions. On Saturday mornings, my parents sent their three older children (my older brother, my sister, and me) to Czech language school, held in the basement of a mission house run by Czech Jesuit priests. The volunteer teachers were kind, I remember, and it was fun to learn to recite Czech poems and perform folk dances in colorful costumes. But I remember almost nothing of the roughly two dozen other Czech-speaking children who attended the school. I was not much interested in them. I recall thinking we had very little in common with each other.

What drives the monumental self-transformation of a child who is born into one language but forsakes it for another? The lines of inclusion and exclusion drawn by peers, who instinctively befriend children of the same social group, are probably not wholly responsible. Nor is the promise of faraway rewards in the form of future earnings. If language is so close to a person's essence, what could induce a child to so drastically alter the fabric of her nature?

Children may be predisposed to think of language as a way of carving up social groups, but these inclinations are surely reinforced by the role that language plays in undergirding the structures of power in their society. The French sociologist Pierre Bourdieu argued that language is not just a communicative tool, but also a system for dispensing symbolic profits in exchange for certain behaviors.[44] In any grouping of human beings, he maintained, there is a tendency for one kind of language to want to claim a monopoly over others, to want to be viewed as more legitimate, more authoritative, and more valuable. If you train to become a scientist, for example, you will need to learn a specific style of scientific writing—one that avoids, among other things, the use of contractions, the pronoun "I," emotional language, and personal anecdotes; if you fail to learn this style, you may find that editors of scientific journals don't want to publish your papers and your peers don't take you seriously. If you want to make a documentary film about a rural Appalachian community, speaking an Appalachian dialect may give you the social and moral authority to ask people to reveal their lives to you on camera—and it may earn you invitations to dinner.

In a grouping as large as a nation-state, a tremendous amount of social activity and effort go toward elevating one "standard" language or dialect over others. Certain forms are endorsed as "correct" or "appropriate" for public use while others are censored. In the United States, English is obviously the public language—but not just any variety of English. The Black dialect of English, known to linguists as African American Vernacular English (AAVE), is often stigmatized as a defective form of English and deemed unfit in the mouth of a national news anchor or a high school English teacher, as are dialects such as Appalachian English and Hawai'i Creole English. Even Americans whose speech is strongly flavored with a regional accent, whether it marks them as residents of Brooklyn, Boston, Pittsburgh, or Tennessee, can find themselves shut out of certain public roles simply because of the way they speak.

The choice of the particular "legitimate" form of language is not coincidental, nor does it have anything to do with the standard dialect being inherently more correct, logical, or beautiful than others. It owes its lofty status to one fact only: it is the language spoken by the most powerful members of the society. As Bourdieu points out, when French language standardization became a national preoccupation after the French Revolution, it was no accident that it was the language spoken by Parisian elites—and not by peasants in Provençal—that became the standard against which everyone's speech was measured. If language is erected as a prerequisite to power, why would the powerful put up any barrier other than the one they themselves are already able to clear?

In Bourdieu's view, all of us, not just minority-language children, are constantly remaking our language in order to reap the symbolic profits—social approval, status, prestige—of whichever environment we find ourselves a part of. Sometimes, these symbolic profits can be traded in for concrete profits in the form of well-paying jobs, or for access to education that will lead to such jobs. For those who are born lucky (such as children of middle-class parents who are native speakers of Californian English), the adjustments that will be required of them throughout their lives may be very slight. For others (the immigrant children, the speakers of Indigenous languages or nonstandard dialects), a great deal of self-transformation is needed if they hope to participate in spheres where the standard dialect holds a monopoly on legitimacy.

Signals about the kind of language that is considered legitimate become part of the ambient noise of a society. They come in all manner of forms: A teacher who marks certain grammatical forms as wrong. A person who cantankerously corrects her friend's use of "I could care less." A political leader who suggests a candidate seeking nomination would do better with accent-reduction training. The uneven portrayal of TV characters with and without foreign accents. A radio station that refuses to hire a young woman because she speaks in the style of voice known as "vocal fry," common among many younger speakers of English today. A journalist's sneer at a president's use of the word "nucular" instead of "nuclear." The question "Why can't they speak English?" uttered by someone who witnesses a family's use of their home language while riding the bus. An educated and articulate man claiming, with no trace of irony, that a certain dialect hurts his ears.

A person comes to instinctively know how a certain utterance, spoken in a certain language or style, will be received by whoever she is interacting with at any given moment. To the best of her ability, she will adjust her language accordingly.

When a form of language bursts into a sphere from which it was previously barred, this is always a sign of an underlying shift in power. This is why it can feel so threatening to those who already speak the standard language and so triumphant to speakers of the formerly illegitimate language. In Spain, where the Basque language had been suppressed during the long years of Franco's regime (1936–1975), radio and TV broadcasting in Basque only began in 1982, three years after the Basque region won the right to elect its own Parliament, enact its own laws, create its own police force, and make its own decisions about culture and education. The language found an eager audience among those previously starved of it; Basque TV programs were even watched by many people who admitted they couldn't understand the language very well.[45] I can imagine that simply *hearing* the Basque language on TV would feel liberating.

Liberated was how many Quebecers felt in 1968 when they watched the premiere of Michel Tremblay's play *Les Belles Soeurs,* a tragicomedy about a working-class woman who wins a sweepstakes. This play is famous for being the first in Quebec to dare to sully the stage with the variety of Quebec French spoken by the working-class majority at the time—in other words, to dare to portray its ordinary characters as speaking as they would ordinarily speak in their homes. Until the 1960s, Quebec was a constrained and stratified society. Education and health care were under the control of the Catholic Church, and most of its economic and political life was dominated by Anglophones and a small number of Francophone elites who differentiated themselves from the downtrodden masses by speaking a version of French they called "standard" or "international"—a variety more closely aligned with that spoken in France than the one that fell from the lips of their fellow Quebecers. The more widely spoken Quebec variety—pejoratively known as *joual* at the time, mimicking the way its speakers might casually pronounce the word *cheval* (horse)—was deemed too vulgar for spaces as culturally pure as theaters and universities. But by the time Michel Tremblay wrote his play in 1965, Quebec was in the throes of its Quiet Revolution, an upheaval that would dramatically reshuffle the power structures within the province, wresting control from the elites and the Catholic Church and elevating the prospects of the millions of *joual* speakers in the province. Not surprisingly, just as hearing this dialect in the theater felt empowering to many, it also felt shockingly inappropriate to others. The elites of the day savaged the play as a linguistic and moral degradation. No matter. Revolution was underway, and soon the Québécois dialect was heard all over the radio, in schools, on television, and even from the premier's podium, issuing from the chain-smoking, *joual*-slinging lips of Quebec nationalist leader René Lévesque. Far from being squelched by the critics, Tremblay's play came to be performed in many languages around the world, including Scots, German, Italian, Yiddish, and English, but never in "standard" French, which Tremblay explicitly forbade.[46]

Quebec was not alone in pushing against the authority of the Catholic Church in the 1960s. In 1964, the Church responded to the growing pressures upon it by decreeing that Catholics around the world could now hear the Mass spoken in their own languages rather than in Latin, a language that very few sitting in the pews could either speak or understand. This decision was part of the seismic set of reforms instituted by the Second Vatican Council, and it heralded a redrawing of the relationship between parish priests and their congregations.

I often wonder what it must have felt like to walk into a church one Sunday to hear your own language filling its airy space for the very first time. I imagine it might have been a bit like the feeling I had as I stood on the platform of that train station in Prague on my first visit back to my native country, hearing an official announcement in Czech over the loudspeaker: first, a jarring sense that this language was being uttered in the "wrong" place; and then a sense of wonder and exhilaration, that I was now in a place where this *was* the right place for Czech.

Judgments about the value of language carry as much force as they do because they are fused with judgments about the worth of the individuals who speak them. The steady drip of such attitudes fills the minds of those who speak low-value languages as well as those who can speak languages of the elite. It's not hard to find scientific demonstrations of their toxic power, many of which can be traced back to a now-classic study showing how stereotypes about a linguistic group can taint first impressions of a person, based solely on the language that comes out of that person's mouth. In 1960, eleven years before my family's arrival in Montreal, psychologist Wallace Lambert and his colleagues at McGill University published an experiment whose results revealed the depths to which the French language had been consigned to poor-cousin status in Quebec.[47] They found five perfectly bilingual speakers of English and French and recorded them reading short passages of text—direct translations of each other—in each language. The listeners, who were either Francophone or Anglophone college and university students, heard the recordings and were asked to imagine a set of personality traits that came through in the quality of the speakers' voices. They were falsely told (and apparently believed) that they would hear ten different speakers rather than five speakers who read in both French and English. The participants rated the English and French samples very differently, despite the fact that they were rating *the same speakers,* uttering *the same content.* Only the language differed between the two "groups" of speakers.

Not surprisingly, the English-speaking students favored the English voices. They imagined the English speakers to be taller, better-looking, and more ambitious, kind, and dependable than the French-speaking counterparts. The researchers were not at all surprised to find this, given the rampant anti-French bias among Anglophones at the time. What did surprise them, however, was that the French-speaking students also heard the English voices as more richly imbued with desirable traits than the French voices—in fact, the French-speaking listeners were even more generous than the English-speaking students in judging the English voices on qualities of leadership, intelligence, and self-confidence, and they were even *less* generous in judging the French voices on these traits, in addition to downgrading their fellow Francophones on their likely good looks, sense of humor, and sociability. This harsh judgment was all the more surprising given that the Francophone students claimed they preferred to socialize with French-speaking students.

The authors of the study found it worth noting that one of the French voice recordings represented a Parisian dialect, whereas the others were clearly identifiable as representing Québécois French. The former—that is, the speaker of the variety that in 1960 would have been granted a place on the stage and in news broadcasts—was judged more positively by both Anglophone and Francophone students than the other French recordings, reflecting the linguistic biases underlying the explosive reactions to the performance of Tremblay's *Les Belles Soeurs.*

This paper provided the template for many others; since then, dozens of similar studies have laid bare the impressions and stereotypes that have come to be stamped into particular languages. The experimental methods all follow the same general pattern: Participants hear or see recordings of people speaking a dominant language or dialect as well as recordings of people speaking a nonstandard language or dialect. Sometimes the speakers of both languages or dialects are the same, as in the Quebec study; sometimes the speakers in the two groups are different people, but closely matched in features such as age, gender, race, and appearance, if they are videotaped. Participants, often drawn from different linguistic groups themselves, rate their impressions of the speakers on a number of attributes.

These studies reveal the generous social dividends that are reaped by speakers of the standard language compared with those who speak other languages or varieties.[48] At times, the results vary in their details. In some cases, participants who speak the low-value language are less biased in their ratings than participants from the prestige-language group, but some prejudice against their own nonstandard language is usually firmly in place. While traits that are linked to professional success (intelligence, self-confidence, and so on) can almost always be heard in the voices of prestige-language speakers, sometimes speakers of the nonstandard languages score higher on traits that make for likeable friends or social acquaintances (warmth, kindness, and so on), especially to members of their own language group. And the chasm between perceptions of the elite language and its underprivileged counterparts is wider in some countries than in others. Studies conducted in the United States have shown that speakers of nonstandard accents, whether regional or foreign, are judged more harshly than in any other country where such studies have been conducted. (In a notable comparison, nonstandard English speakers in the United States were judged with twice the degree of bias that was documented in the allegedly accent-conscious United Kingdom.) But time and again, across many different language groups, in a variety of geographic locations, voices that do not sound like the voices of those in power are judged to belong to inferior human beings—even when, through the cunning manipulations of experimenters, the human beings speaking the disdained languages are actually identical to those speaking the language of power.

Such judgments are not privately tucked away. They leach into personal interactions, into hiring decisions, and into performance evaluations, and they are projected in vibrant color and in larger-than-life size onto the screens we watch for entertainment. TV and movie characters whose speech fails to meet the standard-language ideal often have moral and intellectual failings as well, their "flawed" language an aural embodiment of their personal shortcomings. Researchers who analyzed shows on primetime television found that characters who spoke with foreign or regional accents were grossly under-represented; when they did appear, they were portrayed as dumber, lazier, and uglier than characters who spoke standard American or British English.[49] Even Disney movies, which routinely pack the theaters with viewers who are barely out of diapers, are drenched with linguistic stereotypes. A content analysis revealed that Disney characters who spoke with a foreign accent were depicted as evil or undesirable more often than they were portrayed as good—by contrast, among those with American accents, good characters outnumbered the bad by four to one. And when foreign-accented characters aren't ethically compromised, they are apt to be stuck in small lives, with limited horizons: as amiable servants, shopkeepers, and support staff, rarely as the characters who seize the reins of opportunity and ride off to meet their glorious destiny.[50] On the silver screen, as in life, success—and beauty and goodness—speaks (standard) English.

For children who already speak the dominant language, school is a widening of the family circle, an expansion of the home culture. All of the sounds of home, the familiar songs and stories and sayings, can be heard at school. They are simply multiplied, refracted, enlarged. These children learn that their own language is alive in important books and in the mouths of famous men and women.

For children who arrive in the classroom with a different language or dialect, school is a remaking factory. They learn that school is the wrong place to speak the language they already have. In this lively and regimented building, they learn how to silence their at-home voice and how to manufacture a new one, an outside voice.

Because the dominant language is a public language and not just a private one, a school's mission is to teach children how to buff and polish that language for public consumption, how to wield it for maximum effect. Richard Rodriguez writes:

> I easily noted the difference between the classroom language and the language of home. At school, words were directed to a general audience of listeners. ("Boys and girls.") Words were meaningfully ordered. And the point was not self-expression alone but to make oneself understood by many others. The teacher quizzed: "Boys and girls, why do we use that word in this sentence? Could we think of a better word to use there? Would the sentence change its meaning if the words were differently arranged? And wasn't there a better way of saying much the same thing?"[51]

Such attention, bordering on devotional, is never lavished on the home language. Certainly, it could not be matched for me by those Saturday-morning Czech language lessons held in a church basement by a well-meaning but untrained and slightly ragged parent. I remember receiving a nickel for each vowel-less Czech word I could think of (*vlk, krk, prst,* etc.). I do not remember ever learning how to make a Czech sentence more powerful or more beautiful. I never learned to write a persuasive essay or a business letter in Czech. And though I learned to recite poems written by Czech writers, many of them dead, I was never taught that I could write my own poems in Czech or that there might ever be anyone to listen to them.

School, then, is a place where the relative value of languages can become etched into a child's psyche. Because it is the doorway through which one gains access to the upper tiers of a society, passing through it requires mastering the language of the powerful. By virtue of the school's central mission, which is to prepare children to succeed in the world at large, it also becomes a place that perpetuates a society's definition of *which language* is the most powerful.

Sometimes, this takes the form of an overt, violent struggle, as in the residential schools that forcibly remade the minds and languages of the Indigenous children of North America and Australia, or the Kenyan school at which Ngũgĩ wa Thiong'o witnessed the bloody whipping of a boy who persisted in speaking Gikuyu. At times, the legitimacy of one language over others is chiseled into legislation and policy, in wording that rationalizes its superiority. In a 2012 TV interview, Deputy Prime Minister Bülent Arinç justified the Turkish government's relegation of Kurdish to a subordinate position in Turkey's schools, wielding the cool blade of commonly held biases: "Would education in Kurdish be as effective as education in Turkish? Turkish is a language of civilization, but is Kurdish a language of civilization? Kurdish can become an elective course, but we cannot have Kurdish as the language of education from primary school to universities."[52]

The struggle for legitimacy is most pitched when another language is seen as nipping at the heels of the dominant one. An interesting battle over language has played out in the state of Hawaii, which is exuberantly multilingual, with a linguistic buffet of more than 130 languages, and where 25 percent of the population conduct their domestic lives in a language other than English.[53] Yet, in 1987, the state's board of education singled out *one* of these languages, tagging it for exclusion: it proposed banning Hawai'i Creole from all schools, whether in the classroom, cafeteria, gymnasium, or on the playground at recess. Hawai'i Creole refers to a dialect spoken by about half of Hawaii's heavily multilingual population. It arose historically as a *lingua franca* that stirred together English with elements of the native 'Olelo Hawai'i language and various Pacific Rim and Asian languages, resulting in distinct pronunciations and sentence structures. (It is sometimes referred to as *Pidgin,* though it is in reality a full-fledged language and not a simplified dialect.) Even though—or rather, precisely because—it is so widely spoken, it has a fraught relationship with standard American English, much like the one Québécois French has had with so-called standard or international French. Like Québécois French in the 1960s, it is concentrated among low-income and working-class people, and it has a history of being snubbed in prestigious spaces.

The proposed ban was never achieved, but it revealed the depths to which some held the language in contempt. In a survey conducted by a Honolulu newspaper, citizens who supported the proposal argued that Hawai'i Creole fostered illiteracy (despite the fact that a body of literature exists in that language), describing the language as a "lazy form of speech" and a tongue that promoted "backward thinking."[54]

Although Hawai'i Creole was never officially forbidden at school, its lowly status was readily absorbed by children. In fact, attending school likely strengthened biases against the language, argued Richard Day, who visited children in Honolulu schools to gauge their attitudes toward Hawai'i Creole and standard American English. In his study, which was published in 1980, Day found that children from an affluent neighborhood where most adults held professional jobs had a negative opinion of Hawai'i Creole by the time they entered kindergarten. This was true even though these children were no strangers to the language, speaking it regularly and proficiently with many of their friends. Nonetheless, the children asserted that Hawai'i Creole didn't sound as good as standard American English. The situation was slightly different at a school in a working-class neighborhood: here, the kindergarteners did not yet show a bias against Hawai'i Creole. But first-graders at the same school did. Within the space of one school year, children had learned that Hawai'i Creole, which they used more competently than standard English, was the inferior form of language.[55]

Within many educational systems, attitudes about nonstandard dialects are slowly changing; these dialects may now be acknowledged as alternative languages that happen to be spoken by a group of people who do not represent society's elites, rather than as languages that are defective or broken. More often now, teachers will assure children who were born into such dialects that there is nothing wrong with speaking that way among their friends, at home, or on the playground. But they emphasize that the students also need to learn another way of speaking and writing. In the classroom, among their elders, or when they apply for a job, they need to speak differently—and here, words like "properly" and "correctly" often sneak their way in.

I find it impossible to fault teachers who insist on teaching whatever language is considered to be the standard in their society. Children who do not master this language will inevitably find their lives hemmed in, regardless of whether such constraints are just or moral. But it is important to notice, I feel, that not *all* children who speak an alternative version of English will be required to learn a new way of speaking. Children who arrive in New York City from London, England, or from Sydney, Australia, will probably not be counseled by their teachers to adjust their language in order to succeed in life. Adults will probably find their speech charming rather than inadequate. *Their* alternative language is recognized more as a brother-language: different, but equal. No self-transformation will be necessary.

Parents who speak a stigmatized dialect are often faced with a cruel dilemma: they may feel that, in order to set their children on the road to success, they need to encourage them to emulate other adults, ones who do not resemble themselves, their parents, or their grandparents. This is a very unnatural thing for a parent to do. It runs against the instinct for continuity and connection that is inherent to the very process of having and raising children.

I found myself moved some time ago while watching a documentary film called *Code Switching,* which focuses on the ways in which Black people in the United States negotiate the differences in status between standard English and African American Vernacular English (AAVE). In the film, one Black man, an attorney who grew up speaking AAVE in a poor community of Richmond, Virginia, describes his growing awareness as a child that he needed to learn what was essentially a different language at school. Although he still speaks AAVE with ease, along with standard English, he has raised his own children to become monolingual speakers of the latter. In the film, he admits to spending $60,000 each year to send his four children to private schools where they learn a glossy version of standard English. When his children hear traces of AAVE in their father's speech, they correct him, which he claims to think is "cute." Jokingly, he says, "I'm like, you *ought* to be correcting me, because I'm paying enough for you to be correcting me even though you're in fourth grade." But then his face changes. The laughter leaves his eyes as he considers what they have lost in not speaking his native dialect. His own speech slides further and further toward AAVE as he muses, "They're not getting the benefit of the double language because they have been isolated with their education so they're not going to have that great benefit, I call it, because there's nothing more relaxing and fun than being around your boys, your fraternity brothers or whatever, and jus' drop it all. It's a cultural thing. You jus' feel like that you're able to jus' act Black for a lil' while. And ain't nothin' wrong with that." He continues, a touch defensively, "An' there *is* such a thing as acting Black, cuz I do it almos' every weeken'."[56]

My own experience at school was very different from that of children who come to school speaking AAVE or Hawai'i Creole or a foreign language that carries the weight of damaging stereotypes. Aside from the reactions of my peers to a language they perceived as alien, I felt no specific stigma attached to my home language. Czech was not seen by my teachers as a contaminant of my English. It was simply considered irrelevant. From my teachers' perspective, it was an invisible language, as if I'd arrived at school with no language at all. And as I progressed in my education, there was less and less to convince me of the importance of speaking it.

My family landed in Montreal in 1971, unaware that we'd arrived in the midst of a tectonic upheaval of power in Quebec (thankfully, a more peaceful version than the one we had fled in Czechoslovakia). It didn't take long, however, for the language tensions and debates between Montreal's English- and French-speaking populations to leak into our own lives. My brother began first grade immediately upon our arrival, attending school in English, a language he couldn't yet speak. The other children at school called him a "French frog," assuming he was a Francophone, and he was bullied by the French kids in our neighborhood because he went to an English school.

My parents' decision to send him to school in English rather than French seemed an obvious one: it was not yet clear where in Canada my father would find work, and English was the majority language of the rest of the country. Besides, life in English was seamless in Quebec at the time. There were good English schools and universities. One could easily navigate government and health services in English. And at least in Montreal, English was widely spoken in banks and shops, sometimes to the exclusion of French. Anglophones earned an average of 35 percent more than Francophones and 80 percent of employers were English-speaking.[57] The Canadian dream, just like its southern counterpart, was also an Anglo dream, and Francophones who wanted to pursue it were required to learn English, regardless of the bulk of their numbers in Quebec. In veering toward English rather than French, we were simply following a well-trodden path.

Had we arrived a few years later, our family's language trajectory might have turned out quite differently. Hoping to weaken the gravitational pull of English, the Quebec government passed a law in 1977 restricting access to English schools for children of new immigrants. By then, my older siblings and I had already begun school in English, so the law did not apply to us. Our younger siblings were permitted to follow suit, under the merciful logic that it made little sense to force immigrant families to cope with two different languages of instruction. Then in 1976, the nationalist Parti Québécois led by René Lévesque swept to electoral victory and, in its first legislative act, implemented a set of language laws known as Bill 101. These laws proclaimed French as the sole official language of the province's government and its courts, and they established French as the daily language of public life. Francophones were guaranteed the right to receive a broad range of services in French (with no such guarantees for English). Workers gained the right to speak French at their place of employment and could not be fired or demoted for being monolingual Francophones (again, no such guarantees for monolingual Anglophones). Customers could expect to be served in French. All outdoor signs were to be in French—a clause that was later amended to also allow other languages as long as they appeared in a font that was no larger than half the size of the French text.

Overnight, the French language had elbowed its way into the dreams of Quebecers. It was no longer possible to live a frictionless life without solid proficiency in French. In the wake of Bill 101, many businesses and hundreds of thousands of Anglophones—along with many immigrants who wanted to be able to educate their children in English—left the province for other parts of Canada. The country's economic center of gravity tilted from Montreal to Toronto. The English-language newspapers inside and outside of Quebec published accounts of clashes between business owners and Quebec's "language police" over signage.

Nonetheless, Bill 101 is widely lauded by many language policy experts; without these reforms, they argue, Quebec would have either separated from the rest of Canada under the momentum of Lévesque's nationalist party, or eventually become a Canadian version of Louisiana, with its French heritage swamped by the incursion of English waters. Even the advertisements and signs that make up the linguistic landscape, they suggest, have real effects on people's attitudes and choices about competing languages. Far from being empty gestures, they visibly embody the status of competing languages, advertising the symbolic profits that accrue to each language.

A 1997 study surveyed Francophone high school students in several Canadian provinces and found that the students' exposure to French through road signs, publicity flyers, government notices, and other sources had a dramatic effect on their perceptions of the status of French in their immediate environment. It also had a subtler but still noticeable effect on how frequently they reported using French themselves.[58] Elsewhere, similar observations have been noted. A 2005 study of Spanish-speaking high schoolers in California used the classic technique of asking listeners to imagine personalities attached to recorded voices; the stronger the presence of Spanish in the students' media landscape and physical space, the less likely they were to inflate their perceptions of native speakers of English in comparison with speakers who spoke English with a Spanish accent.[59]

Quebec's census data clearly reveal that Bill 101 has stalled and reversed the province's slide toward Anglicization.[60] Between 1972 and 2011, the percentage of Quebecers who spoke English as their mother tongue dropped from 13 percent to 8 percent. The percentage of native French speakers has remained about the same, dropping very slightly from 80 percent to 79 percent owing to the ever-greater inflow of immigrants who speak other languages. But most dramatic of all are the language choices of Quebecers who were not born into French. In 1972, just a year after we arrived and my brother started school, 85 percent of children known as Allophones (those whose native language is neither English nor French) attended school in English, as we did. By 2012, more than 81 percent of Allophone students attended *French* schools, the remainder qualifying for access to English schools because one or both of their parents were educated in English. Even many Anglophone families, who do qualify for access to English schools, choose to send their children to French schools because they recognize the economic and social penalties that come with not knowing French; such children represented 26 percent of Anglophones in 2012, compared with just 9 percent in 1972. And even when Anglophone parents send their children to English schools, most of them opt to enroll them in French immersion classes that are taught alongside the English classes in these schools. Anglophones, who several decades ago could remain comfortably monolingual despite their tiny numbers, are now overwhelmingly bilingual, and they have lost any income advantage they previously had over Francophones. The small number of people who speak only English (less than 5 percent of the population) is limited to elderly Anglophones who have remained in the province and newcomers who have not yet had the opportunity to learn French.

These statistics give the impression that a complete linguistic transfer of power in Quebec has been achieved. But a closer look at Quebec's still-unfolding story suggests that English does not yield its grip on symbolic power so easily, even in the face of a dramatic—and often traumatic—rewriting of language policy. Francophones still feel the pull of English, perhaps more strongly than ever: among Francophones, proficiency in English rose from 42 percent in 1991 to

48 percent in 2011, with most monolingual Francophones living outside of the city of Montreal. Young Francophones in particular are drawn to English. Despite being barred from English-language primary and secondary school, about a third of native French speakers who go to college choose to go to an English-language one (and almost all Anglophones do). And, while immigrant families overwhelmingly send their kids to French schools, they find English sufficiently attractive to learn it in addition to French, making it their *third* language. As a result, Montreal has the highest concentration of trilingual speakers in North America.

Most startling of all, perhaps, are the results of a study that hint at the difficulty of dislodging a prestige language from its pedestal, and indicate just how long attitudes toward languages can persist even after power dynamics have been transformed. This study, which repeated Lambert's classic 1960 study in 2007, also used recordings from the same speakers in both English and French to test people's attitudes toward these languages. Montreal students from all language groups—Anglophone, Francophone, and Allophone—still judged the English voices to belong to people who were more desirable on all ten traits that were measured.[61] Thirty years after Bill 101, with French firmly entrenched as the language of government and commerce, these students still judged voices in English to belong to people who were more intelligent, more ambitious, more highly educated, better leaders, more dependable, kinder, warmer, more likeable and sociable, and even possessing a better sense of humor than the same voices when they were speaking French.

If it has proven this hard to dispel the asymmetries in symbolic power between English and French in Quebec, I wonder, how could Spanish possibly displace English in the United States? And if this much legislation, infrastructure, and exertion is required in Quebec to bolster a language as powerful as French and keep it from sinking in the Anglophone ocean of North America, what hope is there for the smaller, much less powerful languages of Navajo, Tlingit, or

Stoney Nakoda? What would it take for such languages to be able to dream of survival—much less anything else—when the world around them speaks of success only in English?

I've lived my life keenly aware of its accidental nature, feeling that there is nothing inevitable about how it has unfurled. Like many immigrants, I've seen firsthand how the convulsions of history have a way of knocking a life off its tracks. The life that continues is a reckoning between personal choice and external stricture, and so many different turns are possible. I think often of the parallel lives I never lived—of the one in which my parents decided to hunker down under political oppression rather than flee their homeland, or the one in which they settled in Vienna or Italy instead of launching themselves across the ocean. I imagine too what life would have looked like—and who I would *be*—if they had raised their young family in the remote margins of Labrador, where my father was offered a job as a land surveyor, rather than in the urban hustle of a bilingual Montreal. Or if we had arrived in Montreal a few years later than we did.

If anything, the parallel lives of an immigrant child today have only proliferated. People from more and more countries are arriving in places that have rarely seen immigrants in the past, settling not just in the New Yorks or Londons or Montreals of the world, but in the rural towns and sprawling suburbs of many Western nations. And many find that several of their parallel strands crisscross occasionally or even braid together for periods of time. While some people are still prevented from returning to their original homes—whether because of war, documentation status, or financial constraints—many others travel back and forth to an extent that was unimaginable to me as a child. And more and more often, the newcomers are not committed to living out their lives in the host country, seeing these places less as adoptive homes than temporary residences. (This is the case particularly in Europe, where cross-border work is less impeded than elsewhere.) Even if immigrants do not travel physically back and forth, many aspects of living in more than one country at a time are available through modern technology—news, media, and online communities.

These developments are rewriting the language dynamics within many Western societies. Immigrant stories are less likely to have overlapping plot lines. I might have much less in common with Richard Rodriguez if we were both growing up today, and even less in common with the child of Czech academics teaching for a brief stint in the Swedish university town of Lund. National languages, once assumed to be the soul of a country, now share space with a great variety of other languages. Europe has embraced a new multilingual reality, expecting its children to learn not one but two languages in school in addition to their native tongue. It's had to cede much of its precious intellectual territory to English, increasingly the common language of the knowledge economy. And in a growing number of cities, in Europe and elsewhere, native speakers of the so-called mainstream language are in the minority, with no single ethnic or linguistic group forming a local majority.

Such conditions seem ripe for dramatic shifts in the balance between the various languages that mingle together within a society. They alter the social and economic incentives that draw speakers to them as well as the supports available for languages that are not spoken by the majority. It's too early to predict with any confidence which languages will or won't be spoken by tomorrow's second- or third-generation immigrants, but it will be especially interesting to see what happens in cities where a single minority language has gathered momentum. This has been the case in Vancouver, where about one-fifth of the current population is of Chinese ethnicity at a time when Chinese languages are gaining in global relevance and prestige.

Still, despite the fact that today's cities might look and sound unrecognizable to a resident just one generation ago, some researchers maintain that mainstream languages have a tenacity that persists well beyond their numerical supremacy—an assertion that seems supported by the lingering status bestowed upon English in Quebec. In Vancouver, sociolinguist Ai Mizuta has argued that beneath the rhetoric of Chinese ascendance, there is a bedrock of belief that promotes English as the sole language of the mainstream. For example, she has explored the consequences of a 2011 decision by the Vancouver School Board to open a dual-language Mandarin–English program but restrict admission to children whose primary language was English, under the rationale that children in a bilingual program might not acquire enough skills in English. Not only did this establish English as the indispensable language, it also had the effect of barring children whose parents were recent arrivals from China and spoke to their children in Chinese—a group that was *especially* invested, both personally and culturally, in maintaining the Chinese language skills of their offspring. Herself of Japanese heritage, Mizuta is firmly committed to raising her daughters in her native language, but she describes the subtle pressures that inhibit her from speaking Japanese to them in public. "I am conscious not only of being different," she writes, "but of how my difference might be perceived by the 'native-born' Canadians around me. I do not want people to think we are immigrants who have never learned English." When she finds herself in a shop where there is a group of international students speaking Japanese, Korean, or Mandarin, she is especially conscious of speaking English "rather loudly to show everyone that I am not like 'them.' It is even better if I have my own grocery bags to show that I not only speak English to my kids, but I am also environmentally conscious as a Vancouverite."[62] And, when one of her daughters wins a coveted lottery spot to attend one of the best schools in Vancouver, attended by children whose parents come from all over the world, she is greeted, at the entrance to the elegant, modern building, by a sign announcing: "At [this school], we speak English."[63]

In the United States, no city is in a better position to challenge the supremacy of English than Miami. Although a number of other American cities are also home to many Spanish speakers, Miami is unique in the degree to which Spanish is present in commerce and in the media. It was one of the first cities to receive large numbers of Spanish speakers, when scores of Cubans fled the Castro regime in the early 1960s. Unlike in many other areas of the country, where Spanish-speaking immigrants typically arrive with little in the way of education or financial resources, this wave of immigrants spanned the entire socioeconomic spectrum. Believing that Castro's rule would not last long, they quickly established Spanish-language communities—complete with schools, social clubs, banks, and trade associations—intended to sustain their lives in the United States until they were able to return home. These communities provided a firm foundation for later waves of Spanish-speaking immigrants.[64]

By 1987, the unique character of Miami was apparent to the writer Joan Didion, who observed:

> What was unusual about Spanish in Miami was not that it was so often spoken, but that it was so often heard: in, say, Los Angeles, Spanish remained a language only barely registered by the Anglo population, part of the ambient noise, the language spoken by the people who worked in the car wash and came to trim the trees and cleared the tables in restaurants. In Miami Spanish was spoken by the people who owned the cars and the trees, which made, on the socioauditory scale, a considerable difference. Exiles who felt isolated or declassed by language in New York or Los Angeles thrived in Miami. An entrepreneur who spoke no English could still, in Miami, buy, sell, negotiate, leverage assets, float bonds, and if he were so inclined, attend galas twice a week, in black tie.[65]

By 2010, almost two-thirds of Miami-Dade County identified as "Hispanic or Latino" in the census—a figure that reached 95 percent in some areas of the city. The majority of these residents were not born in the United States.[66] Today, Miami is considered a global Spanish-language hub, with a banking district that is referred to as the "Wall Street of Latin America," attracting investors from Argentina, Colombia, and Venezuela. It has also earned a reputation as the

"Hollywood of Latin America," a home to the largest US Spanish-language television networks, Univision and Telemundo, as well as a number of transnational media companies.[67]

It strikes me that a second-generation immigrant child with Latin American parents should have more hope of retaining fluency in her heritage language than just about any other child in North America. And yet, it's not clear that young people growing up in Miami today will pass their Spanish language on to their children in large numbers. In a study published in 2006, linguists found that although many Spanish-speaking families voiced a firm commitment to raise their children in Spanish, in reality, the amount of Spanish used in the home fell short of their intentions. Moreover, among young bilingual speakers—including those who had recently arrived in the country—conversation often veered into monolingual English.[68]

It appears that while diversity is often very visible on the surface, what is less apparent are the undercurrents that still pull language and culture in the direction of the dominant group. I am reminded of a time when I was out with some companions, enjoying a friend's performance with his band one evening at a café in downtown Calgary. After the band finished, we sat and talked as a new group took the stage and the audience in the café turned over to a younger crowd. Fully absorbed in our conversation—concerned about that day's new travel ban by then president Trump preventing some nonresidents from entering the United States—it was a while before we looked up and took stock of the new clientele. One of us remarked that we were now the only White people in the place. Another commented on the fact that it had taken us so long to register this, and how this implied that being among people of all races and ethnicities now felt so normal that it was almost beyond notice. But as we sat there, it took us even longer to register another fact, which I suppose felt even more normal: in this crowd of noisy, happy people, whose ancestors clearly came from all continents, the only language we heard was English.

Bundled up for a walk, my mother, siblings, and I *(second from right)* learn to love the bitter and beautiful Montreal winters.

Chapter 3

Duality

I remember the first time I became aware of a split vision, of being able to shift perspectives between Czech and Canadian cultures. I was nine years old, and it was Eastertime. Czechs have a rather singular Easter tradition whose origin is mysterious to me: it's customary for the boys and men to make whips out of willow twigs braided together and whip (usually gently!) all the girls and women they meet on Easter Monday. In return the girls give them colored eggs; if they have especially warm feelings toward the male at the operating end of the whip, they attach a festoon of ribbon onto the end of his instrument. In some villages, the females also get a proper drenching when buckets of cold water are thrown on them. In theory, this treatment is supposed to preserve female youth and beauty.

To an outsider, the symbolism of male sexual dominance and female submission sits right on the surface—how could one *possibly* miss it? But like the thumping of one's own pulse, this custom was so familiar to me and my family that its symbolism was invisible. It was, simply, part of life's rhythms, like preparing meals and harvesting vegetables. But I remember very clearly how, the year I turned nine, my father made the willow whip as usual, only to be confronted with the immovable refusal of his three daughters: "We're not doing that anymore, Dad." I was too young to be able to articulate any change in my views of the *meaning* behind the custom. But after living in Canada for several years, a different feeling had seeped into me and my sisters about the nature of a normal relationship between the sexes. All we knew was that our Easter tradition, which had once felt as natural as opening presents on Christmas, now felt deeply weird. My father, cowed, put the whip away.

Many years later, when I visited my father's family in his home village after his death, it was Eastertime, and I was confronted with the view from the other shore. Observing the whipping ritual, I unspooled my adult analysis of this custom for one of my female cousins, who reacted with knit-brow perplexity and suggested that I had been reading too much Freud. When I challenged her to explain the custom, she said, "What's to explain? It's just a nice custom." Yes, in years past, she admitted, the boys would sometimes get carried away, and some of the older women recalled having red welts all over their thighs and legs from overly zealous Eastertime whippings in their youth. But nowadays, the women were treated gently and respectfully. It was nice, she repeated. Later, I witnessed this same cousin receiving guests at her house and turning around at the door to present her buttocks to the visiting males for a gentle swat with the willow whip. When I stopped by the home of another cousin that afternoon, I was similarly swatted by all three of her teenaged sons, none of whom had met me before, but who addressed me deferentially with the formal *vy* rather than *ty,* both before and after my "whipping."

The ritual still felt strange. But it also felt—and this may be hard for a non-Czech to understand—a little *festive,* all the more so for being a bit bizarre. Throughout my visit to my father's village, I was constantly reminded of how my life has been defined by these swings of perspective, of the potential for the invisible and the unnoticed to appear deeply odd, even aberrant, when looked at from a different slant. Of the way that something mundane suddenly leaps into view and demands an explanation. I became aware of the flipping of my own perspectives, from Czech to North American and back again. After a while, it becomes possible to flip between viewpoints at will.

I am far from alone in this. There's a flash of recognition that often passes between those of us who were born on the shores of one world but have planted the leading foot onto the banks of another. What defines us better than the very state of straddling, of divided perception, regardless of which particular worlds bisect our consciousness? As a member of this club, this assembly of migrants, minorities, and other misfits, I immediately recognized the Vietnamese-American protagonist of Viet Thanh Nguyen's novel *The Sympathizer* as one of us, right from the opening lines:

> I am a spy, a sleeper, a spook, a man of two faces. Perhaps not surprisingly, I am also a man of two minds. I am not some misunderstood mutant from a comic book or a horror movie, although some have treated me as such. I am simply able to see any issue from both sides. Sometimes I flatter myself that this is a talent, and although it is admittedly one of a minor nature, it is perhaps also the sole talent I possess. At other times, when I reflect on how I cannot help but observe the world in such a fashion, I wonder if what I have should even be called talent. After all, a talent is something you use, not something that uses you.[1]

Nguyen builds his entire novel around this sense of duality. A bisected nature is the whole soul of the protagonist: Nguyen has imagined him as a product of the union between a Vietnamese woman and a French priest. He is raised in Vietnam but goes to college in the United States. He becomes a North Vietnamese mole embedded in the South Vietnamese army but harbors deep affection for the general and soldiers upon whom he is spying. During the fall of Saigon, he is ejected from Vietnam and sets up residence in Los Angeles, where he is hired as a consultant to provide a Vietnamese perspective during the filming of a

Hollywood movie about the Vietnam War. Even the novel's climax turns on double perspectives, when the protagonist finally grasps the second meaning of an ambiguous sentence.

Another member of the Split Selves Club, along with Nguyen and his two-faced protagonist, is Eva Hoffman, Polish émigrée and author of the memoir *Lost in Translation.* Hoffman's trajectory is eerily similar to my own. She and her family fled their native Eastern European country for Canada when Hoffman was an adolescent. Like me, she completed her education in the United States and launched her career there. Just as familiar to me as the details of her migration is the chronic sense of double vision she threads throughout her entire memoir. In one poignant passage, she describes her Polish and North American selves vying for influence over her major life decisions:

> Should you marry him? The question comes in English.
> Yes.
> Should you marry him? The question echoes in Polish.
> No.
> But I love him, I'm in love with him.
> Really? Really?[2]

Thus ensues a volley between her two halves, with her North American inner voice dwelling on her boyfriend's husbandly qualities and her Polish voice insisting that she feels no "creaturely warmth" for him, warning that ambivalent feelings are not a sign of maturity but a harbinger of impending dissatisfaction in love. Later, the whole dialogue reprises:

> Should you become a concert pianist? The question comes in
>   English.
> No, you mustn't. You can't.
> Should you become a pianist? The question echoes in Polish.

Yes, you must. At all costs.

The costs will be too high.

The costs don't matter. Music is what you're meant to do.

Don't be so dramatic. I can play for myself. For pleasure.[3]

And so it goes.

For those who experience themselves as divided, the separate selves are often anchored to separate languages, as they were for Eva Hoffman. Many people who speak more than one language express the feeling that they are somewhat different people in each of their languages—in fact, when researchers asked more than a thousand bilingual and multilingual people whether they felt this way, two-thirds of them replied that they did.[4]

But does this *feeling*, common as it is, translate into something more tangible? Do bilingual people really behave or respond differently when they are actually using their different languages, and do other people perceive them as different depending on which language they are speaking? And if so, what lies at the heart of this cleaving of the self?

Many bilingual people think of language as a portal into alternative ways of being. They feel that their separate languages are deeply embedded within separate systems of values, behaviors, and emotions—systems that are coherent and larger than the self, but that have somehow become internalized. If this is true, many questions arise: Is there something inherent about the languages themselves that molds their speakers, nudging them into different worldviews? Or is the language simply a container for all of the teachings and attitudes that have been conveyed by those speaking it? Or perhaps the connection between languages and ways of being is somewhat of an illusion—maybe people behave differently in their languages simply because their two language communities happen to have different customs and social norms? In that case, the link between language and the sense of self could be more or less accidental; after all, it's only natural to mirror the norms and expectations of the people around you, regardless of the language they speak. Even monolingual people can have very different experiences of themselves depending on their social surroundings; one can act coolly assertive with colleagues at work but dissolve into an emotional puddle at a family gathering.

The first step to probing these enigmatic experiences of bilinguals is to determine whether there is in fact some meaningful, nonaccidental link between languages and ways of being. To psychologists who are interested in these questions, it's important to extract bilingual people from their social milieu, place them in a more neutral setting, and see whether operating in one or the other language affects their behavior all on its own. One of the first psychologists to conduct such an experiment was Susan Ervin-Tripp, in a study carried out in 1954. Curious to see whether different manifestations of her bilingual subjects would emerge in each of their languages, she presented them with the kind of test they might encounter in a psychoanalyst's office. She had Japanese–English bilinguals complete the Thematic Apperception Test (TAT), in which participants are shown cards depicting scenes of people in ambiguous situations and are asked to spin stories that describe what is happening to the people in these scenes. Like other projective tests, such as the well-known Rorschach inkblot test, the TAT is meant to open a window onto the client's inner feelings and preoccupations. When responding to the TAT in Japanese, the participants created stories drenched in melodrama: people went mad with grief or sobbed over lost love. In English, the stories that were triggered by the same images were less emotional, revolving around a thieving hypnotist or a girl's attempt to complete a sewing project. The stories related in Japanese were preoccupied with family and romantic relationships, dwelling on themes of love, betrayal, and loss; in the cooler English stories, relationships were more distant, if present at all. A similar test of French–English bilinguals also revealed different themes depending on the language in which participants took the test; in French, people were more likely to tell stories in which characters were verbally aggressive to each other or turned their backs on someone after a disagreement.[5]

Since these early studies, some psychologists have tested bilinguals' responses on standardized personality tests, taking literally the recurring claim among bilinguals that they have different personalities in each of their languages. If bilinguals exhibit different personality traits depending on the language in which they take the test, this would be rather striking, because psychologists tend to think of personality, as least as measured by these standardized tests, as something fairly stable and not likely to change very much depending on context. But several studies, using a variety of different tests, suggest that perhaps we should take bilinguals at their word when they claim to have malleable, language-specific personalities.

In one such study, researchers chose a test, now widely used for measuring personality traits, known as the Big Five Inventory. This test groups items under just five dimensions, labeled *Agreeableness, Extraversion, Conscientiousness, Neuroticism,* and *Openness to Experience.*[6] An advantage of the Big Five test is that it is deemed appropriate for measuring stable personality traits across a number of different cultures. In this study, the authors wanted to do more than simply establish whether bilingual speakers of Spanish and English have split selves—that is, whether they respond differently depending on the language in which they take the test. They also wanted to know whether those divided selves resemble the personalities of monolingual Spanish speakers living in Mexico and monolingual English speakers living in the United States. When bilingual participants describe themselves in Spanish, do they do so in a way that resembles how average Mexicans describe themselves, and similarly, do their English-language personalities align more closely with the typical American profile?

Results from three separate groups of Spanish–English bilinguals, located in Texas, San Francisco, and Mexico, confirmed that their languages pulled them in different cultural directions. Monolingual Mexicans had lower scores than monolingual Americans on the dimensions of Agreeableness, Extraversion, and Conscientiousness, and higher scores on the dimension of Neuroticism. This pattern was mirrored by the bilinguals' responses: when they took the test in Spanish, they also scored lower on Agreeableness, Extraversion, and Conscientiousness and higher on Neuroticism than when they took the test in English.

But doesn't it go against the grain of cultural expectations that Mexicans (and bilingual speakers responding in Spanish) would score *lower* than Americans (and bilingual responders in English) on the traits of Extraversion and Agreeableness? Aren't Mexicans supposed to be famous for their warmth, sociability, and easygoing natures? The authors of the study were reassured by the symmetry between bilinguals' responses in their two languages and the responses of monolingual Mexicans and Americans, but they were also troubled by the overall slant of the results, which clashed with common notions of the cultural differences between these two groups. On closer inspection, the results related to Extraversion are perhaps less puzzling—a number of the items bundled under this label are more focused on assertiveness and dynamic social presentation than on a preference for social interaction over solitude, as the term is commonly understood. It's harder to explain away the scores on the Agreeableness dimension, though; here the test items really do seem to align with the Latin American notion of *simpatía,* probing for traits such as kindness, cooperation, avoidance of conflict, and politeness.

The authors argued, in a follow-up study, that the answer to the puzzle is buried in a paradox: at the heart of Latin American *simpatía* is the value of modesty—one is not supposed to blare one's own horn.[7] In fact, because *simpatía* is so culturally valued, a person *claiming* to be agreeable could be seen as rather arrogant—the last trait one should see in a person who is really and truly agreeable! Thus, any attempt to measure how agreeable people are by asking them to report their own degree of kindness or politeness is thwarted by the cultural definition of these traits and by their high value in Latin American society. To really get a sense of whether speakers of Spanish are more agreeable than speakers of English, argued the authors, we'd have to actually see how they interact with others, whether they are in fact more kind, pleasant, cooperative, and polite, and by extension, whether bilinguals who speak both languages behave differently in their two languages.

To test this, the authors recruited a group of Spanish–English bilinguals living in Texas to take part in two simple video interviews, one in English and one in Spanish. Because they wanted to test whether language alone could produce differences in behavior, they went to great lengths to scrub the experiment of other possible influences, which resulted in a rather antiseptic social interaction. Rather than engaging with a living, breathing person in the same room, the participants responded to questions posed by a videotaped interviewer, played back after the fact—the interviewers, speaking in either English or Spanish, had been coached to speak as neutrally and unemotionally as possible, to avoid any inadvertent differences between their presentation in the two languages that might bias the interviewees. The participants' responses were also recorded, and these videos were then watched by two sets of judges, one group from Mexico and one from Texas, who assessed the speakers' personalities using a checklist based on the test items for Agreeableness that are found in the Big Five Inventory. Since people's ratings of speakers' personalities are known to be biased by the particular language or dialect that is being spoken, the videos were played with the sound turned off, so that the judges had to rely on nonverbal cues to evaluate the personality of the speaker.

Admittedly, judges had limited information available to draw conclusions about the speaker's personality. But the tactic succeeded in purging the study of any language-related biases, as none of the judges guessed that the speakers in the videos were using different languages.

When told that the interviews varied between Spanish and English, the judges were unable to reliably discern which of the two was spoken in any given interview. Despite all the constraints imposed on the experimental procedure, the judges, whose ratings were quite consistent with each other, did in fact pick up on differences in the speakers' behavior based on the language in which the interview took place. The interviewees were judged as more agreeable when they spoke in Spanish, despite the fact that these same bilinguals assessed themselves as *less* agreeable when filling in the Big Five Inventory in Spanish compared to taking the test in English.

Perhaps the notion that an agreeable personality can be detected in a person's demeanor is not so far-fetched. At a recent reunion of my sprawling, cross-continental extended family, a Czech cousin claimed that he could immediately identify which relatives were from Canada just by looking at them. The Canadians, he asserted, had kinder faces. I believe him. If you have ever interacted with a Czech official or store clerk, you may have had an inkling, even before any words passed between you, that agreeableness is not a strongly valued Czech trait. It is, however, a cherished Canadian one.

Nonetheless, one might object that a well-scrubbed experimental procedure is a poor representation of the rich and subtle realities of bilingual life. Researchers who study human interaction are always caught between competing scientific values. In order to be able to isolate the likely cause of a certain behavior, the experiments they design may be artificial and stripped of context. What they gain in control over critical variables they lose in naturalness, and their experiments may bear very little resemblance to the kinds of interactions they are ultimately trying to explain. It helps when tightly controlled experiments, such as the one that tested Spanish–English bilinguals, produce results that are echoed and elaborated by studies that allow for less sterile interactions. In one of these, researcher Michèle Koven settled on a design that is almost the polar opposite of the study of agreeableness among Mexican-Americans: where the former study used an interaction almost denuded of its social nature, Koven deliberately designed her study to be as natural and socially rich as possible. Rather than using videotaped strangers as interviewers who asked impersonal questions, she had French–Portuguese bilinguals tell personal stories to peers who were also bilingual, first in one language, then in the other. Instead of relying on standardized personality tests, she performed a detailed analysis of their linguistic choices in each language and had bilingual judges (who did not know the participants) create a character sketch of each speaker based on their Portuguese and French storytelling. This method leaves much more room than the previous study for contaminating biases and competing explanations, but it provides a more authentic and nuanced picture of how bilingual people express themselves in each of their languages.

Koven noticed stark differences in how her participants chose to tell the same stories in French versus Portuguese. For example, one young woman related a story about a frustrating experience she'd had with a Portuguese bureaucrat. When she told the tale in Portuguese, she chose an emotionally distant stance, using fairly neutral expressions in describing this clerk, and reported the clerk's speech indirectly rather than repeating her exact words. In French, she didn't hold back from expressing her scorn for the same bureaucrat and quoted her directly, in a cartoonish manner and with an exaggerated voice that portrayed the clerk as absurdly unreasonable. These two versions were perceived very differently by the judges, who remarked that it was hard to believe that the two accounts were told by the same person. In Portuguese, they felt she came across as a polite, calm, and respectful person who was forced to deal with an inflexible, uncooperative clerk. In French, they saw her as angry, aggressive, vulgar, even explosive—but also as more dynamic and funny. Another participant, who told a story about fending off an unwanted kiss by a dark-skinned boy, was perceived as somewhat racist when speaking Portuguese and more preoccupied with traditional values of feminine virtue; in her French version, she was described as an open-minded, assertive young woman who held modern notions of sexual consent and who could express herself clearly in a charged situation. These narrators obviously projected very different personalities in their two languages.

Particularly intriguing are experiments showing that people's actions and choices can tilt in different directions depending upon the language of the moment. A fascinating example comes from the Netherlands, in a study in which bilingual Dutch subjects played a variant of the famous Prisoner's Dilemma game.[8] In this game, players are thrust into a choice between cooperative and cutthroat actions, the desirability of each hinging on whether they believe their partner will veer toward a cooperative strategy or a selfish, competitive one. The original version of this game asks players to imagine that they have been charged with a crime, together with a partner, and are offered the following deal: If both the player and their partner confess (each kept in the dark about the choice of the other), both will serve a term of, say, two years in prison. However, if the partner confesses and the player denies responsibility for the crime, the player will be set free but the partner will be locked up for five years. Conversely, if the player confesses but is betrayed by their partner, the player alone will be thrown in jail for five years. The authors of the Dutch study were professors of economics and business, and they were mainly interested in how language might affect business decisions, so they altered the game accordingly. Their version of the game was set up so that a participant was placed in a fictional business situation: he reaped the highest profits if both he and his partner in the game chose a cooperative strategy of keeping prices for products high, and the lowest profits if he himself acted cooperatively but his partner chose to undersell him. Half of the participants played the game in English, and half played the game in Dutch. Language did indeed have a strong influence: English nudged participants toward a more competitive strategy, but only if they had lived in an Anglophone country for at least three months, a point to which I will later return. Among these players, those who played the game in Dutch played cooperatively 51 percent of the time, while those who played it in English did so only 37 percent of the time, choosing to betray their partners more often than not.

Studies like these add substance to the feeling that language can divide the self in two, making it hard to dismiss as illusory or coincidental. A cascade of implications follows. What are the origins of such a division? How does one live as a split self? And what happens to someone who abandons a childhood language, eager to become absorbed in a new culture? Is that person destined to live a life of incompleteness, of psychic amputation?

There is a beautiful notion that a language is the soul of a people, that it is infused with the essence of a culture, and that one can partake of that soul, or merge with it, or ingest it in some way, if one learns the language of that people. Czechs apparently have a proverb, which ironically I have only ever heard in English: "Learn a new language, get a new soul." There are many beliefs about the various flavors of linguistic souls; no doubt you have heard it asserted that Italian is a swooningly romantic language, or that French is a tongue that promotes logical thought, or that some languages are delicate while others are harsh, some are more orderly or precise or nuanced than others, and that these traits can be transferred to speakers of these languages, perhaps even to new learners. Upon seeing evidence that bilinguals toggle between different ways of seeing, or that some aspects of themselves alter their shape depending on the language they're using, it's tempting to attribute such shifts to the languages themselves. Perhaps there is something intrinsic to those languages that subtly colors the way speakers view their world, as if they wore differently tinted glasses.

If you give voice to such ideas in front of a linguist—who is, after all, paid to take an analytical view of claims about language, even beautiful ones—you're apt to get in response a wistful sigh, slightly upturned corners of the mouth, and a challenge to identify exactly *what it is* about a particular language that gives rise to a certain defining trait. What, for example, makes Italian romantic—does eroticism reside in its rules for combining sounds, in its system of marking tenses on verbs, in the fact that it distinguishes grammatically between the genders of inanimate objects such as tables and spoons? And what *exactly* is it about French that makes it so impervious to fits of irrationality? Surely you aren't about to claim that it is exempt from exceptions in its verb conjugations, or that it lacks its share of paradoxical expressions—such as the idiom *sans doute,* which literally means "without a doubt," but which is typically used when one is speculating—used, in fact, to admit that doubt exists.

And if you were to bravely venture some offerings—suggesting, for example, that the sounds of Italian and the way it alternates vowels and consonants make the language flow in a pleasing and musical way, or that its system of verb conjugations allows many opportunities for rhyming, which has allowed for the flourishing of poetry—the linguist may smile again and suggest an experiment that seems ugly. She might suggest that we invent a language (we'll call it Blickish) that has an Italianesque ratio of consonants and vowels in its words, or that has the same proportion of rhyming endings. We'll recruit participants to come into the lab and learn this new language. And we'll test to see if people report feeling more amorous, or are more inclined to arrange the words into poems, compared to another invented language (let's call it Geblian) that does not have these properties. And, of course, this feels like a very wrong way to think about languages and their souls; it feels like it is missing the whole point. Surely, a language born in the lab would have no soul at all.

Linguists truly do think about language like this, and their obsessions with linking claims about cultural differences to *specific*—and often arcane and mechanical—aspects of languages' sound systems, grammars, or lexicons have helped sharpen hypotheses about the nature of linguistic souls, should anyone wish to examine them more closely.

Every now and then it is possible to find some ingredients in a language that behave like a mirror to its society's important customs. In Korean, a cultural preoccupation with hierarchy and politeness does indeed seem to have settled into the very bones of the language. Its speakers are required to express respect for elders or social superiors in a myriad of ways: in their use of specific pronouns, in choosing "polite" versions of certain nouns and verbs (for example, the plain form of the word for house is *cip,* but in speaking with an elder you would have to use the word *tayk* instead), in attaching special endings on the ends of some verbs and nouns, and in uttering bits of sound at the end of a sentence whose sole purpose is to convey a deferential bow—or rather, subtle variants of a deferential bow, as speakers must differentiate among six different levels of politeness.[9] It is wildly implausible that a language would go to such lengths if its users were *not* concerned with social distinctions.

Other languages contain features that are culturally important, even if these do not drench the whole language in the same way as Korean honorifics. Vocabularies of kinship, for example, can proliferate in ways that would bewilder a typical Anglophone. To Brij Lal, a trilingual Indo-Fijian historian, the many Hindi words for family members are laden with subtle meanings. "English is my language of work," he writes, "but it is inadequate in expressing my inner feelings, in capturing the intricate texture of social relationships which are an integral part of my community." The trouble is that English lacks Hindi's nuanced way of marking the very particular roles assigned to family members. The word *uncle,* for instance, encompasses either a mother's or father's male sibling, whether the uncle is older or younger than the parent, and whether the relationship is by blood or by marriage. According to Lal, this is woefully inadequate. In Hindi, a father's younger brother is *Kaka;* his older brother is *Dada;* a mother's brother is *Mama;* a father's sister's husband is *Phuffa.* This vocabulary is not merely decorative: "In Hindi, each has its own place, its own distinctive set of obligations. We can joke with Kaka, be playful with him, but our relationship with Dada is more formal and distant. A Dada can be relied upon to talk sense to one's father, with some authority and effect; a Kaka, knowing his proper place in the order of things, cannot, at least not normally."[10]

When glancing over at another language from the perspective of our own, the words that it seems to be *missing* often jump out at us, like gaps in a set of teeth. It's tempting to grasp at some meaning for these gaps and claim that the lack of a word devoted to a certain concept must show something profound about the mindset of its speakers. Sometimes it does, but often it does not. For example, in writing for the *New York Times* about the sexual shenanigans of former Italian prime minister Silvio Berlusconi, Rachel Donadio pointed out: "It is not always easy to translate between Italian and American sensibilities. There is no good English word for 'veline,' the scantily clad Vanna White–like showgirls who smile and prance on television, doing dance numbers even in the middle of talk shows. And there is no word in Italian for accountability. The closest is 'responsibilità'— responsibility—which lacks the concept that actions can carry consequences."[11] The Italian word *responsibilità* lumps together meanings that English prefers to slice up into different words such as *responsibility, accountability, guilt,* and *liability.* The journalist is implying a connection between Berlusconi's antics and the Italian lexicon. Other commentators have drawn similar links much more blatantly. In a blog post, the economist Frederic Sautet described a lecture given by Graham Scott, who served as secretary of the New Zealand Treasury between 1986 and 1993, a period of important fiscal reforms in New Zealand. Scott noted that the word *accountability* had no direct translation in a number of languages, including French and Spanish, and that the words one would use in its stead were "less precise." Sautet writes: "In Scott's view, the concept of accountability is at the core of the public management reforms in New Zealand. But its absence in many other languages may limit (and perhaps has already limited) the adoption of similar reforms elsewhere. Or it may lower the quality of their results. This would show the power of language in shaping institutions."[12]

From a scientific point of view, such casual observations almost always skate on wafer-thin ice. First of all, languages have many tools other than *words* to express concepts, so one shouldn't be too struck by the fact that a language doesn't delegate the task to a free-standing word. Language *A* may use a suffix, a manner of phrasing, or even just a rising tone laid over a vowel to accomplish what Language *B* encodes in a separate word. It's far too easy to notice a misalignment of an unfamiliar language with one's own and instantly leap to an explanation based on a shallow understanding of the culture of its speakers. Too often, these explanations rely on ignorance about how the language actually works as well as on flimsy cultural stereotypes.

In a witty essay, Amy Tan playfully mocks a version of the *no-word-for-X* reasoning she finds in an article whose author marvels at the fact that Chinese has no words for *yes* or *no*. The author of the article ventures that this is because Chinese people are so discreet and modest that they would not risk a loss of face by asserting themselves too emphatically. In her short essay, Tan briskly dismantles stereotypes of the meek Asian, misconceptions about the Chinese language, and simplistic links between vocabulary and culture. Just think, she scoffs, "of the opportunities lost from failure to evolve two little words, *yes* and *no,* the simplest of opposites! Genghis Khan could have been sent back to Mongolia. Opium wars might have been averted. The Cultural Revolution could have been sidestepped."[13] As it turns out, Chinese speakers have every opportunity to decline, reject, or deny. It's just that these actions are achieved differently than they are in English. In English, the word "no" hovers like a hazy cloud over the general area of the question, leading to ambiguities in what, precisely, is being denied. (What does it mean if someone replies "No" to the question: "Did your wife come back to you because you promised to stop beating her?") In Chinese, assertions and denials are instead intertwined with the phrasing in which the question was posed. This allows speakers to be more precise, not less, about exactly what is being accepted or denied:

> Ask a Chinese person if he or she has eaten, and he or she might say *chrle* (eaten already) or perhaps *meiyou* (have not).
>
> Ask, "So you had insurance at the time of the accident?" and the response would be *dwei* (correct) or *meiyou* (did not have).
>
> Ask, "Have you stopped beating your wife?" and the answer refers directly to the proposition being asserted or denied: stopped already, still have not, never beat, have no wife.
>
> What could be clearer?[14]

Even if a language does entirely lack the dedicated machinery for expressing a specific concept, this doesn't mean that its speakers fail to grasp or experience it any more than a non-German is immune to *Schadenfreude* or a non-Czech unmoved by the feeling of *lítost*. Human reality is far richer and more textured than can ever be expressed in human vocabulary or grammar, and the *ineffability* of it, the absence of a straight line between experience and language, is probably the main reason we have poetry and novels, which use language to come at experience sideways. To a surprising extent, the forms that a language takes are somewhat arbitrary, and we are all constantly struggling—through metaphor, imagery, narrative, allusion, and all manner of inventive devices—to escape the strictures of our particular language.

Still, the notion that differences in language can lead to different ways of experiencing the world has long captivated linguists and anthropologists. Edward Sapir and his student Benjamin Lee Whorf are jointly credited with advancing this idea, now known as the *Sapir–*

Whorf hypothesis. Perhaps it was a natural question for these scholars to ask, given that their work was steeped in the study of Indigenous North American peoples, whose languages are as starkly different from those spoken by Europeans as their ways of seeing the world.

By scrutinizing the structural differences between languages and their possible effects on how we think and perceive, the many studies inspired by the Sapir–Whorf hypothesis have led to a deeper understanding of the ways in which language is—and is not—intertwined with thought. Some of these investigations have led to dead ends. For example, some languages, like Mandarin, do not have a linguistic tool for conveying that a situation is hypothetical but false in the actual world. Where an English speaker might say, "If he had been there, he would have cried," a Mandarin speaker has no way of linguistically distinguishing this idea from the one in the English sentence, "If he was there, he cried." An initial study suggested that Chinese speakers had more trouble reasoning about hypothetical situations than English speakers.[15] But this was quickly followed by a flurry of counter-studies that pointed out defects in the original study, and upon fixing them, found no differences between speakers of English and Mandarin—in the end, this particular hypothesis was discarded.[16] In some cases, claims about grammar's imprint on the mind remain hotly contested, as with the provocative idea that languages that distinguish grammatically between present and future tenses are somehow linked to behaviors that are self-defeating over the long term, such as eating too much food or saving too little money.[17]

There *are* a number of studies, though, that have made a credible case for links between specific components of a language and some aspects of its speakers' way of thinking about or perceiving the world. These insights are rarely of the type that we think of as defining the essence of a language or the soul of a people, and they are unlikely to explain any of the findings about shifted personalities or altered choices among bilinguals. Nonetheless, they are fascinating.

A vast amount of scholarly energy has been decanted over a minute detail of language: the vocabulary of color. Many languages of the world (largely from societies that were, at least until recently, nonindustrial) have a sparse collection of words to express color, some as few as three. Colors that English speakers label with distinct words are happily conflated: Yupik has a single word for green and blue; Lele assigns one label to yellow, green and blue; Gunu refers to red and yellow with the same word.

It is easy enough to dispatch with the notion that speakers of these languages fail to perceive the difference between, say, red and yellow.[18] To see how implausible this is, you need only consider the limitations of our English vocabulary when it comes to scent. Aside from a smattering of vague words like *dank, acrid, putrid, fragrant,* and so on, we have almost no words that capture smells as abstractions, disembodied from the objects that emit them. Yet that doesn't stop many people from identifying very specific smells—popcorn, gym socks, gingerbread—with remarkable accuracy. Nor does it stop them from talking about these smells. "This cheese smells like gym socks that have been sitting in a locker for months," you might assert. And this is the strategy used by many speakers whose language has almost no words for colors as *abstractions*. "This shirt is the color of a ripe lemon," a speaker of Gunu might declare.

However, is it possible that a profusion of color words might help someone make very subtle distinctions, perhaps in the same way that a sommelier's acquisition of terms for specific flavors in wine (*buttery, crisp, baked*) might plausibly help to refine his perceptions of them? A number of modern-day studies have found some evidence for this. The most convincing among them rely on technologies that were not in existence at the time that Sapir and Whorf speculated about the interplay between language and thought. For example, one study recorded reaction times, down to the millisecond, to determine how quickly English and Russian speakers make decisions about the similarity of subtly different shades of blue. In Russian, one *must* distinguish, using different words, between a light blue, like the color of a robin's egg (*goluboy*), and a darker blue, like the hue of a ripe blueberry (*siniy*). English obtusely allows just one word—*blue*—to describe both, despite the fact that they clearly evoke different experiences. If Russian speakers are shown squares of two very similar shades of blue that most of their compatriots would describe using the separate words *goluboy* and *siniy*—to imagine the experience, think of shades that hug the boundary between English's *blue* and *green*—and then are shown a third square and asked to identify which of the two other squares it matches, they are about a tenth of a second faster than English speakers to match the right squares. (And notably, Russian speakers are *not* faster to distinguish between two slightly different shades of dark blue, which they would label with the same word. This shows that their superior color discernment is restricted to colors that are labeled more precisely in their language.)[19] Greek is also a language that enforces a verbal distinction between light and dark blue (*ghalazio* and *ble*). When researchers used an EEG machine to compare the electrical activity in the brains of Greek versus English speakers, they found that Greek brains responded differently from English brains to visual sequences of light and dark blue. Neither language, however, demands that a similar distinction be made between light and dark green; when viewing different shades of green, the activity of Greek brains matched that of English brains.[20]

Using the sensitive tools available to modern language scientists, quite a few other studies have been able to detect subtle ways in which bits of language leave their imprint on how people perceive or think about concepts that are yoked to those pieces of language. For example, when English speakers describe movement, they can select from a juicy assortment of verbs that depict the precise manner of motion; a boy can *walk,* for example, but he can also *amble, saunter, trot, plod, skip, stride, scuffle, march,* and so on. But to express where a person or thing is headed, they usually have to tack on an extra phrase like *up the stairs* or *down the street.* In languages like Spanish and Greek, it's the path of the motion that fuses with the verb, while the manner of the motion dangles off on the side. A functional Spanish translation of the English sentence "He walked into the house" would be "*El entró en la casa caminando*"—literally, "He entered the house by walking." Since in all of these languages verbs are mandatory in a sentence but dangling adverbial phrases are optional (they are only included if the information they encode is crucial), English speakers always have to pay attention to the manner of motion (and sometimes its path), whereas Spanish and Greek speakers always have to pay attention to the path of the motion (and sometimes its manner). Researchers have found that Greek and English speakers distribute their attention differently while preparing to describe videos involving objects and people in motion; Greek speakers spent more time gazing at the endpoints of the motion, whereas English speakers spent more time looking at the visual details that would allow them to identify the manner. For instance, in looking at a video of a boy skateboarding into a soccer net, the Greek speakers gazed longer at the net, while the English speakers focused on the skateboard.[21]

These fascinating studies show that specific aspects of language—how words claim their territory on the color wheel or how a language parcels out the labor between verbs and adverbs—can indeed tune human perception in subtle ways. For language scientists, knowing the details of how language insinuates itself into attention or perception is important for understanding how different systems in the brain interact with each other. But it's hard to know whether any of this affects people's subjective experiences beyond the laboratory walls in any meaningful way. It is telling that many of these studies rely on very precise tools of measurement such as eyetrackers, EEG machines, and computers that record reaction times down to the millisecond, tools that can tap into mental activities that escape the notice of the humans engaged in them. Do Russian speakers have any awareness at all that their sensitivity to shades of blue is slightly enhanced compared to their perception of shades of green? Would a speaker of Lele, whose language conflates blue and green, experience Monet's painting *The Water Lilies* just a touch less vividly than a speaker of English? And if that person knew both languages, would contemplating the painting while describing it in English rather than in Lele nudge her toward a slightly richer appreciation of its colors? Would such a speaker ever say, "I feel more artistic in English," solely because English has a more extravagant color vocabulary?

As the linguist John McWhorter argues, if these studies "are showing anything like different lenses on life, then the difference between lenses is like the one between two lenses that your optometrist shows you during an exam for glasses or contacts when you have to have her alternate between them several times to decide whether you see better through one or the other, because really, the chart looks the same through both."[22] It's possible to find a measurable difference, perhaps, but it makes little difference to your life whether you end up with one set of glasses or the other.

And yet. There is that persistent sense of split selves among bilinguals, the unshakeable feeling that different languages really do conjure up different realities. For many bilinguals, the mother tongue is redolent with fragrances, flavors, sensations, and images that are absent from a later-learned language. M. J. Fitzgerald, an American writer who was raised in Italy, writes: "The word *candy* does nothing to my taste buds, whereas the word *caramella* brings instantly back the sweet crunch of the teeth through the shell, softened by sucking for as long as possible, to the soft center." She claims that even colors have a different quality in Italian than they do in English, describing "a sea whose intensity of blue can only be contained in the Italian word *azzurro*. The word *blue,* an anodyne descriptive term, does not convey that childhood sea, but *azzurro* brings it all back with a violence in memory that invariably hits me like a punch in the stomach."[23]

Fitzgerald's experience of *azzurro* versus *blue* clearly has nothing to do with Italian and English vocabulary—both have similar inventories of color terms. Nor is it likely to have much to do with the sounds of the words, despite the energy that seems to ripple through the *zz* and *rr* of the Italian word; I counter Fitzgerald's impressions with my own sense that English *blue* is anything but anodyne, capturing the moodiness, stillness, and deep, sad *blueness* of the color far more aptly than the Italian word, which to me, is just a word despite its sonic razzle-dazzle. Fitzgerald and I do seem to be experiencing color differently in these two languages, but it has more to do with our own relationships to Italian versus English, and with our private encounters with the color blue, than anything that resides in the languages themselves.

When we learn a language, the words we speak become entangled with the life we've lived in that language. Just like the taste of a madeleine dipped in tea in Proust's *In Search of Lost Time,* which triggered for the protagonist a reel of youthful recollections, language can stir to life the memories that are associated with it. And at times, language itself can be stirred to life by a fragment of life that is attached to it. I had my own Proustian moment when I sampled a persimmon, an unfamiliar fruit that I'd bought as a university student when they first became available at ordinary grocery stores in Canada. As soon as I tasted its silky flesh, I found myself transported to a small Viennese kitchen; the strange word *kaki* sprang into my mind. The image and the word were so eerily vivid, and so linked with the taste of the fruit, that I immediately called my mother to ask her whether she knew of a fruit by the name of *kaki*. "Yes!" she cried, "I remember eating one for the first time in Vienna!" Evidently, that is how the fruit was called by Austrians. A remnant of that knowledge remained in me, dredged up when tasting the fruit itself. (The durability of this memory for both me and my mother is not as far-fetched as it may seem; anyone who has grown up in a Soviet bloc country seems to have at least a few detailed fruit-related memories, as almost no imported fruit was ever available in those countries. I still remember the startling, creamy sweetness of the first banana I ever tasted.)

Though Eva Hoffman is not a language scientist, she is a wonderfully astute observer of language, offering some of the most lucid commentary I have ever read of the experience of learning a new language. She was aware of a stark difference in the emotional texture of words in Polish, her native language, in contrast with their much blander translations into English. She is correct, I think, in blaming the flatness of English on the poverty of her own memories in her new North American life. She writes: "'River' in Polish was a vital sound, energized with the essence of riverhood, of my rivers, of my being immersed in rivers. 'River' in English is cold—a word without an aura. It has no accumulated associations for me, and it does not give off the radiating haze of connotation. It does not evoke."[24]

Her musings are echoed by scientific demonstrations of the bonds between language and memory. Paul Kolers, a psychologist, documented how, for a bilingual person, a word in one language can indeed trigger associations that are very different from those sparked by the same word translated into the other language, evidence that these doppelgänger words have led different lives and consorted with different friends.[25] Several researchers have found that, when bilinguals relate a personal memory, their accounts are more plush with detail and emotional color if they describe the memory in the same language in which it was lived.[26]

In one especially precise study, Russian–English bilinguals were asked to describe a personal memory that sprang to mind when prompted with a specific word—such as *birthday* or *blood,* for example—with separate interviews taking place in English and Russian. People were more likely to relate a memory that had taken place in a Russian-speaking milieu when interviewed in Russian, and similarly, more English-milieu memories when the interview took place in English. The researchers then wanted to understand the connection between language and memory more precisely: does the recall of a particular memory rely upon hearing a specific word that is embedded with that memory itself, or can that memory be brought to the surface simply by hearing the language associated with it, regardless of which specific words are uttered? To put it another way, in order to loosen Eva Hoffman's sensual memories of Polish rivers, would she need to hear the Polish word for *river,* or would it be enough to simply converse in Polish and then hear the English word *river*? To find out, the researchers repeated their experiment, but included situations in which the general interview took place in one language, but the prompt words were offered in the other, as well as situations in which the entire interview, prompt words and all, took place in Russian or English, as in the first version of the study. The psychologists discovered that the ambient language of the interview *and* the language of the specific prompt word each played a role in dredging up a memory that had taken place in the matching language. Although a memory that took place in Russian was most likely to be recalled if a Russian prompt word was offered during a Russian interview, simply using Russian with the interviewer helped transport participants to Russian places, and to the events and the people that populated them, even if the specific prompt was uttered in English.[27]

These studies explain how early memories can be so tightly bound with a first language, even for people who fully master another language later in life. They help to explain why, for the writer Richard Rodriguez, family intimacy could not easily be replicated in English, and independence could not be forged in Spanish. When one lives such different lives in each language, language keeps the different aspects of the self at arms' length from each other, mirroring and reinforcing their division of labor within society.

In her book *The Bilingual Mind,* Aneta Pavlenko discusses the fusion of language and memory in the writings of Vladimir Nabokov, who fled the Russian Revolution in 1919 and arrived in the United Kingdom when he was twenty years old. By the time Nabokov wrote his memoir *Conclusive Evidence* in 1951, he'd been writing in English, his adopted tongue, for many years. Yet he struggled with this particular text, most of which focused on his childhood and youth in Russia, complaining that his memory was tuned to the "musical key" of Russian rather than English. Soon after its publication, he translated the memoir into his native tongue. Working in his first language seems to have prodded his senses awake, leading him to insert new details into the Russian version: A simple anecdote about a stingy old housekeeper becomes perfumed with the scents of coffee and decay, the description of a laundry hamper acquires a creaking sound, the visual details of a celluloid swan and toy boat sprout as he writes about the tub in which he bathed as a child. Some of these details eventually made it into his revised English memoir, which he aptly titled *Speak, Memory*. Evidently, when memory speaks, it sometimes does so in a particular tongue.[28]

Because language is so yoked to memory, bilingual people whose lives have been cleaved by language can develop lopsided relationships with the languages they speak, relationships that reflect the phases of life in which each of their languages took center stage. Eva Hoffman was a teenager when she emigrated from Poland, where she had fallen in love with a boy for the first time. She found herself later having trouble expressing her love for an American man in English. To her, English was the language of her schooling, an abstract and disciplined language; in such a tongue, she writes, "terms of endearment came out as formal and foursquare as other words. In that neutral and neutered speech, words were neither masculine nor feminine; they did not arise out of erotic substance, out of sex. How could I say 'darling' or 'sweetheart,' when the words had no fleshly fullness, when they were dry as sticks?"[29]

Not so for Thomas Laqueur, whose childhood language was German but who shifted into English very early in life. For him, it is English that is the erotically charged language, not his mother tongue: "My German is, first of all, a connection with a pre-Oedipal me. I have never made love in German; I know no words for matters sexual, and few slang words of any sort. I would not know what it would mean to feel sexual in German." In fact, he notes, so sparse and narrow are his experiences in the German language that many of its words remain tethered to idiosyncratic emotions and memories, as if fixed in the amber of his own childhood memory. For example, "the word for caraway seed, *kümmel,* is an adjective for a kind of bread on which one eats corned beef or chopped liver; i.e. rye bread; for me, it describes a man who terrified me as a small child, *der kümmel Mann,* a beggar with a pock-marked face who stood outside our Istanbul apartment. Too little has happened to me in German to make the regular public uses of words mean what they should."[30]

For me, Czech has all the Proustian qualities of the beloved foods of my childhood, of which we had almost enough, and much of my pleasure in hearing it comes from the memories that marble the language. These language-drenched memories are what make Czech irreplaceable to me, why losing the language feels like the loss of a portion of my life. Like the food itself, Czech words and phrases awaken sensations and memories that attest to our parents' heroic efforts to manage the strains of migration: of cozy spaces, almost always too small for the number of people occupying them, but filled with the smells and the warmth of my mother's cooking; of the eloquent melodies of my father's voice; of the companionable, chaotic sense of being one segment in a large family, and the feeling of a ramshackle security erected against the unpredictable and overwhelming world swirling outside the door. English has many, many resonances for me, but it is lacking in these particular ones. In my mind, the English phrase "pork with cabbage and dumplings" refers to a *concept,* the national dish of the Czechs. But hearing the Czech phrase *vepřo-knedlo-zelo* induces salivation and foresees contentment; it evokes the fragrance of roasting meat, pillowy dumpling loaves being pulled steaming out of a tall pot and sliced with sewing thread, and the clink of the nice china as the table is dressed for Sunday dinner, the ritualized fulcrum of every week in my childhood home.

If this is the soul of a language, it is one that has to be earned by the life that accompanies it. It is not enough to learn the words and grammar, just as eating someone else's favorite childhood food will not transport you into the landscape of their childhood.

On my first visit back to the Czech Republic, I recall going to a restaurant with my academic advisor. The menu offered *vepřo-knedlo-zelo* and, hearing my gasp of delight and my rhapsodic description of the dish that my mother had made on special Sundays (especially the *knedlíky,* ohmygod, the spongy, porous dumplings that sop up every drop of sauce or meat juice—a staple of Czech cuisine and replicated almost nowhere else), my advisor ordered it. In eager anticipation, I watched as he cut off a small piece of dumpling, speared it with a fork and chewed it. "It's very good," he assured me, in his earnest, Midwestern manner of wanting to please. But I could tell. To him, it was just boiled bread.

For many people, a language learned later in life retains the quality of boiled bread. It is nourishing, practical, but lacking the symphony of memories that give *knedlíky* their incomparable texture. In her memoir, Eva Hoffman writes at length of the desolation she felt in the early phase of her migration, which she blames in part on the bleached quality of the words she now had to use in daily life. She lamented that "this radical disjoining between word and thing is a desiccating alchemy, draining the world not only of significance, but of its colors, striations, nuances—its very existence. It is the loss of a living connection."[31]

When Aneta Pavlenko and Jean-Marc Dewaele, in the course of their research, asked multilingual people which of their languages seemed most strongly imbued with emotion, an overwhelming majority chose their earliest languages.[32] Many claimed that they could be more tender with their loved ones in their native language, or that this was the language they automatically tumbled into during an argument. For some, the coolness of a later-learned language could be a refuge, offering liberties that were not possible in their mother tongue. Some could not bring themselves to swear or express anger in their first language because these words felt too explosive or forbidden. Or perhaps they preferred, in order to limit the possible damage, to do domestic battle in their more recently learned language, as this language allowed them to slide into a calmer, more rational skin.

Some writers may even feel liberated by an exact reversal of Nabokov's fruitful re-entry into his native Russian while translating his memoirs. Jerzy Kosinski, a writer whose childhood was far less idyllic than Nabokov's (he grew up fleeing the Nazis in Poland, studied under the authoritarian regime of Soviet Russia, and then moved to the United States in his twenties), describes the freedom he felt in expressing himself in English. "It seemed that the languages of my childhood and adolescence—Polish and Russian—carried a sort of mental suppression," he observed. "English, my stepmother tongue, offered me a sense of revelation, of fulfillment, of abandonment—everything contrary to the anxiety my mother tongue evoked."[33] In this language of adulthood, he claimed, he was able to escape the involuntary associations that were soaked into his native tongue.

Alongside the lyrical reflections of multilingual writers and the recurring reports of bilingual speakers, there is a bundle of scientific papers that have tested such claims about the leaching of emotion from later-learned languages. Many of these papers describe measurements of the most technical and biological sort, perhaps to reassure fellow scientists that the topic of emotion can indeed be objectively studied by rational methods, or to provide a counterweight to the intensely personal, often literary flavor of the firsthand accounts.

Swear words or words that are taboo are among the most emotionally potent words in any language—in fact, expressing and arousing strong emotion is a curse word's entire purpose in life. But many people claim that swear words seem rather washed out in their second language—and even more so in a third, and yet more in a fourth.[34] A person who can't bring herself to swear in her mother tongue may have no such inhibitions in another language. (I can't help but recall the Québécoise grandmother of my childhood friend, who would casually say, "*C'est tout fucké,*" but who strictly forbade us from uttering the word *tabernacle* in her presence—a word that for me barely registered above the boiled-bread level.) In fact, it is because of the sheer primal force of this form of language that I felt so linguistically deprived when I realized how ignorant I was of any Czech swear words, due to my parents' aversion to them. I felt denied one of the very most intimate and visceral connections one can have with words, a connection that couldn't be fully replaced by the forbidden words of another language.

And a visceral connection it is. The feelings evoked by such words can be located—and yes, measured—in the body. Using a device to detect how easily a person's skin conducts electricity (which is exactly the same technique used to detect heightened emotion in a lie detector test), researchers usually find that skin conductance rises for several seconds after a person hears or reads a swear word or some other emotionally charged word. But this effect may be dampened in bilinguals using their second language. In a study of native Turkish speakers who learned English as adolescents or adults, the participants revealed a strong emotional response to taboo words and reprimands of the sort one might hear as a child (*Go to your room!*). But the effect was stronger when the words or phrases were in Turkish; in particular, reprimands in English seemed drained of their emotional voltage compared with the Turkish rebukes. A number of the participants later told the experimenters that, when they read these phrases in Turkish, they could hear the scolding voices of their elders reverberating in their minds.[35] A similar study with Spanish–English bilinguals also found blunted emotional responses for the second language, but only among speakers who had learned it later in life; those who had learned English in childhood responded as strongly to the loaded English phrases as they did to the ones in their native Spanish.[36]

Calculating the dilation of pupils is another sophisticated measure that has been used to test the emotional force of first and second languages. Pupils become larger when we are emotionally aroused (as well as when we're thinking more intensely), a link that researchers from the University of Glasgow decided to exploit in their experiments. They measured bilingual participants' pupils in response to a variety of words and phrases, some of them meant to be rather dull (*civil receptionist*) and others designed to provoke a negative reaction (*hostile terrorist*). The aggressive phrases did indeed cause the participants' pupils to widen, but again, the response was tempered when these occurred in their second language (English) as compared with their first (either Finnish or German).[37]

Not all such studies do reveal a subdued emotionality for the second language, a fact which some researchers attribute to the variability in participants' histories with their second language. Many factors could affect the emotional weight attached to a language: the age at which it is learned, how proficient the person is with the language, whether they've been speaking it long enough to accumulate rich memories in it, and whether they learned it in a social setting saturated with emotionally rich experiences or within the sterile confines of a classroom. But despite disagreements about its universality and underlying cause, there is overall a fair bit of convincing and objective evidence that native languages are—at least for many bilingual speakers—embedded in a richer network of memories and emotions than languages learned later.

Other researchers have pushed this idea even further, asking whether the emotional coolness of a second language translates into a more dispassionate style of thinking. In a research study led by psychologist Albert Costa, volunteers were confronted with a moral dilemma known as the "trolley problem": Imagine that a runaway trolley is speeding toward a group of five people standing on the tracks, too stricken with fear to move. Next to you is a switch that can transfer the trolley to a different set of tracks, thereby sparing the five people but killing one who is standing on the side tracks. Do you pull the switch?

Most people agree that they would. But what if the only option for stopping the trolley is to shove a hefty stranger off a footbridge into its path? People are more squeamish now, and very few of them admit to being willing to do this. However, in both scenarios, one person is sacrificed to save five; from a strictly rational point of view, one is hard-pressed to say why the sacrifice would be moral in the first case, but immoral in the second. It simply *feels* more violent to put your hands on the body of a person and throw him off a bridge, in a way that flipping a switch does not.

Costa and his colleagues found that when participants heard these versions of the dilemma described in a second language they had learned as adults, they were less affected by the violent feeling of the second version. In their second language, more than half the participants said they would be willing to push the sacrificial person off the bridge, in contrast with the fewer than 20 percent who said they would do so when queried in their native tongue. (Both native Spanish- and English speakers were included, with English and Spanish as their respective foreign languages. The results were the same for both groups, showing that the effect was linked to the use of a second language, and not bound to one or the other language—that is, it does not appear that complacency in the face of physical violence is baked into the soul of either language.)[38]

In another study, researchers found that people's moral verdicts shifted when they used a foreign language. The participants read descriptions of acts that appeared to harm no one, but that many people find reprehensible—for example, stories in which siblings secretly enjoyed entirely consensual and ultra-protected sex, or where someone cooked and ate his dog after it had been killed by a car. When confronted with such stories, people often struggle to explain *why* these acts are wrong, but they feel they are deeply—and self-evidently—depraved. However, when bilingual participants read these stories in a foreign language (either English or Italian), they judged the actions to be less immoral than those who read the stories in their native tongue.[39] In their second language, their moral judgments were more "logical," lacking the visceral feeling of their native language.

These studies are accompanied by a flurry of others showing that, when using a later-learned language, people are somewhat immune to a range of biases that can seep into reasoning and decision-making. In their native languages, they are prone to responding very differently to descriptions of two scenarios that are logically equivalent but whose wording evokes different feelings in the gut (for example, a scenario in which 20 percent of people will die as a result of a certain action, compared with an equivalent scenario in which 80 percent will be saved). In their second languages, these differences in wording have a softer impact.[40] These results are not without controversy. Not all have been replicated easily, and researchers are embroiled in discussions about how to explain the differences across languages. While some argue that later-learned languages have less emotional baggage attached to them, others argue that the effects are simply due to differences in language proficiency or even to the effects of switching to an unexpected language. Nonetheless, they add an intriguing thread to the tapestry of observations about the duality experienced by many bilingual people.

If languages absorb the flavors of the lives in which they are lived, it is perhaps no surprise to find that early languages are steeped with shame, tenderness, bliss, outrage, or fear. When we learn a language in childhood, it is by throwing our full selves—bodies, emotions, familial entanglements, social duties, and all—into the task of learning the language. A language learned much later is sheltered from the emotional weather of childhood, all the more so if it's learned within the walls of a classroom, under the tutelage of a trained professional, in docile progression through a predetermined curriculum. In a later language, you may have never tasted bitter humiliation or been cut by betrayal; perhaps no one has ever brought your rage to a boil or stroked your hair while murmuring words of love.

As children, we have little in the way of analytic skill to bring to the learning of a language. As adolescents or adults, we find it harder to simply inhabit a language, to be present in it without running it through the analytical procedures we've come to rely on. We strain to avoid the hilarious or inappropriate errors of language that adults find so adorable in children—and perhaps we rightly discern that we will not be so easily forgiven for them. This too may add to the sense of emotional remoteness from a language, a feeling that it is a rented piece of clothing rather than a skin that envelops our own bones and meat. Irene Ulman, a Russian-born translator and journalist who migrated to Australia at the age of twelve, describes how she often felt a bit of an imposter when uttering casual or idiomatic phrases in Australian English: "To avoid looking and sounding fake, I have done things like use a deliberately fake voice, or an exaggerated Australian accent, as if quoting someone else or using someone else's voice. It's as though I were borrowing something before deciding to appropriate it. And speaking of borrowing and appropriating, I'm aware that some of my favorite phrases and expressions have a specific source. Sometimes I even visualize the people to whom I owe some of my language when I say something that I associate with them."[41] Such self-conscious use of language, she writes, left her feeling distanced from herself, disembodied, as if aware of a certain time lag in conversations.

Over time and with immersion in real life, even a later-learned language can become seasoned with the immediacy of experience. Gradually, it can come to feel like a second skin. One slowly comes to resemble native speakers when using it. Recall the study from the Netherlands in which Dutch people behaved in a less cooperative manner when speaking English than when speaking their native language. The authors of the study attribute this to their participants' close encounters with Anglophone culture rather than any property of the language itself or the participants' use of a less-familiar language: only those who had lived in English-speaking countries behaved differently in their two languages. For those who had not lived outside the Netherlands, English did not—regardless of their level of proficiency with the language—become infused with the individualistic norms of Anglophone life.[42]

And with time, perhaps, the self-consciousness abates, the analytic observer within steps aside, and the speaker fuses with the language. For Eva Hoffman, who arrived in North America at the age of thirteen, it was not until after she finished her graduate studies in literature and had begun teaching at a university that she felt able to breach the last barrier between herself and the English language. Though she had a longstanding love of English literature, it was a love that sprang more from the intellect than the senses. But one day, upon reading T. S. Eliot's *The Love Song of J. Alfred Prufrock,* she became aware that English had finally worked its way into her body:

> Over the years, I've read so many explications of these stanzas that I can analyze them in half a dozen ingenious ways. But now, suddenly I'm attuned, through some mysterious faculty of the mental ear, to their inner sense; I hear the understated melancholy of that refrain, the civilized restraint of the rhythms reining back the more hilly swells of emotion, the self-reflective, moody resignation of the melody. . . . I read, tasting the sounds on the tongue, hearing the phrases somewhere between tongue and mind. Bingo, I think, this is it, the extra, the attribute of language over and above function and criticism. I'm back within the music of the language, and Eliot's words descend on me with a sort of grace. Words become, as in childhood, beautiful things.[43]

IN THE SCIENTIFIC pursuit of explaining how and why it is that language runs like a fault line through the self, brain scanning machines continue to whir, the diameters of pupils continue to be inscribed in electronic files, and psychologists continue to wordsmith scenarios that are meant to engage the thinking and feeling parts of the brain to different degrees. All the while, though, something else has been happening in the quiet rooms where people give voice to their pain. Psychotherapists use no fancy instruments or tightly worded scripts, concentrating instead on the minute changes of emotional weather as registered in gesture, tone, face, and language. With their bilingual clients, they have long noticed—for almost as long as there has been psychotherapy—that these atmospheric changes are linked to shifts of language. Many practitioners have remarked that their clients seem more emotionally withdrawn when using a second language. In a paper published in 1949, psychoanalyst Edith Buxbaum voiced her suspicion that clients were using language defensively, retreating into a nonnative language as a way to avoid confronting repressed memories that might float to the surface more readily in the language of childhood.[44] Her suspicions are directly confirmed by the words of a bilingual client of another psychoanalyst, Ralph Greenson, as described in his 1950 paper titled, "The Mother Tongue and the Mother." During therapy, Greenson's client, a native speaker of German, admits in English to her analyst, "I have the feeling that talking in German I shall have to remember something I want to forget."[45] Buxbaum and Greenson believed that, in order to resolve the inner conflicts that originated in their childhoods, these patients needed to undergo analysis in their mother tongues.

And indeed, these and other authors have reported breakthroughs that came about after introducing their client's native language into therapy. RoseMarie Pérez Foster writes of her therapeutic work with a client she calls "Anna," a Chilean dance student studying in New York who was referred for alarming weight loss and depression. Although Anna knows that the therapist speaks Spanish, her own native tongue, she arrives at the office requesting that the sessions be conducted in English, ostensibly to improve her proficiency in English. The therapist mentally raises an eyebrow but follows Anna's lead, noting that her client has revealed almost nothing about her inner life after a month and a half of regular sessions. One day, as

Anna prepares to leave, she drops her wallet, spilling her coins all over the office carpet. Without thinking, the therapist blurts out, in Spanish, "Oh dear, you've dropped your change!" Anna stares at the therapist as if she's seen a ghost, bolts from the room, and cancels the next two sessions, claiming to be sick. When she returns, she lashes out at the therapist for not supporting her desire to learn English—perhaps, she ventures, the therapist does not *really* want her to succeed in this country. But something has cracked; Anna begins to release her emotions, crying in therapy for the first time and admitting her homesickness, claiming that the only way she has been able to survive in New York is by never speaking Spanish and becoming "*duro como un gringo*" ("hard like an American"). She even begins to speak of her mother, who had begged her not to leave Chile and has hinted darkly that she might die if Anna abandoned her. Anna's native tongue has pried open a floodgate, allowing her to begin therapy in earnest.[46]

The accounts of the distancing effects of a second language are echoed by more extensive research studies, including one in which 182 multilingual clients were queried about their experiences in therapy. One client remarked that the therapist's probing into childhood memories seemed "irrelevant"—until the client began mixing in some words from the native language, and suddenly, these experiences became more immediate and pertinent to the concerns of the present. Many who responded agreed that talking about emotional experiences, especially those colored by trauma or shame, felt less intense in a nonnative language.[47]

In another study, when bilingual patients who had suffered a childhood trauma were evaluated for symptoms of post-traumatic stress disorder (PTSD), their psychic wounds were apparent to different degrees, depending on the language in which they filled in the assessment questionnaire. Patients rated their symptoms as more intense and described their traumatic memories with greater vividness and immediacy when using Spanish, their first language. When they were later interviewed about troubling childhood memories, a number of them coolly related their memories in English, as if these events had happened to someone else. But they wept or trembled when describing them in Spanish, and related them in more vivid detail. One woman could not at first think of any upsetting memories from her childhood during the English interview, and eventually remembered a serious car accident that she and her family had been in. But when she related the experience in Spanish, details of the memory came flooding back to her: the sight of her bloodied father in the ambulance with her, her fear that he was going to die. She became overcome with emotion and had to stop speaking for some time. Upon recovering, she remarked, "It was like I was seeing it, right there in front of me—the accident. It wasn't like that when I was speaking in English."[48]

A multiplicity of languages complicates therapy. It can erect borders that separate a patient from the therapist or from important aspects of herself. The barriers may be involuntary, created by a misalignment of languages between clients and therapists. Clients who have no choice but to take part in therapy in a language that is effortful for them may always feel as if they are speaking to their therapist through the time lag of an internal translator. Even when they do speak the therapist's language with ease, there may be a sense that some parts of themselves are not invited into the room. Or, they may hide behind the screen of their second language, unconsciously obscuring their true selves and slowing their progress in therapy.

But multiple languages also create opportunities that are seized upon by both clients and therapists who feel free to shift between languages in their therapy sessions. For some patients, a second language can create the opportunity to repair the effects of trauma by approaching their trauma sideways, softening the emotional impact of the memory until it becomes bearable to face it head-on in the native language. For some people, the cultural norms associated with their mother tongue may make it impossible to talk about sex or to express anger at an older relative. When they are emotionally stuck, flipping between languages can allow clients to explore alternative viewpoints and get a fresh understanding of a situation, as if from outside of themselves. And, as Pérez Foster writes, a shift into a native tongue can rearrange the therapeutic relationship, as when her client Anna abruptly re-enacted her relationship with her mother upon hearing her therapist inadvertently slip into Spanish. The patient then begins to speak from a different aspect of the self: "My signal that this phenomenon has taken place is not only the music of the new language, but often my own transformation in the presence of the patient, who somehow in a linguistic instant can sculpt me into another."[49]

But perhaps the greatest indication that therapy needs to encompass the entire fragmented, complex, divided self of the multilingual patient is the stated desire of many of these patients for a therapist who also speaks multiple languages, even if they are not the same languages spoken by the client.[50] Perhaps these clients feel the flash of recognition that passes between them and the therapist; they are fellow members of the Split Selves Club.

If multilingualism is an audible sign of membership in the club of divided souls, it is possibly a misleading one. Or rather, what is misleading is the assumption that the monolingual's *absence* of alternate languages points to a unified self. In reality, no one is undivided. William James, one of the founders of the field of psychology, brushed off as a fiction the idea of a coherent, unitary self. Since one's identity arises from interactions with others, he wrote in his 1890 volume *Principles of Psychology,* a person has as many social selves as there are individuals who form an opinion of him. Because these individuals tend to cluster in distinct groups—teachers and mentors, peers of the same gender, peers of a different gender, fellow hockey enthusiasts, fellow bird watchers, speakers of a common language—it is natural to let loose different sides of oneself within each group. A boy who is demure and intellectual with his teachers may swear and swagger with his friends. This, argued James, inevitably partitions an individual into several distinct selves, a division that may be "a discordant splitting . . . or it may be a perfectly harmonious division of labor."[51]

Language, then, is not so much a source of schism as a tagging of it. It is harder to maintain the fiction of an undivided self when one's cohabiting sub-selves sculpt their thoughts into mutually incomprehensible sentences. Perhaps, by providing distinct linguistic uniforms for these personalities, language makes visible—thereby reinforcing—their separateness. But more than anything, it exposes an essential condition of human nature, one that is becoming more and more inescapable as cultural change accelerates everywhere.

In her memoir, Eva Hoffman reflects on her own immigrant story of lingering psychic fragmentation, contrasting it with the triumphant memoir *The Promised Land* by Mary Antin, a Russian Jew who arrived in Boston at the age of fourteen in the 1890s. When Antin wrote of her rise, as a young woman, from squalid poverty to literary pet of the Boston elite, it was within the frame of the familiar Immigrant Success Story. It was a tale of never looking back, of embracing the culture of her new country and seizing all the opportunities it had to offer. To Hoffman, what is so striking is the utter lack of ambivalence in the memoir. Only Antin's preface hints at the pain of dislocation and the straddling of two different worlds, a pain that is quickly swept aside by the author's steadfast assertion that she would rather forget the past entirely. The book comes across as a story of joyful assimilation in which one whole self is simply exchanged for another whole self, and it is without question a good bargain.

But Hoffman arrived in North America in 1959 and came of age during the 1960s and 1970s, a time when the cultural ground shifted beneath the feet of all North Americans. She wonders what it would even mean for her to assimilate to the North American culture of her time. Is her own fragmentation really that different, she asks, from that of her American-born friends? She notes the disruptions and

ambivalences in their lives—in their marriages, divorces, reloca-
tions, indecisions about career, inner conflicts over love and work
and life—and decides that they too constantly swim in waters that
are cut by crosscurrents, they too are constantly pulled in opposite
directions by competing perspectives and values. "A hundred years
ago," she muses, "I might have felt the benefits of a steady, self-assured
ego, the sturdy energy of forward movement, and the excitement of
being swept up into a greater national purpose. But I have come to a
different America, and instead of a central ethos, I have been given
the blessings and terrors of multiplicity." What, then, does one assimilate *to* in a splintered society? To multiplicity itself? Perhaps the
immigrant success story is no longer one of total transformation so
much as one of a nondestructive splintering. In the end, concludes
Hoffman, perhaps "a successful immigrant is an exaggerated version
of the native."[52]

I recognize that the narrative of selves that are neatly split by the
event of migration, along linguistic fault lines, is too simple for me.
It is easy to attribute all inner conflicts to the rupture between old
world and new. Not that these conflicts aren't there. When I returned
to my deceased father's village for a prolonged visit, my uncle and I
settled down at his kitchen table, and one of his first questions to me
was, "Why did you abandon your mother?" I was taken aback, and
it took me a while to realize that he was referring to an entire series
of events that would, in North America, be described not as abandonment but as the trajectory of a successful child: moving out of
the family home to attend university in a different town, then going
to the United States after earning a spot at a top PhD program in my
field, and eventually taking a job at an Ivy League university, a good
day's drive away from where my mother lived. My uncle's question
brought back for me some of the tensions that had colored my relationship with my father: the sense that assimilation to North American life so often implied a betrayal of my father's values; the dogged
tug-of-war between aspiration and family ties.

As I spent more time with my Czech relatives, I realized how strange my autonomous and nomadic life must seem to them against the continuity of their own lives, lived in such close proximity to family members. They were so unaccustomed to moving that, upon hearing how my sister recently sold her house and bought a new one in the same city, they asked: when you sell a house do you have to sell the furniture with the house as well, or do you get to keep it? My uncle still lives on the family compound that has housed Sedivys for several hundred years. His son and his son's family live in an apartment in the compound just above his own; one of his daughters lives a few streets away, and another literally in his backyard, on a section of the family land on which he had let her build a house when she married. One of his sons-in-law was busy building several houses in the same village for his own young daughters. When he proudly showed me where his children would live once they established their own families, I shook my head and said, "That would never work in Canada. I could build a house for my kids, but chances are slim they would ever choose to live there."

But the splintering has breached the homeland as well. The tides of globalization have lapped its shores, reaching as far as the family village. It turns out that one of those lovingly built houses is bereft of the daughter for whom it was built; she is now in Africa, where she works as a dentist for an NGO. One of her cousins has spent years travelling and working in the United States and now Australia. Many others of that generation are fanning out into the rest of Europe, wherever they can find good work. They are meeting and falling in love with people who come from different worlds than the ones they themselves entered as infants. They are now confronted with the same decisions and conflicts that riddled my own upbringing. Even those who stay behind in the village feel the effects; the call of alternative lives, lived outside of the traditions and structures of the long-time family home, is always there.

I suspect the greatest legacy of a life spent straddling cultures is not the splintering of identity itself—which has become, as Hoffman points out, a condition of contemporary life—but the conscious feeling, so widely shared among migrants and minorities, that the splintering has become an essential part of oneself, that duality is not merely a condition of life but *the* defining trait of one's character. So it is for Eva Hoffman and for the two-faced protagonist of Viet Thanh Nguyen's novel *The Sympathizer,* whose sole talent is to be able to see any issue from both sides. And so it is for me. When I look back at the choices I've made in my life and work, I see that I'm drawn, like a moth flinging its body against a light bulb, to in-between spaces and intersections, to hyphenations, to situations in which there will always be two sides. This is, for me, where all the heat and light can be found.

When I applied to PhD programs to study psycholinguistics, I was most interested in a program that allowed students to combine studies in both linguistics and psychology. Despite its compound name, the field of psycholinguistics was at that time largely segregated between the two disciplines, with very few people trained in both. The two subfields had different methods, assumptions, and sociologies. But it seemed to me that the best way to understand the workings of language in the human mind was by flipping between these perspectives, using one to illuminate the other, and back again. I had two academic advisors, one a psychologist and the other a linguist, and I had office space in both departments. And though my program encouraged much greater integration between the disciplines than most, I still felt that I spent some days as a linguist and others as a psychologist, switching between the two as I would with different languages. As with different languages and cultures, the friction between the two disciplines caused certain habits and patterns of thought to leap into attention and demand an explanation. Practices taken for granted in one discipline looked a bit odd from the viewpoint of the other. When I entered the academic job market, one of the most common questions people asked me was: "Do you consider yourself a psychologist or a linguist?" Fortunately, I found a place at a university that was in need of a faculty member split between the two disciplines. The psychologists and linguists in my department had each requested their own position but were told that they would have to share one. Much of my work there over the next twelve years involved translating the linguists and psychologists to each other, a practice that had many fruitful effects on my own research.

More recently, I've been drawn to combining literary writing and science, once again lured by the productive friction between the two, the tension between the objective distance of one and the subjective stance of the other, their competing aesthetics, and clashes of language. In my spare time, I run a political discussion group in my community, where conservatives and liberals read books together and explore the strangeness of each other's viewpoints. Like Nguyen's sympathizer, I find dualities in my life at every turn; evidently, I too am being used by the ability to see every issue from both sides. How could it be otherwise? A single self, after all, seems like not nearly enough of a self.

In a collision of cultures, my mother and I don traditional Czech dress to celebrate Halloween, a holiday then unknown in our native land; in a further departure from Czech tradition, I am wearing clothing intended for men, and my father accompanies us dressed as a space alien.

Chapter 4

Conflict

I spend much of my working time on the top floor of Calgary's spectacular Central Library, where I can settle into a swivel chair, plug in my laptop, and soak up the prairie sunlight that ricochets around the office towers on soaring display outside the library's windows. The murmur of conversations around me is an antidote to the overdose of solitude that can come with writing—I'm glad that utter silence is not enforced here. But today, a man is playing music, very loudly, from his laptop, and a staff member comes over to ask him to turn it down. The man explodes. "Why do *I* need to turn it down? *I'm* only playing my music to drown out the sound of all these *people* in here yammering in all these *languages*. Why don't you tell them to turn down all their *languages*?"

There are, in fact, many different languages spoken in the library. On any given day, I might hear Punjabi, Mandarin, Russian, Arabic, Spanish, Cantonese, Tagalog, Hindi, French, Farsi, Bengali, Turkish, Korean, Urdu, Vietnamese, Italian, or any other of the 140 mother tongues that are claimed by local residents. Calgary is a growing city, reliant on immigration to shore up its labor supply, and the library offers an all-you-can-eat buffet of services for newcomers. As someone who has had to repeatedly wiggle my way into a language from the outside, there is something familiar and almost comforting about being enveloped by a language I don't understand. When I need a mental break from the manuscript I'm tapping out on my computer, I make a game of trying to identify the languages around me. Sometimes I can only recognize the language family, not the specific language itself. Russian, Polish, and Slovak (and of course Czech) are clearly distinct to me, but I can't distinguish among the Slavic languages (such as Bulgarian, Slovenian, and Croatian) that are at the outer reach of my experience. If the language is known to me, such as French or Spanish, I try to peg the regional or national variety. For me, the instinct to peer into a neighboring language is as irresistible as the temptation to gaze, from the shadows of a sidewalk on a wintry evening, into the glow of a brightly lit room where people are sharing a meal.

But this man's explosive response reminds me that not everyone shares this feeling—what many hear instead is an undertone of threat lurking within foreign languages. Although this particular man in the library was less restrained than many of his fellow Canadians, it is not rare, even in a cosmopolitan city like Calgary, to witness a twitchy unease that is triggered by the sounds of other languages. *They always sound angry,* someone might say about speakers of a certain tongue. Or: *I think they talk about us, knowing we can't understand.* I'm struck by how often I hear people voicing the suspicion that speakers of other languages use their mother tongues to secretly discuss others who are present (as if the private conversations of strangers were anybody else's business at all). In fact, this suspicion is so widespread as to seem almost instinctive. Among speakers of Shoshone, whose language is at risk of imminent extinction, politeness norms bow to this sensitivity and require that Shoshone be set aside in the presence of even a single person who does not speak it, lest that person feel that you are talking about them in secret.[1] In conversation, Shoshone speakers must approach strangers linguistically disarmed, palms out and facing upward: *look, no plotting, no gossip, no hidden weapons.*

The man in the library reminds me of how my classmates' shoulders would stiffen when they heard me and my siblings speaking Czech. He brings to mind all those laboratory studies that reveal how children reflexively distance themselves from those who speak another language. To this man—as to the child who believes language to be the permanent, immutable stuff out of which a person is made—an unfamiliar language signals a difference in *kind*. At the very least, it says: *You and I have had different life experiences and teachings; my values, motives, loyalties, and hatreds are as unknown to you as the contents of my conversation.* It is true that two speakers of the same tongue may also have lives that are so different as to seem alien to each other. But a foreign language announces this difference from the very first syllables that are spoken.

Why don't they speak English is another remark that is often prompted by the sounds of a foreign language in public. In fact, the people in question may well know English, may well speak it with robust (if accented) competence at work, and they may well speak it with the majority of the people they encounter each day. But here, with their families or close friends, they want to speak a language that smells of a home they left behind, a language in which jokes are funnier, and a language that binds them closer to each other.

The inescapable truth is that a language both binds and excludes. To those who don't speak it, a language is a wall encircling a community to which they don't belong. Because language is such a potent sign of difference, the swift assimilation of immigrants to English and even the extinction of most of the world's languages can look like progress to many people—an indication, perhaps, that humanity is outgrowing its attachment to tribal linguistic allegiances and coming together. They may even see it as a reversal of the biblical curse of Babel, when a monolingual humanity cooperated so well that God felt threatened by it, and smashed the language shared by all humans into countless shards, many of which are spoken today in Calgary's public libraries. The resulting linguistic mayhem, as the story goes, put an end to humanity's grandest ambitions. Perhaps converging upon a small handful of common languages could help restore our shared aspirations.

Still, I want to hold out for an alternative to both the mayhem of Babel and the mythical uniformity that preceded it. I find the same impulse in the writings of Robert Bringhurst, a scholar who has translated epic works of poetry from the Haida language, now spoken natively by a mere handful of people off the West Coast of Canada. Bringhurst describes his vision of a society in which multiple languages and cultures are allowed to intertwine, much as voices do in the European polyphonic music of Bach's fugues or Josquin's motets:

> In polyphonic music, two or three or more melodic lines, independent of each other yet respectful of each other, move in the same space at the same time, sometimes contradicting one another, sometimes dancing with each other, but never giving up their independence, never falling into line and shouting slogans or marching down the street. The non-Aristotelian physics of classical Haida sculpture, where two creatures can indeed occupy the same space at the same time, is very close to polyphonic space. In both arts, there are discords. Things can bump against each other. But the discords pass, and because they pass, they contribute to the shapeliness and wholeness of the whole. It is hard to imagine how, in a world rich with Haida sculpture and polyphonic music, there could be such things as suicide bombers, or even their comparatively harmless but equally pitiful academic and journalistic equivalents.[2]

As a fellow lover of polyphonic music, I'm enchanted by Bringhurst's vision. I imagine how it might have felt to a listener in the late Middle Ages to hear this bewildering new form of music. In comparison, the earlier Gregorian chant in which all voices moved in unison must have sounded a bit flat—much as a monolingual city now sounds rather flat to me. But along with the complex and ethereal beauty of this music, the metaphor reminds me of the extraordinary skills of composition that are needed to achieve it. One does not get gorgeous polyphonic music simply by gathering a group of singers together and having them vocalize. It takes compositional genius, a sense for tonal contrast and balance and a recognition of just the right degree of dissonance but no more than the ear can tolerate, to allow several melodic strands to move in the same space at the same time. In the hands of an unskilled composer, the same voices quickly become the cacophony of Babel rather than the sublime sounds of Bach, and they risk provoking a fierce nostalgia for the monophonic lines of Gregorian chant. I can't help but wonder whether our modern, complex, increasingly multicultural societies will have the compositional skills needed to pull it off. What would it take to achieve a truly polyphonic society?

Daniel Abrams and Steven Strogatz are mathematicians who have applied their expertise to an omnivore's sampling of real-world questions: Why do crickets chirp in unison? How did a crowd of people unknowingly synchronize their movements so as to cause London's Millennium Bridge to wobble on its opening day? Why has evolution not weeded out the small minority of left-handed people who continue to be engulfed by a right-handed supermajority? In 2003, Abrams and Strogatz attempted a mathematical explanation of the mass extinction of languages occurring around the world. They published a model that simulated the results of competition between two languages within a single pool of speakers.[3] Based on the assumption that people are motivated to learn a language if it is spoken widely enough and if it carries sufficient status (perhaps in the form of economic value), they concluded that when two languages vie for the same set of minds and hearts, one will inevitably, over time, smother the other to the point of extinction—although the authors suggested that this process may be slowed by taking measures to hoist the status of a minority language, citing as an example the resilience of Quebec French within the mass of English speakers in North America. The Abrams and Strogatz model was a toy imitation of the real world, built on the simplifying assumptions that individuals could not speak more than one language and that every person had exactly the same number of interactions with all other members of the population. But the paper inspired an industry of similar models that added or tweaked assumptions to provide a more detailed and realistic mirror of real-life language communities: What happens if we allow people to be bilingual? What if we set the model so the social habits of our speakers vary? What if we make it easier for one generation to bequeath the minority language to the next (for example, by setting up schools that teach the minority language)? To what degree can the death of one language at the hands of another be forestalled?

The underlying premise of all of these models is elegant and unsettling: that languages compete with each other to occupy the minds of individuals. It is unsettling because, in a world that is cross-hatched with connections, and where a handful of super-languages dominate, the survival of the smaller ones depends precisely on the possibility of multiple languages co-existing in the same mind. When the costs of not speaking the dominant language are too steep, smaller, local languages have no chance of winning minds and becoming their sole occupants; they must pin their last hopes on bilingualism. This means that building a polyphonic society in which multiple languages can co-exist—or even answering the question of *whether* we can or should build such a society—can only start with an understanding of the polyphonic mind. And there is a deep psychological truth to the notion that languages struggle for dominance within individual minds, even if the struggle is not as absolute as the one-language-per-mind constraint of the original Abrams and Strogatz model. Languages can and do co-exist within a single mind, but they tussle, as do siblings, over mental resources and attention. Like a household that welcomes a new child, a mind can't introduce a new language without having some impact on the languages already living there.

Language scientists now believe that as people learn a new language, it is impossible to completely sequester the new one from the old; the new language exerts pressure even if the first one continues to be spoken on a daily basis. Try uttering a word in your native tongue, and the newcomer language jostles elbows with the original occupant. Saying anything in either language becomes an exercise in ignoring the cries of "Pick me!" of the language you weren't planning to speak in that moment. Even while quietly listening to someone speaking in one language, we find it difficult to muffle the other, as one laboratory study vividly demonstrates. In this study, Russian–English bilinguals followed instructions spoken to them entirely in Russian.[4] The participants, whose eye movements were being tracked, were asked to move familiar objects around on a tabletop; when asked, for example, to move the stamp (*marku* in Russian), their eyes often flitted over to a marker, whose similar-sounding English name they were unable to mentally suppress. The record of their eye movements offered visible proof of the way the English language tugged at their attention even when they knew to expect only Russian.

When a new language is added, the native tongue no longer enjoys the undivided attention it once had. There is a measurable loss of efficiency in daily use of that language. Even when speaking their native language, bilinguals are a touch slower to fish words from memory compared to monolingual speakers, due to regular crosstalk from the competing language.[5] The slowdown of the native language can become apparent after just one semester of study abroad in young adults.[6] After three years of immersion in a second language, words in that new language may spring to mind more quickly than words in the language that was spoken from birth, even for people who are still far from proficient in the new language.[7] And bilinguals are more often plagued than monolinguals by those maddening tip-of-the-tongue states, when a word or a name is known to the speaker but dances elusively just beyond consciousness's fingertips.[8]

It is quite apt to think of the different languages inside a multilingual person as being like the different voices woven into a polyphonic motet, all occupying the same moment in time and space, all vocalizing at once. This means that some part of the mind must always play the role of conductor, encouraging one language to sing more assertively, another to sing with greater restraint. A perfect balance is rarely achieved. One language often insists upon singing more loudly than is appropriate for the situation. When the mind's conductor is not in full control, as in moments of fatigue, stress, or drunkenness, it may be impossible to tone down the loudest language. Words that leap to mind in one language may have to stand in for the misplaced words of an intended other. And in conversation, a dominant language may drown out one that requires slightly more time or effort to process, an experience that is vividly described by Nancy Huston, an Anglo Canadian who moved to France as an adult, but retained English as her dominant language:

> I experience this virtually as a physical combat in my brain—and the mother tongue invariably comes out on top, whether I like it or not. A few months ago, I had lunch with a francophone friend at Schwarz's, a famous Jewish deli on Saint Lawrence Boulevard in Montreal. She was confiding to me in a low voice about the problems of her first marriage—but halfway through the meal, four hefty middle-aged men came in, evidently regular patrons of the restaurant; they sat down at the next table and started talking loudly in English. Despite my ardent desire to concentrate on the fragile, precious, hesitant, trembling, tearful story of my Québécois friend's marital disaster, all I could hear now were anglophone inanities. "Hey waiter! Could you bring me the head of the bread? Just tell the cook it's for me, he knows I'm crazy about it. The head's the best part you know. Never eat anything but the head of the bread." At the end of the meal, I realized to my despair, that I would never know the details of my friend's marriage; it was not the sort of story that you can ask someone to repeat.[9]

Despite its best efforts, the mind's conductor has only so much control over the comparative volume of its voices. But their volume is by no means fixed. The loudness or softness of one language or another responds to the linguistic milieu of the moment. Spend some time in a monolingual environment, and the mental volume of the language spoken there is soon turned up—which is why flying from Calgary to Lyon is the best method I know for quickly improving my French. I seem to make miraculous strides after just a few days there, due less to a sudden spurt in vocabulary growth than to the relative quietude of my English in an all-French environment. It is in Montreal—where I can never know for sure if the person I'm about to speak with prefers English or French or an exuberant mixture of both—that I most strongly feel the active combat between languages. And sadly, in most of the environments in which I live my daily life, it is my own mother tongue of Czech that has the greatest trouble making its voice heard, nowhere more than in a mostly monolingual English-speaking city like Calgary.

The lesson is clear: do not learn a new language unless you are prepared to alter the one you already have. Some changes are visible almost immediately after a new language is introduced into the learner's mind. For example, many researchers have reported that bilinguals produce and perceive the sounds of their native language in ways that are subtly different from monolingual speakers of the same language, even if they have only recently begun to learn their second language. In one of the most dramatic demonstrations of this effect, known as "phonetic drift," linguist Charles Chang studied adult native speakers of English who had just begun to learn Korean.[10] These learners were enrolled in a six-week intensive course that took up four hours of each weekday, but they had no other contact with Korean in their daily lives on an American university campus. Their English was firmly entrenched and, one might think, impervious to the influence of such a late interloper in their linguistic psyche. Nonetheless, Chang found that just a couple of weeks after the course began, the students' pronunciation of certain English consonants and vowels started to drift over toward the Korean style of pronouncing these sounds. The students were beginning to acquire a very subtle Korean accent, even after decades of a life lived in English and only weeks of learning Korean a few hours a day in a classroom. Their accent, to be sure, was so subtle as to be undetectable to most ears, but it was distinct enough to be picked up by precise acoustic measurements.

Such studies show that no language has ever settled into its final shape in the mind, even if it's been the sole tenant there until adulthood. When pressed up against other languages, its contours shift in response; when the other languages withdraw, the native language aspires to its original form. For multilingual people who move back and forth between their language environments, the tidal pull of the ambient language on their own speech can take on a cyclical rhythm. Researchers Michele Sancier and Carol Fowler documented these cycles in the speech of a Brazilian graduate student enrolled at an American university, recording her in her native language of Brazilian Portuguese after four months of US residence, then again after a two-and-a-half-month sojourn in Brazil, then again four months after her return to the United States.[11] When native speakers of Brazilian Portuguese listened to the recordings of her speech, they discerned that she had sprouted a foreign accent after living in the United States for four months; after her brief stay in Brazil, her speech once again sounded native-like to her fellow Brazilians; another four months after her return, her American accent was audible once more.

In addition to ruffling the sounds of a native language, the new language can reach deep into its lexicon to rearrange the concepts that underlie a person's understanding of the words of their native tongue. Speakers of Greek, whose language enforces a distinction between light and dark shades of blue by labeling them with different words (*ghalazio* for light blue and *ble* for dark blue), are slightly faster than English speakers to visually distinguish between shades that sit on opposite sides of the *ghalazio / ble* border. But after several years of life in an English-speaking country, this advantage disappears.[12] Evidently, the Greek distinction loses a touch of its crispness when it shares a mind with English, a language that is more cavalier about describing blueness.

It would appear that the only way to preserve one's native language in its pure monolingual state is to avoid even the slightest exposure to learning another. In a stunning demonstration, psychologist Barbara Malt and her colleagues showed that native English speakers who spent a mere twenty minutes learning how to name various beverage containers in Russian began using the English labels for these objects differently as a result.[13] In English, most drinks come in containers that are called *glasses, cups,* or *mugs,* and membership within these categories, as with all words, is somewhat murky. (If you use a container that has a handle and is made of glass for drinking tea, is that a glass or a mug? If you use the same container to drink milk, *now* is it a glass or a mug?) In Russian, ten different words are available to name the assortment of objects that are covered by the English *cup / mug / glass* trinity. And while Russian *stakan* translates roughly to English *glass,* and Russian *chaska* to English *cup,* the alignment is far from perfect—for example, Russian speakers would call an object with no handles that is made of paper or Styrofoam a *stakan,* whereas most English speakers would consider it a cup, not a glass. After participants successfully learned how to apply the Russian labels in a single session in the language lab, their English category labels wobbled in the direction of Russian, with the glass category now absorbing objects that were previously deemed to be cups. Given that the research participants resumed their normal monolingual lives upon leaving the lab, this wobble may have been a temporary distortion of their English usage after being bombarded with a small set of foreign words, looping repeatedly for twenty minutes in one sitting. But it mirrors the more permanent changes that were found, in a separate study, to have settled into the minds of native Russian speakers who relocated to the United States. The boundaries of their Russian labels for drinking vessels revealed a distinctly English-like shape. Presumably, these immigrants had learned the English pattern over time by sharing beverages with native speakers rather than by being drilled on the English names for beverage containers.[14]

Linguists are familiar with the dangers of language attrition, especially for children who are transplanted from one language environment to another while very young. But they had long assumed that a native language nurtured to adulthood would resist the incursion of a later-learned tongue, especially if the native language continued to be used as the dominant language. Results like these, which show how readily a native language changes when it shares a brain with a newcomer language, have prompted researchers Monika Schmid and Barbara Köpke to suggest that some of the same tensions that lead to outright language loss are at play to some extent in the mind of every bilingual. They have even gone so far as to assert that "every bilingual is an attriter" of language.[15]

This statement sparked howls of protest among some of their colleagues.[16] These colleagues rushed in to point out that, after all, if a new language is learned in adulthood, its influences on the native tongue remain quite subtle, even if the native language is sorely neglected for decades. Yes, people may take longer to unearth words they haven't spoken in years, and they may be prone to using simpler sentence structures, and a smaller variety of them, but their native language doesn't *crumble;* for the most part, they continue to speak in grammatical sentences. Moreover, although learning a new language undeniably leaves an imprint on previously learned languages, its effects are not indiscriminate. Not all aspects of the earlier languages will be altered. An American student who goes on to study Korean to the point of achieving fluency in it, all while continuing to live in the United States, will not suddenly begin swapping *r* and *l* in her speech—at most, her very proficient English will take on the slightest coloring, so that discerning ears may pick up on something "extra" in her clearly native-like English. It is important, argue these researchers, to distinguish between the accommodations made by a native language as it moves over in the mind to make room for a new one, and the beginnings of one language devouring another. It is true that competition between languages becomes a permanent fact of life for any bilingual. But the competition need not be a fight to the death—regardless of the results of the toy model built by Daniel Adams and Steven Strogatz, in which languages battle for sole occupancy of speakers' minds. The constant tug of one language at another within the mind of a bilingual person may gently reshape certain consonants and vowels, and it may result in an extra fraction of a second of rummaging around before words can be pulled out of memory and launched off the lips. But to say that these changes are the same as outright language *loss* is overly alarmist. It risks stoking an unwarranted fear of bilingualism. It can give the mistaken impression that a language securely lodged in the mind is vulnerable.

As new research reveals the pliability of a native language in the presence of a second one, these critics worry that the benefits of bilingualism may, in the public's perception, become overshadowed by unwarranted fears of its costs. They point out that a reflexive distrust of other languages can quickly rise to the surface, creating an exaggerated sense of their threat to an established language. Let us be careful, they seem to be saying, not to enflame the anxieties of the man who, fearful of the sounds of other languages in the public library, pines for monophony.

Polyglots have probably existed for as long as language has, and linguists often assert that more than half of humans currently living on our planet speak more than one language. However, a scientific understanding of how languages share mental space has barely hatched. Lack of firm knowledge, though, has rarely stopped anyone from holding—and voicing—passionate opinions about the blessings or terrors of multilingualism. Language is too enmeshed with culture and identity to allow neutrality much of a chance.

These opinions have had a way of leaching into the scientific study of language itself, so that research has at times reflected society's attitudes toward multilingualism more than it has guided them. The first half of the twentieth century, at least in the English-speaking world, is rife with scholarly writing that oozes concern about the harmful consequences of bilingualism for children unfortunate enough to be burdened with more than one language. One expert wrote that "mental confusion is seen to exist in bilingual children to a higher degree than in monoglot children."[17] Another opined that "the use of a foreign language in the house is one of the chief factors in producing mental retardation."[18] Yet another suspected that being divided between two languages, and hence, two conflicting identities, "can lead to split personality and, at worst, to schizophrenia."[19]

It wasn't until 1962 that a landmark research study by Elizabeth Peal and Wallace ("Wally") Lambert of McGill University began to turn the tide of scholarly opinion about the psychological effects of bilingualism.[20] (Wally Lambert is the author of another groundbreaking study, discussed in Chapter 2, that revealed the stigma attached to speakers of French in Quebec. His own children were raised as French–English bilinguals.) Peal and Lambert's paper offered a blistering critique of the methods used by earlier studies purporting to show serious mental deficits among bilingual children. In some of these studies, the school performance of poor immigrant children had been compared to that of monolingual children from prosperous homes, making it impossible to tell whether the performance gap between the two groups was the result of bilingualism or (more plausibly) a consequence of poverty. In some cases, children of different ages were tested, their performance then compared with each other. Or, children with minimal English skills were assessed—in English— with researchers attributing their poor performance to bilingualism rather than to a poor grasp of the language in which they were being tested! Once Peal and Lambert controlled for these crucial variables, they found that, overall, bilingual children performed as well as or even better than monolingual children on various tests of nonverbal and verbal intelligence.

In hindsight, it may be hard to believe that so-called language experts once held such bleak and biased beliefs—especially if you belong, as Lambert did, to a middle-class professional family in which dinner takes place in more than one language. But at the time of their writing, their conclusions must have seemed like common sense, their results merely confirming the obvious. Particularly in North America, the great majority of bilingual children were immigrant children, many of whom lived in squalor. Their parents were generally uneducated, and the children's own schooling may have been splintered by dislocation, poverty, or war. The evidence was there for anyone to see: the children who spoke a language other than English were not doing as well as the children who were raised speaking only English. Added to these demographic realities was a general feeling of besiegement among many settled North Americans. The early twentieth century in the United States was a time of backlash against waves of immigration in the late 1800s and early 1900s; two world wars did nothing to calm fears of foreigners, whose loyalties were constantly suspect. It was a time when the sounds of other languages must have seemed particularly sinister. In historical context, it's perhaps not so surprising that those early, sloppy studies of bilingualism were not scrutinized too closely—until these studies encountered the eyes of researchers like Peal and Lambert, whose own experience of bilingualism clashed with what they saw in published reports.

In contemporary cosmopolitan circles (and certainly among affluent parents clamoring to enroll their children in dual-language school programs), it is Peal and Lambert's results that seem to align with common sense. Multilingualism, in fact, is often touted as a cognitive tonic. But given what scientists are learning about the incessant competition between languages, a realist is perfectly justified in questioning how it is possible for several languages to be stuffed into the brains of children as successfully as is claimed by enthusiasts of multilingualism.

At the most basic level, languages compete with each other for time and opportunities to speak them. We now know that it takes an enormous amount of contact with a language to learn it properly; monolingual children who are included in too few conversations in their early years enter school at a disadvantage compared with their peers from verbose households.[21] Surely, a child whose time is divided between two or more languages will feel each language pinched for practice time—much like a child who takes up both violin and piano, and who is less likely to progress in either as quickly as children who devote themselves to a single instrument.

And indeed, these realities are apparent. Elementary school children who are learning two languages have vocabularies that are as large as those of children who speak one—but their vocabularies are split between their languages, so that each language contains fewer words than the single language of a monolingual child. In theory, this could have devastating consequences for scholastic achievement. There is very clear evidence that vocabulary size is a strong predictor of success in school. It's well known, for example, that children from poor households often enter school with smaller-than-average vocabularies; this drawback is linked to a gap in school performance that only yawns ever wider as the child advances through the grades.[22] If a child is divided between a home language and a school language, then lower proficiency in the school language might be expected to have similar disastrous results.

But it does not appear to. Once we account for the effects of poverty, which is indeed a fact of life for many bilingual children due to their families' trajectories, maintaining two languages does not dim their long-term academic prospects. The achievement gap of bilingual children narrows rather than widens over time.[23] Nor is being *taught* in two languages an impediment; a thorough survey of dual-language programs in North America reached the verdict that once enough time is allowed for students to reach proficiency, students who learn in two languages do as well in school as students who are taught in only one.[24] Bilingual education does not even disadvantage children who have language-specific learning disabilities. These children struggle in school more than children without a disability, but they do not struggle any more as a result of knowing or studying in two languages. Even these children have room in their minds for more than one language.

There seems to be a stark difference, then, between a diet that is deficient in language overall as opposed to a diet that divides its nutrients between two languages. Unlike linguistic deprivation, linguistic time-sharing doesn't hinder the efficiency with which a child learns language. There is some carryover of skills that offsets the competitive tensions between the languages—just as we would expect that cross-training between two sports would have some advantages for overall strength and stamina, and that these advantages would offset some of the costs of dividing one's training time between two very different types of movement.

In some cases, skills that are more easily learned in one language can act as scaffolding for the other. This is certainly true of learning to read.[25] English is saddled with one of the most opaque alphabetic systems ever inflicted upon schoolchildren, with famously loose connections between individual sounds and symbols. How in the world is a child supposed to learn the sound that the letter *g* makes when it inserts itself into words such as *girl* and *gin* but also *cough* and *dough*? The lucky children who are born into writing systems that are more transparent—such as Spanish or Czech—typically learn to sound words out at a younger age. And so it was for me. I first picked up the rudimentary skills of reading in Czech rather than English, without any actual memory of being taught—no doubt Czech's compulsively regular orthography made it easier to connect specific marks on the page with particular sounds, or even to have the *aha!*

realization that words are composed of separate sounds, each of which can be recognized as an individual with its own visual avatar. From there, it was a happy experiment to extend the same alphabetic avatars to the sounds of English. I recall being able to read simple words in English well before my peers in school learned this skill from the curriculum. Upon discovering this, my kindergarten teacher trotted me out to the staff lounge to demonstrate my ability to the other teachers, who were equally astounded by the reading ability of this immigrant kid who still spoke broken English. I enjoyed the attention, which was lavished on me as if I were a genius. I doubt the teachers thought to credit the orthographic tidiness of my native language for my precocious reading.

Some of the skills that support language learning may even be strengthened by exposure to more than one language. Simply extending the range of sounds and structures that children hear in different languages may have the effect of sharpening their attention to them. In some situations, bilinguals learn new words more quickly than monolinguals.[26] They may be more sensitive to very fine distinctions in speech sounds.[27] (And those inclined to collect languages will be encouraged to hear that experience with two languages can make it easier to break into an unfamiliar third—as shown, for example, by a study in which English–Mandarin bilinguals had an easier time than monolingual English participants in learning the difficult "click" sounds of Ndebele, a language spoken in Zimbabwe.[28]) Because bilinguals navigate two grammatical systems, often with wildly different opinions about how to assemble words and sentences out of linguistic parts, language's underlying structure becomes more visible to them.[29] Learning two languages, then, may offer similar benefits to those who learn to play more than one musical instrument: what one loses in technical fluency with a single instrument, one gains in a deepened musicality, an understanding of how music is put together and how each instrument contributes to the overall effect.

All of this helps to explain why bilingual children are ultimately much less hobbled in school than one might predict, based on the state of their vocabulary knowledge as they enter their first classroom. But there is something else behind this surprising resilience. Vocabulary gaps in the language of instruction don't necessarily reflect inadequate time with the language (or "time on task" in school parlance). They also reflect the fact that children's languages are beginning to specialize, to divide the labor of life in a predictable way. A group of psychologists who studied bilingual children in preschool and elementary school found that their early vocabularies were being sorted into different language bins.[30] In their home languages, the children knew more words that related to objects and concepts one would talk about at home: words like *squash, ladle,* or *camper.* In English, their school language, the children knew more words for concepts discussed at school, like *astronaut, penguin, rectangle,* or *vowel.* In fact, the bilingual children knew about as many English school-related words as the monolingual children did, which helps to explain why a vocabulary that straddles two languages may be much less of a handicap for scholastic achievement than one might think. To a large extent, their English vocabulary lacked certain words simply because these words were not very relevant to the school environment in which they used English; as a result, it was not a major threat to their academic progress.

Adults who speak multiple languages are well aware of the division of labor between them. For most of us, none of our languages is entirely complete, all the more so if they have been learned on different continents and in different periods in our lives. Eva Hoffman, who left her native Poland at the age of thirteen, writes of the resulting gaps in her native tongue: "In Polish, whole provinces of adult experience are missing. I don't know Polish words for 'microchips,' or 'pathetic fallacy,' or *The Importance of Being Earnest.* If I tried talking to myself in my native tongue, it would be a stumbling conversation indeed, interlaced with English expressions."[31]

Most of the time, this fragmentation does not cause us any trouble. At home, we learn the language needed for loving, cooking, and fighting. And we are perfectly articulate when we love, cook, and fight. At work, we learn the language of our profession. And we are not hampered by our inability to give effective presentations or evaluate employees in our home language. At times, this separation can be a blessing, allowing us to draw a curtain between the different rooms of our lives. When I was a graduate student, I worked closely with a fellow student who, like me, could speak Québécois French. At the end of a long day, we would sometimes go out to drink beer and speak French. For both of us, this was a social language, the language learned on the streets and spoken when hanging out with friends. It was the fun language. It was not a language to exert oneself in. We would have been hard-pressed to have highly abstract conversations in it, and it would have been impossible for us to hash out the details of the experimental procedures we were working on. Speaking in French enforced relaxation and made it impossible for work to bully its way into our leisure time.

But seen through a monolingual lens, such splintering appears pathological or, at the very least, deficient. Achievement is still always measured against the monolingual norm, not against the expressive needs of the bilingual person whose life takes place in two languages. (Never mind that monolinguals themselves vary widely in their mastery over vocabulary and grammatical styles.[32]) If maintaining two languages means that a person can grow up to be able to speak to her grandmother—without jeopardizing her prospects in an Anglophone economy—what does it really matter if she takes an extra tenth of a second to retrieve a word in English, or if her English vowels are unusually shaped, or if she uses certain words in ways that may startle a native speaker?

But this is not the way we tend to talk about language in the English-speaking world. Achievement in *English* seems to be all that matters—to a level that is indistinguishable from that of a monolingual Anglophone—whether attaining this level of achievement is valuable to the individual or not. This plainly frustrates many of the researchers who have conducted studies on the effects of bilingualism. In many of the papers, alongside the conclusion that bilinguals are as good as, slightly worse than, or slightly better than monolingual English speakers on this or that particular skill or test, there are plaintive reminders: but let's not forget that the bilingual subjects *can speak another language*.

When a child considers taking up a second sport, or a second musical instrument, we weigh the costs against the child's goals. Is her goal to win international competitions in the sport? Does he want to become a violin soloist with a world-class orchestra? We recognize that most people who set out to learn a skill are not reaching for these heights, and that there is immense value in being able to enjoy multiple sports or pick up and play any one of a number of instruments. The benefits of knowing another sport or being able to play another instrument are prominent in the deliberations. But even within the scientific literature on bilingualism, the spotlight is so often fixed on preserving English mastery rather than on the pragmatic trade-off between English virtuosity and knowing another language. This speaks volumes about the assumptions lodged deep within our monophonic society: bilingualism is acceptable as long as it has no impact on English.

Through a multilingual lens, other things come into focus. To many who speak more than one language, the combat between them is one of the *blessings* of bilingualism, not just a tiresome side effect. As with polyphonic music, the beauty lies precisely in the fact that the mind is split between different voices whose melodic paths must all be pursued at once. There is also beauty in the moments of dissonance, startling clashes, pleasurable unsettlings. (What would jazz be, after all, without its blue notes?) The details of one's native language and culture are at their most vivid when they strike a discordant note with another language or culture.

My inner poet is constantly delighted by the chronic intrusion of English into my other languages. When I utter the vowel-less word *blb* in Czech, it is *because* English insists on its simultaneous translation—*idiot*—that I become aware of just how phonetically perfect the Czech version is, with its two bumbling consonants holding up the lurching simpleton between them. The too-elegant English word is no match; it simply doesn't capture the same degree of *blb*-ness. To many French speakers, the phrase used to describe love at first sight, *un coup de foudre* (meaning: *a lightning strike*) may sound like a tired cliché, but its metaphorical force claps me in the ear every time I hear it, due to English piping up with its far blander, more literal expression. And I'm delighted by the contradiction between English's *falling in love* and Czech's *se zamilovat,* whose literal translation is something like *to enamor oneself of.* This tension between accidental love and self-inflicted love enthralls me, and it strikes me that there are times when the Czech phrase is far more apt than the English one. When one language is constantly accompanied by the running commentary of another, it's harder to treat it with the indifference doled out to the familiar objects in one's life.

As many will confirm, some of the best things about being bilingual come from the very fact that languages are not quarantined from each other in the mind. When bilinguals talk to each other, they often mix their languages, not simply to evade moments of lapsed memory but to wring the greatest expressive power from them. The internal polyphony of languages makes it possible to pick and choose between one vocal stream and another. When a woman says "*Je veux pas avoir des* dishpan hands" ("I don't want to have dishpan hands"),[33] it's not because she can't think how to describe the effects of dishwater on her hands in French. It's because French does not have a ready-made phrase for just this condition—in French, dishpan hands are not *a thing* the way they are in English, and when she inserts this English phrase into her French sentence, she pulls in with it all of the social judgments and connotations that are part and parcel of the phrase.

In a market economy in which competition is allowed to flourish, choice is made possible, along with the mental work that choice sometimes entails. In the same way, knowing multiple languages—and the cultures they drag with them—makes it possible to choose between competing phrases, competing social habits, and competing values, all of whose merits and defects are illuminated. It becomes possible to escape the limits of monopoly.

These liberating effects have long been described by speakers of more than one language, who feel that the rewards of their inner linguistic battles far outweigh their mental costs. But in recent years, it's become possible to find echoes of these sentiments even within scientific papers on bilingualism—many of which, I suspect, are written by researchers who speak more than one language themselves. Struck by evidence of how languages constantly wrestle for attention, these researchers have proposed that, alongside the uninvited intrusions and the words that melt on the tip of the tongue, such competition can have value for speakers. They have suggested that this linguistic conflict can exercise the mind, perhaps strengthening it not just for language, but for other mental activities that involve a clash between impulses.

The Canadian psychologist Ellen Bialystok has been especially influential in this new area of research. She has concentrated on the heavy demands that bilingualism places on the mental capacity known as executive function—that is, on the metaphorical conductor that modulates the volume of each language in the mind and directs it to sing in turn. She argues that regular practice in directing languages spills over into other areas of cognition. As a result, bilinguals should generally be better at squashing distractions that are irrelevant to a task at hand, since they must constantly be shushing an intruding language or skillfully switching back and forth between languages.

In 2004, Bialystok and her colleagues published a paper in which they used a simple but maddening procedure called the Simon task to measure executive function among their participants.[34] In the Simon task, participants have to press one of two buttons depending on the color of a square that appears on a screen—for example, the left button for a blue square, the right button for a red one. Sometimes, the square itself is on the same side as the button that needs to be pressed. Not surprisingly, when this happens, participants press the correct button very quickly. But when the location of the square clashes with the location of the correct button—the left button to confirm the blue square on the right side of the screen, for example—participants can easily get confused, either pressing the wrong button or taking longer to press the correct button. This game serves as an analogy for what presumably happens in the mind when a bilingual person is trying to retrieve a word in one language while dealing with the distracting effects of a word from the other language that is clamoring for attention. In fact, the argument is that the tasks require the same skills and draw on the same circuitry in the brain.

Like many tasks that lean heavily on executive function, the older the participants, the harder they find it to press the correct button on the clashing trials. This aligns with the experience of many older people, who complain that age has made it more difficult to retrieve words or to pay attention to two things at once, such as trying to cook dinner while carrying on a conversation. But Bialystok and her colleagues found that older participants who were bilingual performed better than their monolingual counterparts. The researchers suggested that a lifetime of managing the clashes between competing languages had, to some extent, spared executive functioning from the usual ravages of aging. Later studies extended the research to young adults and children, and some have reported similar advantages of bilingualism on various tasks that demand that irrelevant information be suppressed.[35]

Of course, these results are only interesting if they reflect something meaningful about how people conduct their real lives. But trying to measure performance on a real-world activity is much harder than measuring performance on an artificial task controlled and timed by a computer. For example, if you were trying to measure whether bilingual people have an easier time cooking dinner while having a conversation, how would you control for the differences in cooking skills among the various participants? An expert cook might be able to prepare food while talking *and* tap-dancing, simply because of the time he has logged in the kitchen. His prowess could not be compared fairly to the ineptitude of someone who struggles to assemble a meal in the best of circumstances, regardless of how many languages either of them spoke. And surely the topic of conversation— how absorbing it was, or how demanding—would affect cooking performance, but how would you take this into account in your measurements? A simple, uniform task that measures performance in milliseconds offers a much cleaner method for scientists, but its relevance depends on whether it can predict a person's ability to function in the messier day-to-day activities of life. To date, there is very little clear evidence for this.

There are, however, reports that bilingualism may have some dramatic consequences for people's lives: things became quite interesting when Bialystok and her colleagues examined the medical records of patients who had been referred to a memory clinic and were diagnosed with Alzheimer's disease.[36] They found that patients who had used two languages throughout their lives were an average of four years older when they were diagnosed with the illness than those who spoke a single language. Bilingualism, they suggested, helps delay the onset of Alzheimer's disease. And this has tremendous implications: as researchers continue to struggle to find any pharmaceutical treatment for the illness, the best advice that medical practitioners have to offer is to try to stay as mentally active as possible, as this appears to stave off the disease to some extent. If being bilingual truly does postpone the illness by four years, this would make it one of the most effective preventive measures that we know of.

These results lit up the bilingualism research community. Media outlets eagerly reported the findings. To many people who speak more than one language, such results are a vindication, an acknowledgment of the subjective value that they themselves place on the tug-of-war they experience between their languages. But a celebration would be premature: more recently, a number of studies have failed to find a bilingual advantage on common tasks that measure executive function. The conflicting reports have sparked a vigorous debate, still ongoing, about whether the cognitive benefits of bilingualism are real, or whether they are the result of flawed methods and a general bias in favor of publishing exciting, novel results over humdrum failures to document any differences between monolinguals and bilinguals.

Some of the controversy around the bilingual advantage may reflect a problem with tossing all bilingual people into a single category. In reality, bilingual people come in many varieties. No two bilinguals deploy their languages in exactly the same way. Some experience their languages as sharply divided by time and space—they may use one language in their country of residence and the other when they visit their ancestral land, much like the Brazilian graduate student whose accent vacillated depending on her location. They may speak one language at home and the other at work. Or they may spend their days around other bilinguals who shift between languages without a moment's warning and even blend the two languages in the same sentence. Each of these situations places very different demands on the mind's conductor. Competition is most strident when both languages operate at full volume, but when there is a clear separation between languages, the other will not intrude as forcefully. And if one language has, over time, become much more dominant than the other, the quieter language may not compete very assertively at all. Such mild forms of conflict may not offer much training of their speaker's executive function. In a new wave of studies, researchers have already begun to sort and identify some of these variations in the bilingual experience.

Adding to this complexity is the fact that, in many societies, people who are bilingual inhabit different social and economic realities than people who are monolingual. Throughout most of the history of the United States, for example, bilingualism has been confined to immigrant communities, often filled with people who were poorer than those in more settled, monolingual communities. In other countries, particularly where immigration rates are much lower, the situation may be very different. There, residents who speak more than one (or two) languages may be among the highly educated and internationally mobile elite. Such population differences could either exaggerate or mask differences that rightly belong to bilingualism; much like the early researchers who argued for the damaging effects of using two languages, those who now argue for its salutary effects need to be careful not to mistakenly attribute these effects to bilingualism if what they really reflect are differences in socioeconomic status or education.

It may take years or decades before the debate is settled, but it is unlikely—to me at least, at the time of writing this book—that the bilingual advantage is a complete mirage. There are enough positive results to persuade me that at least for some bilinguals, under some conditions, speaking more than one language strengthens certain brain functions—though it's not known whether these changes can be felt in real life or whether knowing two languages offers some special advantage that other complex mental activities (such as playing a musical instrument in an orchestra) cannot replace.[37] But regardless of how the debate resolves itself, the sheer energy and resources that have been poured into these studies reveal an important shift in how scientists now think about bilingualism. The friction between languages is no longer seen only in a negative light. Competition between languages *is* real, in ways that those early researchers in bilingualism may not have imagined. But it need not be unduly disruptive. Almost every human mind is able to accommodate the internal combat that comes with knowing two languages—even if a great deal of care and support are needed to keep one language from dominating the other. And more importantly, the debate over the bilingual advantage introduces a new idea. It reaches beyond the question of whether the value of knowing another language offsets the unavoidable tensions that come with being bilingual; it raises the possibility that the conflict *itself* has benefits.

Perhaps anxieties about the conflicted mind of the bilingual person have always really been about a different kind of fear: the fear of conflict among speakers of different languages. And perhaps, in reality, it is this fear—whether or not it is openly acknowledged—that has driven much of the educational policy in Western countries.

It's not that Western societies don't promote multilingualism—modern language departments are a staple of every university, and public schools devote vast sums of money to the teaching of other languages. Many school districts require that students learn at least one language in addition to their mother tongue; in Europe, the expectation is that all students will learn at least two. European professionals are often bilingual by necessity even if they never leave home, given that more and more businesses and academic environments rely on English as a *lingua franca*. Almost no one would disagree with the idea that knowing multiple languages is an asset, a way of broadening one's options in life. And generally, this idea is not especially threatening.

But languages have value for people aside from their sheer usefulness, or we would all converge in these post-Babel times upon a single language. This value is starkly apparent in Quebec, where Francophones have fought to preserve their language despite the many impracticalities of maintaining a French-speaking society nestled inside a massive English-speaking region. Their motivation is eloquently captured by blogger Stéphane Laporte, who wrote the following in the Montreal paper *La Presse,* which I've translated from the original French:[38]

> For more and more people, a language is nothing but a code.
> An interchangeable tool. If it's more practical to speak English,

let's speak English. If it's more practical to speak Chinese, let's speak Chinese.

A language is not just a set of sounds and symbols that allows one to talk on a cell phone or send texts. A language is an imprint on the heart of those who speak it. It's the repertoire of thoughts, emotions, experiences, and dreams shared by a community. Our language is not better than other languages, but it is ours. It's our lived experience. It is to us that it speaks, in more than words. Our laughter, tears, and hopes have a French ring to them. And if we're proud of what we are, we're proud of the language that has allowed us to become what we are. It is in French that we've named our reality.

It is precisely this entanglement of language with emotion and personal identity that quickens the blood. Cool, practical arguments offer only a partial view of language; they do not trigger swells of loyalty, or fear of annihilation, or dogged resistance to change, or a sense of affront and outrage. These things are accomplished by the hot welding of language with self.

It is telling that Western societies seem most comfortable with multilingualism when it's wrapped in cooler arguments and when it does not intrude too much on emotional terrain. Many North American linguists, for example, express frustration that students' first introduction to a language other than English is often delayed until middle school or high school—*after* the period during which children are most receptive to learning new languages. But perhaps this delay is not mere obtuseness; perhaps it is also a way of keeping other languages out of the landscape of early childhood, that time of life when language is etched into some of our most powerful memories. Maybe it is a way of permitting other languages to enter our children, but to keep them from settling too deeply in their bodies and emotions, lest that fundamentally change who they are.

When sociolinguist Ai Mizuta studied the launch of a new dual-language Mandarin–English kindergarten in Vancouver, she noted that the program was open only to children whose first language was English, excluding children whose parents spoke to them at home in Mandarin. In detailed interviews, she discovered that Chinese parents whose children were eligible to enter the program had very different reasons for wanting their children to learn Mandarin than parents whose children were excluded because they spoke the language at home. The eligible parents, who were more deeply assimilated into their Anglophone environment, saw the Mandarin language as *useful* for their children, a way of opening career options in a world where China's global influence was on the rise. The excluded parents, however, saw the language as a way of preserving and expressing who they were. Regardless of the stated reasoning behind the admissions policy, it had the effect of weeding out families for whom the Mandarin language was a badge of identity and of welcoming families for whom it was a sensible tool.[39]

In Europe, more and more nations have been adopting English as the language of instruction at the university level. It is a practical solution that allows these universities to recruit experts from around the world and to position themselves within a global community of researchers and academics. As a result, access to English in public schools is important for gaining entry into higher education. All of this is acknowledged. But as important as it is for children to learn English, I imagine that a proposal to extend English as the main language of instruction down into the childhood years would create an unholy furor in just about any European country. So far, there is reassuringly little evidence that the youth of Germany or France view their native languages as too bothersome to maintain once they've mastered English, or that they decide to speak English instead of their native languages to their own children. If they did embark upon such a trend, I have no doubt that it would trigger a national crisis of the highest order. Amid the rhetoric proclaiming the need for citizens to know other languages in order to thrive within a mobile, cosmopolitan Europe, and the tolerance of English as a language that connects people of different nations, there have been no calls to abandon separate national languages in order to forge a common *identity*. For many Europeans, the various languages they speak play very different roles in their lives. For all its usefulness, English cannot possibly replace the language imprinted on their hearts and woven throughout their national culture. Their languages operate on separate planes of existence, a multidimensional reality that forestalls the inevitable monolingualism of the mathematical models of Abrams and Strogatz that I introduced earlier in this chapter.

It is interesting how utilitarian arguments can smooth the way for a language that is met with passionate rejection on grounds of identity. In Cyprus, an island nation that was partitioned into the Turkish-speaking north and the Greek-speaking south after the armed conflicts of 1974, using the Turkish language came to be seen as an egregious act of disloyalty to Greek Cypriots in the south, despite its being one of the official languages of the republic. In 2003, Turkish was introduced as an optional language into Greek-Cypriot high schools. Initially, official ministry documents promoted the teaching of Turkish on the grounds that this would help the country overcome its ethnic wounds; it emphasized the bonds between the two groups as a result of their shared 400-year history, evident in the many streaks of Turkish in the Cypriot Greek language. But this justification was seen as an affront by many teachers and prospective students, who still heard Turkish as the language of the enemy. Gradually, the ministry's rhetoric shifted to frame Turkish as a useful "foreign" language. Teaching this language was portrayed not as an act of political reconciliation, but simply as one part of the grand multilingual project that is the new Europe. This restatement moved the issue from the hot zone of identity to the cooler realm of economics.[40]

But what of languages that struggle to justify themselves on utilitarian grounds? It's easy enough to make a case for Mandarin or

German or Turkish as major players in the global economy, but the story is very different for the vast majority of the world's languages, spoken by fewer people and bolstered by no grand institutions or commercial networks. Without clear economic reasons to learn smaller languages, their value to potential speakers rests on a sense of identity and belonging. And identity only becomes compelling enough if that language permits a way of being that no other language allows, or if it offers the embrace of a community of people who see themselves as set apart from the dominant culture.

And therein lie the seeds of conflict. Languages tend to feed on a sense of apartness. This point was made by linguist Salikoko Mufwene in his observations of the resilience of Gullah Geechee, a language spoken by fewer than half a million speakers in the United States.[41] Historically, the Gullah language, which is concentrated on the coasts of South Carolina and Georgia, grew out of a version of English spoken by African American slaves; Gullah began to diverge from English over the course of the eighteenth century, as the plantation industry segregated slaves from most White Europeans and their descendants, so that the two groups had very little contact with each other. Gullah has resisted being extinguished or absorbed into standard English, despite its small number of speakers. It has survived the arrival of many English-speaking newcomers into the area, and the daily presence of standard English in local schools and in the media. In his 1997 paper, Mufwene argued that the language has been preserved because the Gullah-speaking community remained sharply segregated. Newcomers did not settle in the Gullah communities. They instead moved into neighborhoods physically severed from Gullah communities by highways and tracts of undeveloped land. Gullah speakers rarely encountered non-Gullah residents except in grocery stores, and there they rarely had much in the way of meaningful interactions. Children in the Gullah community learned standard English at school, and if they left the community for college, they might not speak Gullah at all for a number of years. But upon their return to their home communities, they picked up where they left off and continued to speak Gullah with their families, friends, and neighbors. To do otherwise would have been socially risky; Mufwene reported that a number of Gullah speakers told him they feared being judged as snobbish if they spoke English to their family and neighbors, and that failing to speak Gullah would have been a barrier to making friends in the local community. To not speak Gullah was seen as disloyal, a rejection of one's roots and community and of the distinctness that separated Gullah speakers from other locals. The community language was preserved in part because those who did not speak the language were not granted full membership as insiders—the costs of exclusion were too hard for many to bear.

Particularly for communities that have been looked down upon by the dominant culture, language can offer comfort and solidarity. Speaking their own language is a way that people can say to each other: *Here among us, you belong. Here, you do not have to deny who you are. Here, we will look out for each other—you will not be left at the mercy of the outside world, which does not fully see you as you are. Here, you do not have to transform yourself to be like everyone else on the outside.* But often, the flip side of this solidarity is the message: *Here, you must embrace who we are and agree that we are not like those on the outside. You must align yourself with us by speaking as we do, and not as they do on the outside.* The community's warm embrace clarifies the value of the language, as does its implied threat of disownment.

For some, separation may be an acceptable price to pay for keeping a language alive, and with it, a cultural heritage. For example, Ray Castro, a research associate at Harvard University, published a paper in 1976 that reads like a manifesto in favor of monolingual enclaves.[42] In it, Castro argues that countries like the United States should foster language diversity by allowing—and even encouraging—monolingual communities whose residents, for the most part, speak *only* Spanish or Navajo or Mandarin. These communities should be officially recognized as places in which *all* business within the community—

work, school, medical services, law enforcement, and so on—takes place in the local language. Certainly, there might be some people within each monolingual community who are bilingual and whose lives are lived in contact with the outside world, but visitors to the community would be expected to function in the community language. Castro's vision for a multilingual America is that of a nation containing many miniature Quebecs, or perhaps a nation hinting at a preindustrial Papua New Guinea, with many autonomous communities preserving their languages and cultures but fused together into a single nation with the help of multilingual citizens who resort to English as the common language.

It's an interesting vision, driven no doubt by Castro's own sense of loss of his ancestral language, a loss that seeps into the scholarly language of his article. He admits that a community's monolingualism might limit the mobility of some of its residents but claims that mobility is an advantage that benefits primarily the wealthy. "For the rest of us," he declares, "mobility has been little more than a mixed blessing, which has destroyed families and created a loneliness heretofore unknown in this world."[43] Yes, there would be barriers to the opportunities that come with fluency in English; these, he claims, would be offset by the opportunity to live a more authentic life in one's own language and culture. "No just society," he argues, "can demand the renouncing of history, cultural heritage, grandparents, or self as the price for equal participation."[44]

As passionately as it is argued, Castro's vision is a hard sell for many. It defies the philosophies that undergird the enormous projects of nation-building that have taken place in recent centuries. A collective of people as vast as a nation presupposes some grand, shared identity that binds them together. It's what makes people in one town willing to send resources to fellow citizens they will never meet in a town they have never seen, and even to volunteer to go to war to protect them. Would people be less likely to do these things for others who speak a different language, one that springs from a different history and cultural heritage? Could a collection of diverse language communities be bound up into a nation?

The intimate link between language and identity leads us to a paradox. On the one hand, it is precisely because language is so intertwined with the self that it has so much power in our lives. Language's link to identity is what drives people to preserve their languages—if this link weakens, smaller languages have little chance of surviving in competitive ecosystems. On the other hand, can we truly say that segregation and sharply bounded identities—both of which promote the survival of languages—are good for individuals or for the societies in which they live? Are we left with a conundrum in which what is good for our languages can act as a poison to our societies and even to our own souls?

Europe's official languages appear to be inseparable from their national identities, but until very recently, these languages could hardly be described as the common fabric from which their nations were cut. Linguistic fragmentation was the norm.[45] In 1860, for example, what is now the standard French language was foreign to about half of the nation's children, who spoke an assortment of other languages and dialects at home. In the same year, no more than 10 percent of Italians spoke the Tuscan dialect that would eventually be named "Italian." French and Italian emerged as national languages largely because of focused, deliberate efforts to unify a collection of language communities and local cultures. Typically, the preferred tool of homogenization was to run children through a system of mandatory, standardized education. Occasionally, governments resorted to more brutal attempts to suppress local languages.

In current times, we are apt to question the striving for linguistic uniformity. The languages of established nation-states seem perfectly capable of swallowing the migrant languages that flow into them, and a feeling has grown among many that multilingualism within a nation should be seen as a valuable resource in an interconnected world, and not simply as a threat to national unity. Some countries that rely very heavily on immigration, such as Canada and Australia, are conducting experiments in multiculturalism as overt policy. In many cities, signs in a variety of languages pop up in storefront windows, and families can choose to send their children to publicly funded schools taught in their heritage language.

But there is no denying that language can erect walls or, at the very least, chain-link fences. Language has partitioned humans into groups since very far back in our evolutionary history. Given how language broadcasts identity, it's not unreasonable to ask whether promoting a polyphony of languages is at odds with nurturing a sense of national unity. If the goal is to encourage people to think of themselves as a single community despite being spread out over an expanse of geography, it's not crazy to think that obliterating language distinctions among them—or more passively, doing nothing to prevent the loss of some languages—might further this goal. This, of course, was the *assumption* that guided the nation-building experiments of the nineteenth and twentieth centuries. But it remains to be seen whether this assumption founders in the face of evidence and today's realities, not merely those of nineteenth-century Europe—if indeed the assumption that monolingualism built nations was true even back then.

A clearer understanding of the blessings and terrors of diversity is one of the most pressing questions of our age. But although it's a growing preoccupation among serious scholars, there is still very little we know about how language diversity—and with it, a profusion of separate identities—affects the health of a society. There are some sobering findings, though. Several researchers have reported that regions split among many different linguistic or ethnic groups are more prone to violent conflict or have more sluggish economies than homogenous regions.[46] (Although one can obviously speak a language without belonging to the ethnic group of its native speakers, the two are so frequently entangled that the number of languages spoken in a region is commonly taken in these studies to be a proxy for the number of different ethnic groups.) And in 2007, political scientist Robert Putnam captured the media spotlight when he published a paper, based on a sample of more than 30,000 Americans, in which he argued that public trust was lowest in America's most ethnically diverse neighborhoods—with public trust encompassing many different relationships, including trust of strangers, one's neighbors, members of a different ethnic group, or even members of one's own group.[47] He suggested that daily friction between people of different backgrounds causes them to pull back from the community and retreat into their own private spheres. There is less carpooling, fewer acts of random kindness, less engagement with community volunteer groups. There is lower trust in government and lower voter turnout (but more participation in protest marches). People have fewer friends, and they spend more time in front of the television. To Putnam, the reaction of the man confronted with all of those *languages* in the Calgary Public Library is a typical human response to being surrounded by people from other backgrounds: overwhelmed by foreign sounds, this man retreated into his own bubble of privately selected music, heedless of the comfort or needs of those around him.

Over the last two decades, dozens of studies all around the world have investigated whether regions that are splintered into separate groups (with language often used as a way to count the number of groups) tend to show diminished social trust or other ill effects. The majority of these studies have found such symptoms, leading the authors of a review published in 2018 to "cautiously" conclude that the overall evidence does indicate that social trust is lower in the presence of diversity.[48] But finding evidence of such a link, they hastened to add, is different from being able to say that diversity *causes* the dissolution of social bonds. One can't simply point at the problems that are apparent in high-diversity regions and conclude that these problems are due to the lack of a single, shared identity—that would be akin to pointing at the poor school performance of American children who speak languages other than English and arguing that multilingualism leads to cognitive problems. Other factors may be at play, and these need to be untangled and separately evaluated. For example, some regions may have a long history of competition and conflict, which may be why people have retreated into tightly knit ethnic groups in order to defend their interests. Thus, present-day diversity may be the *result* of historical conflict rather than the root cause of it. Similarly, linguistic diversity could be the result of a poor economy, and not the cause of it. One could argue that this is the case in Africa, which is host to many different languages. Here, linguistic diversity is fostered in part by societal inequalities in which the majority of the people are excluded from reaping the benefits of speaking the dominant language—after all, when only the privileged few have access to good education and good jobs, why bother learning the elite language? Or, tensions could arise because certain groups are excluded from positions of privilege and power, in which case the linguistic or ethnic differences may become symbols of injustice, even though they are not the primary sources of the conflict—the exclusionary practices are. Another consideration is that in the United States and other Western countries, neighborhoods that are ethnically diverse are often the poorest neighborhoods. Is weakened social trust in these communities the result of seeing people unlike yourself, or is it the result of living in a poor, crime-ridden area with substandard schools?

It's no easy task to pull apart these competing explanations. But serious attempts to do so—for example, by statistically factoring out the effects of poverty or income inequality—have shown that the link between diversity and distrust does not readily evaporate even when these are taken into account. Unlike the illusory connection between bilingualism and poor school outcomes, the worrisome relationship between fragmentation and social distrust has thus far withstood closer scrutiny.[49] And the bird's eye correlations reported by number-crunching economists and political scientists align with what some psychologists have seen at close range among real people who en-counter members of another group. In one study, psychologists sent Spanish-speaking accomplices into a suburb of Boston that was al-most exclusively White and Anglophone.[50] The Spanish speakers simply showed up at a local train station at the same time each day and rode the commuter train for two weeks. Commuters on this train were then surveyed about their attitudes regarding immigration from Mexico, and their responses were compared to those of people who rode on trains that had not been assigned a pair of Spanish-speaking interlopers. People who rode on the same train as the Spanish speakers and presumably had overheard them speaking in Spanish favored harsher immigration policies than people who rode their train in the comforting lull of uniformity. (It's worth noting, though, that this difference diminished after ten days of exposure to the pair compared with just three days of riding the same train. Thus, hostilities might soften as one becomes more familiar with people of a different back-ground, a point to which I'll return shortly.)

Despite the challenges that come with diversity, it would be a mistake to conclude that a country that allows a multiplicity of iden-tities to flourish within its borders is setting itself up to become a breeding ground for discord. As political scientists James Fearon and David Laitin take pains to point out, violent conflict between groups is not as frequent as our doomscrolling habits may lead us to believe. Violence breaks out between ethnic groups in only a tiny portion of the situations in which different groups must share territory; these researchers calculate that the actual occurrence of violent outbreaks in Africa as a percentage of *potential* violent events is so low that it "hovers around zero."[51] They suggest that a good theory of inter-ethnic relations needs to explain why relative peace and cooperation between groups is far more common than conflict. It also needs to explain why difference breeds distrust in some situations but not in others. As the data set grows, it has become clear that, although a general link between diversity and distrust can be gleaned from the sum of the studies we have to date, it does not extend equally to all places, situations, or social habits. At times, this link is entirely absent or even reversed.

For example, diversity and distrust are more closely linked in the United States than in most other Western nations. Some other, far more diverse societies fare surprisingly well. In Indonesia, which is home to more than 700 different ethnic groups and 300 languages (with the national language of Bahasa Indonesia spoken at home by less than 20 percent of the population), the situation is especially complex. In the 1970s and 1980s, more than two million people agreed to relocate to newly created villages in the Outer Islands, with an almost random mixing of ethnic groups. These circumstances make the country an ideal laboratory for studying the consequences of hyperdiversity without deeply rooted regional histories or resentments—and in fact, a study published in 2019 found that regions in Indonesia that contain very large numbers of different groups actually enjoy *higher* levels of social trust.[52] It is in the regions where most people belong to one of a small number of groups—resulting in a polarization of powerful groups, rather than sheer diversity—that one sees the worst symptoms of social retreat: in these regions, people are less willing to contribute taxes for public goods such as schools or libraries, are less altruistic, participate less often in neighborhood activities, are less likely to trust their neighbors to watch their children, and so on. Moreover, the degree of segregation within communities turns out to be important; when Indonesians of different ethnicities are clustered together into tight knots rather than spread out and intermixed within their communities, they are less trusting of each other. This is true whether they live in super-diverse regions populated by many different groups or in areas that are dominated by a few larger groups. The authors argue that daily, meaningful contact is a balm to the tensions that flare up between members of different groups—a view that is shared by a group of economists who have shown that countries where linguistic groups can readily interact with each other do better than more segregated countries when it comes to public health, education, and citizens' average income.[53]

There is much evidence to feed the hope that social trust can thrive in the midst of diversity provided there is real engagement across groups—not just spotting other-group members at the train station or trading a few words over the cash register at the grocery store. Superficial encounters between strangers who belong to different groups may actually trigger feelings of threat. But having genuine conversations with each other or working together toward shared goals can build social trust. Intermixed communities may offer the opportunity for contact between people of different backgrounds, but unless people seize these opportunities and actually talk to each other, living in them is unlikely to foster greater trust, as documented by a detailed study of Canadian and American residents and their social lives.[54] This study confirmed the general trend: trust was lowest in diverse neighborhoods, and in fact, trust was lowest of all among people who lived very close—even right next door—to neighbors of different ethnic or racial backgrounds. But distrust prevailed only among people who rarely or never talked with their neighbors. Those who did socialize with their neighbors felt no such reticence. This study (which is echoed by others that draw similar conclusions) supports the notion that while *seeing* people who are different may trigger a feeling of threat, actually having relationships with them can dissipate that threat.

Of course, one challenge is that the very people who are most allergic to seeing someone of a different culture or ethnicity are precisely those who are the least likely to seek contact with them. Like the man in the library, their tendency is to cocoon and to rebuff. One might even wonder whether such individuals are impervious to the warming effects of human contact with an outsider. But in fact it appears that it is precisely the most entrenched and prejudice-prone individuals whose attitudes are most dramatically transformed when they do have friendly interactions with other-group members.[55]

All of this suggests that a multiplicity of languages and ethnic backgrounds is not a death-knell for national unity or community cohesion. Even Robert Putnam, whose revelations of the bleaker side of diversity have been so widely cited, voices optimism that societies are capable of managing differences. Not all differences are divisive, he notes, and even ones that are can shift over time to become more benign. As an example, he points out how attitudes have changed regarding religious affiliation. He recalls that in his adolescent years in a 1950s Midwestern town, dating across religious boundaries was seen as objectionable, making it important to keep track of who was a Catholic, who was a Methodist, and so on—and keep track he did, musing that although he has forgotten the names of some of his classmates, he can still remember which churches they attended. Religious affiliation was not just a part of your identity. It also determined your social network and how close you could get to someone. But this has changed, and while religion is still important to people's personal identities—according to Putnam, his data show religion to be even more central than ethnic background to people's sense of self—it no longer divides people into groups as sharply as it once did. That is, while religion is still *personally* relevant, it has become much less *socially* relevant. Perhaps the same can happen with ethnic or linguistic identities, he suggests.[56]

Putnam envisions a route to societal harmony that does not revert to the monophonic ideals of eighteenth- and nineteenth-century nation building. And indeed, there is reason to doubt that bulldozing linguistic or ethnic distinctions is necessary or even helpful. Such attempts, when forcefully made, tend to backfire. The strangling of the Basque language in Franco's Spain arguably mobilized Basque resistance; threatened with cultural annihilation, many Basques embraced violence. In the end, Franco's policies made language *more* socially divisive, not less. Similar arguments can be made about the suppression of Kurdish in Turkey. Heavy-handed attempts to eliminate differences—inevitably, by insisting that the minority group transform itself to become more like the majority—may reassure the majority, but it often does little to truly integrate the minority.

It seems clear that the best way to temper the tensions between speakers of different languages is to reduce the social barriers between them. But this raises a thorny question: can this be done while still preserving the languages themselves, particularly the smaller ones? If one of the bulwarks against language loss is the segregation of groups and the sense that there is an *us* that is separate from a *them,* as appears to be the case for Gullah Geechee, what will happen if the boundaries between language groups become more porous, and linguistic identities become less socially important? Will smaller languages eventually wither for lack of a tight-knit community that regards language as the price of admission to the group?[57] Indeed, the Indonesian study I cited earlier is not reassuring in this regard: although public trust was highest within intermixed communities rather than segregated ones, it was precisely under these conditions that people were most willing to abandon their native languages. The same environments that fostered a feeling of neighborliness and social cohesion also encouraged people to raise their children in the national language rather than in the tongue spoken by their ancestors.

Bill Labov, a sociolinguist, presses on this point in his discussion of African American Vernacular English, the dialect spoken by many African Americans in the US.[58] Labov notes that AAVE is a thriving language, but he believes that this is largely because of America's long history of racial segregation—a segregation that is the root cause of many problems that hobble African American communities, including soul-crushing poverty, shoddy schools, and substandard housing. His research revealed that in Philadelphia, one of the most sharply segregated cities in the United States, the distinctive features of AAVE were most pronounced among speakers who rarely had contact with White people. If integration were to lift up an endangered people but endanger their distinctive language, he suggests, it would be a bargain worth making.

Yes, but let us make sure that any choice to relinquish a minority language truly is a *choice,* made by its speakers on the grounds that this language no longer serves an important purpose in their lives, and not because they are penalized for speaking it or because their language is dismissed as having no value. In the end, I suspect that a society's ability to nurture a healthy multiplicity is knotted together with its ability to nurture healthy *individuals* with multiple identities.

Can we resist forcing people to choose between versions of themselves? Can we support their ties to family, community, and language, without shutting them out of mainstream society? Can we cultivate their languages, not just as useful economic assets, but as irreplaceable facets of who they are? Can we truly make space for people who are of two minds, the translators, the in-betweens, those who live and remember their lives in two languages, whose loyalties are generously spread beyond a single group? If we can, perhaps we'll be able to reap some of the riches of diversity while avoiding the worst of its dangers.

Individual psyches—not just nations and communities—suffer when language becomes the symbol of a society's fault lines, dividing privileged from marginalized, wealthy from disadvantaged, settled from newly arrived. These divisions not only keep the speakers of opposing languages at arm's length, they also create a deep rift in the selves of those whose lives must straddle these cleavages. A person who feels split between language communities that are at odds with each other can feel like a child of divorced parents, pressured to align exclusively with one or the other. Many bilingual writers have articulated this particular pain, giving shape to an experience that countless others have lived. It is a tension that is threaded throughout the memoir of Richard Rodriguez. On the one hand, full membership in mainstream American society demands that he renounce his native Spanish language. On the other hand, his neighbors and family are affronted by his inarticulateness in Spanish, taking it to be a repudiation of them and their culture:

> It surprised my listeners to hear me. They'd lower their heads, better to grasp what I was trying to say. They would repeat their questions in gentle, affectionate voices. But by then I would answer in English. No, no, they would say, we want you to answer us in Spanish. (. . . *"en español."*) But I couldn't do it. *Pocho* then they called me. Sometimes playfully, teasingly, using the tender diminutive—*mi pochito.* Sometimes not so playfully, mockingly, *Pocho.* (A Spanish dictionary defines that word as an adjective meaning "colorless" or "bland." But I heard it as a noun, naming the Mexican-American who, in becoming an American, forgets his native society.)
>
> Embarrassed, my parents would regularly need to explain their children's inability to speak flowing Spanish during those years. My mother met the wrath of her brother, her only brother, when he came up from Mexico one summer with his family. He saw his nieces and nephews for the very first time. After listening to me, he looked away and said what a disgrace it was that I couldn't speak Spanish, *"su proprio idioma."*[59]

When language becomes the banner of identity that distinguishes a marginalized group from the majority, it can be especially hard on those who, like Rodriguez, try to make their way in the majority culture. And when the mother tongue gives way to the majority language in that person's life and its volume inevitably becomes muffled, such a person may find that it has become impossible to ever truly go home. Monika Schmid, a German researcher who studies language attrition, writes of her own experience:

> For the first twelve years of my life, I was a speaker of the Southern German dialect of Swabian; after that my family

moved to a city near the Dutch border and I quickly lost my Swabian dialect (since it turned out to be a source of great amusement for my new classmates) and became a speaker of a fairly standard variety of German.

A few years ago, I returned to the city where I was born to attend the funeral of a relative. All family members who still live in the region, including a cousin that I was close to when we were little, continue to speak the dialect. To my amazement, I found that it had become virtually impossible for me to communicate with my relatives—not because I had any problems understanding them, but because I could not find an appropriate speech mode. Speaking my usual standard variety of German made me feel like I was trying to be posh or show off—Ms. Ph.D. demonstrating that she's better than the little people. On the other hand, while I could probably have managed a passable imitation of the dialect given a bit of practice, that would have made me feel like a fake, an imposter—or worse, like a bad comedian 'doing the voices'.

There was no way out of the dilemma. I simply kept my mouth shut.[60]

Growing up with two languages or cultures does not, despite the gloomy warnings of the past, make one schizophrenic. But psychological research does point to certain risks of a life divided between cultures. More specifically, it's not that *being* bicultural leads to suffering; rather problems ensue when a person *relinquishes* one or both of their cultures. Psychologists who study the mental health of people who grow up in a bicultural context report that some of their subjects do better than others. For the most part, and especially in the United States, people who assimilate completely to the dominant culture, losing most traces of their heritage culture or language, or those who take shelter in their minority culture by avoiding the mainstream culture do not thrive as fully as others who have achieved a stable duality. People who choose one culture at the expense of the other are more likely to be plagued by depression, anxiety, and loneliness; they do not perform as well in school or rise as high in their careers, and they are more likely to have run-ins with the law; they have shakier social networks and support systems, and generally suffer from weaker psychological and social adjustment. And those who distance themselves from *both* of their cultures, feeling they belong to neither, do worst of all.[61]

A Bulgarian colleague who now holds an academic position in Calgary once startled me by saying that the most painful inner conflict she experienced in her life was the task of reconciling her identity between her mother's side and her father's side of her family. Both of her parents were Bulgarian, but their family cultures differed in ways that she long believed to be irreconcilable. She told me that it came as a happy epiphany to realize that she could hold both family cultures within herself, that she did not have to choose between one or the other. I was deeply struck by her remarks. For me, of course, they echoed the conflict I felt in growing up with a family culture that often jarred with the culture of my friends and mentors. In her case, identity conflicts on a familial scale overshadowed even her task of adapting to a new national culture. (Or perhaps, the process of building an identity that wove together both of her ancestral lineages smoothed the way for similar challenges in her immigrant life later on.) But her story also reminded me that reconciling the discordant aspects of one's identity is a vital task for most people, whether or not their lives are divided across different languages, nationalities, and ethnicities. A person rooted in a single culture might still be torn between competing family loyalties or experience a clash of identities, such as that between nurturing mother and successful professional. We take it for granted that a child who becomes alienated from one or both parents is in greater psychological danger than a child who maintains warm relationships with both. And so it is with all of the elements that make up our origin story or that define us as the person we feel ourselves to be.

In truth, almost all inner lives involve chasms of some form that must be bridged, and it is precisely this work that is the key to happiness—the work of coming to be at peace with complicated allegiances, of gracefully moving between competing frameworks or fusing them in unique ways, of holding within the self seemingly contradictory values and aspirations, of calling upon the norms of one culture to rein in the excesses of another. Key to the well-being of people who are bicultural, according to psychologists, is the belief that, although their two cultures may be in tension with each other, they are not fundamentally irreconcilable, that it is possible to contain both of them in one person. It's even better if the two voices inside the person can be in conversation with each other and not simply take turns delivering a monologue. In short, it is healthy to be as hyphenated a citizen as possible, hazardous to be a cultural amputee. Individuals who give voice to each part of themselves experience less of the anguish that runs through Richard Rodriguez's memoir, and they are often proud of their dual or multiple selves, seeing their complicated backgrounds as a strength rather than a source of pain and loss. In an interview with psychologists, one such person—born in the United States of one French parent and one Lebanese and later transplanted to Montreal in childhood—described his multi-faceted identity like this: "I am like a Swiss army knife. Multiple tools, and you can pretty much deal with anything, if I need a screwdriver, it's in there. So if I need to be American, I'm in there."[62]

Indeed, several researchers claim that bicultural people tend to be more creative than those who are raised in a single culture, perhaps precisely because they can't easily slide into preordained patterns of thought and behavior. The friction of competing worldviews constantly rubbing against each other demands that they become adept at creating new solutions, at finding ways out of paradoxes.[63] Acknowledging these findings, Robert Putnam, the researcher known for his work on how diversity threatens public trust, made a point of emphasizing the benefits of diversity as well as its challenges. For example, he observed that immigrants to the United States win major international awards (such as the Nobel Prize) three to four times as often as native-born Americans—and if one counts second-generation immigrants among the award winners, immigrants take home an even larger share of such prizes.[64]

There is also evidence that people who embody two different cultures can serve as bridges between their communities, soothing animosities between groups locked in opposition. Aharon Levy and his colleagues refer to dual-identity groups as "gateway groups," and they suggest that bicultural people can defuse tensions between their communities of origin simply by offering proof that blended identities are possible. In one of Levy's studies, White participants looked at headshots of people under the pretense that they were taking part in a memory study; half of the participants were shown faces of Black and White people, and the other half saw faces of biracial individuals (which were identified as such) in addition to faces of Black and White people. They then answered a survey about their racial attitudes. Those who had seen pictures of biracial people voiced opinions that were more sympathetic toward Blacks than the other participants. Surprisingly, seeing the photos of biracial people had the strongest impact on participants who'd been flagged as being especially prone to prejudice.[65] In another study, Jewish Israelis were more hesitant to endorse aggressive policies against Arabs living in Israel after reading an article that profiled a number of Israeli Arabs who were described as people who identified with both Israel and Palestine and who didn't necessarily see a contradiction between these two identities.[66]

If the attitudes of one group toward another can be shifted by even such fleeting and superficial exposures, then imagine the consequences of more meaningful encounters with people whose identities are layered, blended, or intertwined. Perhaps people who have succeeded in merging two or more identities can more easily see connections and commonalities between the two cultures, and they can articulate these to others. Perhaps they are able to serve as translators or mediators, explaining what the view looks like from the other side. Having resolved many arguments in their own heads, they may have the tools to resolve disputes between others. At the very least, they are living proof that even cultures with some fundamental disagreements can live side by side. If cultures can live alongside each other within the same mind, then surely they can do so within the same community or nation.

These are powerful arguments for dual identity. People who have been shaped by two cultures flourish best when they are not forced to choose between them; if they are able to stay grounded in both, perhaps they can also help knit fragmented societies together. And in the end, it may be that fostering duality is the only viable path to preserving language diversity in complex societies, one that does not depend on treating language as a symbol in a tug of war of exclusive loyalties. But I don't think this can be accomplished without meaningful changes in our societies.

Whether a bicultural person is able to maintain a dual identity depends on the degree to which each of their cultures and communities accepts their complicated identity. Hearing that they are "too ethnic" on the one hand or "too assimilated" on the other undermines the whole process. Unfortunately, cultures that are embroiled in conflict tend to demand a purity of identity among their members. But such demands can be toxic, as the external conflict plays out as an unwinnable battle inside the person.

Any country that is home to immigrants, refugees, Indigenous peoples, or any variety of ethnic and linguistic minorities has to grapple with the challenges of creating something whole out of many pieces. But rather than demanding that minorities assimilate to the majority culture and language—which risks pulling groups apart into a more intense standoff—such countries might serve their own interests, as well as those of their citizens, by making it easier for them to cultivate complex identities. Aside from helping their citizens thrive, it could also soften the threats to public trust that come with diversity. Making the boundaries between groups more blurry and more complicated—whether these boundaries are defined in terms of race, ethnicity, language, or religion—could be a powerful way to transform the loaded social meanings attached to these differences into something more benign. But it requires the courage to abandon the sheltering comforts of uniformity.

Although I was fortunate enough as a child to be spared the stark discrimination and hostility that are heaped upon many members of marginalized groups, I can't say that I ever received much support in cultivating the Czech side of my identity. The tacit rule was that Czech was to be laid down at the entrance to most of the rooms that made up my life—the halls of learning, the places of worship, the chambers of commerce—and confined to the cramped, dark quarters at the back. I understood that in my teacher's eyes, I'd arrived at school somehow less *formed* than my English-speaking peers, and I hurried to constitute myself. If I were an immigrant kid today, there is a chance I might experience something different, at least in school. A growing number of education specialists are calling for an approach that encourages children to bring their various languages with them into the classroom. This approach (which bears the trendy name of *translanguaging*) flows from the recognition that languages do not need to be kept isolated from each other—in fact, their natural state is to comingle within a person's mind, to be swirled together when communicating with other bilinguals, and generally, to want to occupy the same space at the same time.[67] Its proponents make arguments that are both warm and cool. On the warm side is the acknowledgment that children thrive when their full backgrounds, origin stories, and language skills are seen as valuable, and that it is healthy to "close the gap between students' different lifeworlds."[68] On the cool side is the argument that all children, regardless of language background, need to learn to function within an increasingly multilingual world. A classroom in which all communication takes place in a single language is becoming less and less of a realistic model of the world outside of school.

In practice, translanguaging as pedagogy can take many forms, depending on the mix of languages that enter the room. In a dedicated dual-language school, rather than separating languages and assigning them to specific subjects, classrooms, and periods, teachers draw upon both languages as it suits their purposes. A teacher might present a concept in Spanish, then send students off to the internet to research the topic, encouraging them to draw on articles in English as well as in Spanish. Another teacher might move between English and Spanish texts to illustrate various literary devices or to discuss the contrasts between literary cultures and their respective conventions. The goal is to encourage students to bring all of their linguistic skills to bear on a task, as well as to teach them to consciously notice and analyze differences between languages, an ability that sharpens awareness of *any* language.

The approach is advocated even for schools where instruction takes place in a single language but where students speak a variety of languages that may or may not be familiar to the teacher. In such a case, there are many ways in which a teacher might create space for other languages. She might encourage children to write Mother's Day poems in their home language, or to create dual-language stories in collaboration with each other, or to write an English book report about a text written in any language of their choice. Children who speak the same home language could be permitted to use that language to help their friends understand what is being said, or to discuss a group project together. The teacher could call on students to provide examples that draw attention to interesting commonalities and differences between languages.

These scenarios are so different from my own school experiences that it's hard to imagine how they might have felt to me or what effect they might have had in forestalling my neglect of Czech. At the very least, they might have prompted me to read and re-read the Czech books we did have at home, and perhaps to involve my parents in my homework—a situation that *never* arose as our English acquisition quickly outpaced theirs. In today's digital world, I imagine that such pedagogical practices could lead to some children delving very deeply into the resources that can now be found online in their native languages, shoring up the literacy skills that seem to guard against language attrition, and connecting them with their ancestral culture.

In practice, of course, inviting multiple languages into the classroom comes with some challenges, as acknowledged by a number of German and Dutch teachers in interviews with researchers.[69] Devoting time to explicit cross-language comparisons takes time away from more traditional curriculum content, and for some students (and teachers), it can be tiring to constantly switch between languages rather than have a space in which the volume is turned down on all but one. Having a mix of languages milling about the classroom also makes it harder for teachers to keep the lid on classroom mischief or monitor for verbal abuse—as in one case in which a student, under cover of the Polish language, referred to a teacher as a whore. If students switch to their home languages to explain concepts to each other, the teacher may have no way of knowing whether they are passing on accurate information. And students of a common background might use their language as a way to deliberately exclude those who don't speak their language, devolving into linguistic cliques.

But perhaps the challenge of translanguaging is really the point. Maybe the most valuable thing that students can learn in these

classrooms—provided that teachers are adequately trained and supported—is not how to compare and contrast languages, but how to
work through the day-to-day frictions that arise between speakers
of different tongues. They might learn that Babel can be built despite a proliferation of languages and the misunderstandings they
harbor, and that forward movement doesn't grind to a halt simply
because not everyone speaks the same language with ease—one can
still find ways to make use of everyone's expertise. They might learn,
from the very fact that cross-language tensions are permitted in the
classroom rather than being pushed into the private homes and psyches
of those who speak a minority language, that society is willing to
shoulder some of the costs and burdens of multilingualism, confident that the rewards will be worth it. Perhaps these classrooms are
a training ground for students and teachers in how to move from a
gauzy, romantic ideal of multilingualism to the steady, repetitive work
that is required to achieve it. Perhaps the greatest benefits arise not
in spite of the conflicts, but because of them.

In many ways, the story of language conflict, internal and external,
is the story of my life. The languages in my head have always vied
for supremacy, with some of the early and neglected ones subdued
into near silence as English saturated my adulthood. And my life in
North America began at the epicenter of some of the continent's
greatest language conflicts, at the precise moment when tensions over
language and culture were at their most pitched. Mere months before our family landed in Montreal, members of the separatist group
Front de Liberation du Québec (FLQ) kidnapped a British diplomat and
Quebec's deputy premier, eventually murdering the latter. The incident capped a seven-year period during which the FLQ had deto-
nated more than 950 bombs, many of them placed in mailboxes in
the well-heeled community of Westmount, which, with its sump-
tuous homes perched on the southwestern slope of Mount Royal, was
a neighborhood that to many epitomized Anglophone dominance.

The bombing reached a crescendo when explosives set off at the Montreal Stock Exchange in 1969 injured twenty-seven people. As children, my siblings and I had no stake in the language wars; but because we quickly absorbed both French and English, we were often lumped together with either Francophones or Anglos—branded as "frogs" or "*maudits anglais,*" as the two groups called each other. Mixed allegiances were rare among our childhood friends.

Five decades later, Montreal feels like a very different place. Language no longer cleaves society the way it used to—it is less and less possible to predict someone's religion, culture, social class, and place of residence based on whether they speak English or French. A growing number of people speak both. And immigration has convoluted the identities of all Quebecers, but especially its French speakers, as Quebec's language laws dictate that immigrants send their children to French schools, thereby seeding the Francophone community with a miscellany of ethnicities and ancestries. Many young people growing up in Montreal find it impossible to sort themselves into a single linguistic or cultural community. And they are increasingly comfortable with their complex identities, a comfort that is reflected in Montreal's popular culture. Its rap musicians, for example, have made this art form their own by rapping in lyrics that suture together French and English—and often also Spanish, Haitian Creole, Jamaican Creole, and other languages. Francophone groups like the Dead Obies confound Quebec arts funding agencies, which require that at least 70 percent of their content be in French. How does one categorize lyrics like the following?

> Dough to get
> I got more shows to rip
> Dead-O on the road again, c'est mon tour de get
> Sous le spotlight, viens donc voir le dopest set
> We just gettin' started et pis t'es captivated
> Looking at me now, thinking: "How'd he made it?"

J'suis tellement plus about being felt que famous
Que même moi, j'sais plus what the hell my name is.[70]

This joyous language mixing has not only cost the group grant money, it has also raised the ire of self-appointed defenders of the French language in Quebec. Journalist Christian Rioux, among others, has given the Dead Obies a vigorous pen-lashing—perhaps reminiscent of the contempt once heaped upon the speakers of *joual*—claiming that their mongrel language is a form of linguistic suicide that, if indulged in more widely, will plunge Quebec's French language into a debased form that is incomprehensible to speakers of either English or French.[71] But so far, there is no evidence that this is happening, or that French is being contaminated by being stirred together with English. Shana Poplack, a linguist who has studied language mixing in Canada for more than three decades, argues that every bilingual community ever studied has been found to blend their languages—far from being evidence of linguistic ineptness, it is speakers who control both languages very well who are most likely to switch between them, often for rhetorical or aesthetic effect. She and her colleagues claim that even in communities where French / English mixing is most rampant, such as in the Ottawa Valley, which straddles the border between Quebec and Ontario, the practice doesn't seem to be leaving a permanent imprint on the French language.[72] The languages don't seem to be fusing and losing their individual identities—instead, they are doing the tango.

I can see why Christian Rioux would experience the lyrics of the Dead Obies as threatening. But I find them to be a source of deep pleasure, aesthetically *and* existentially. They strike me as a celebration of the conflicts intrinsic to a multilingual life. Never are two languages in more intense competition in a speaker's mind than when they are being blended together in the same sentence; both languages are invited to step into the spotlight and neither is expected to defer to the other. The listener, too, is invited in, encouraged to feel the jolts and lurches from one language to the other, a bumpy ride that requires both English and French to be on high alert, ready to jump in without notice. It is a music that refuses to choose, that says no to either/or and to enforced purities of language and identity. I find it immensely heartening that so many of Montreal's young people have found creative ways to broadcast their layered identities. It speaks to a growing confidence among Francophones that they do not feel the need to segregate their language from others. Perhaps I'm wrong to be so optimistic. Perhaps the French language alarmists are right to be worried. It may ultimately turn out to be the case that among those with convoluted identities, the bonds to French will not be strong enough to withstand the force of English. But at least for right now, Montreal seems to me the most polyphonic society that I've experienced.

I suspect that some degree of language conflict will always be a part of Montreal's identity. Skirmishes between businesses and the bureaucrats charged with enforcing Quebec's language laws continue; in 2013, a particularly zealous language inspector demanded that an Italian restaurant remove from its menu items such as *pasta* and *calamari,* replacing these with their French translations. This incident, nicknamed "Pastagate," aroused scorn and disbelief from all corners of the internet. And even now, English-speaking friends and family members sometimes describe encounters with store clerks or officials whose disapproval at their inability to speak French wafts about them like an aggressive cologne. Some journalists continue to rail against the threats to the French language by an encroaching bilingualism. But these incidents are not bombs in mailboxes. And over time they feel less and less like a true characterization of the regular rhythms and linguistic exchanges between Montrealers. They are backdrops— ones that change between various scenes and acts—more than they are the fabric of daily life. Far more frequent than the bristling moments of linguistic anxiety are the stretches of peaceable negotiation between languages. Most of the time, strangers meet on a pragmatic and generous ground, willing to grope around in the bag of linguistic competencies they carry with them in order to forge an understanding together. The exchange might swing back and forth between languages until the pair settles on the one best suited for the occasion. Imperfections are inoffensive, grammatical gaffes are forgiven. Self-consciousness is laid aside.

Maybe it's just my own permanent state of multiplicity that has habituated me to conflict. But to me, Montreal's moments of linguistic friction seem a bit like the spicy notes that create sparks of dissonance in a gorgeous motet. It's as Robert Bringhurst wrote, in his ode to polyphony: "The discords pass, and because they pass, they contribute to the shapeliness and the wholeness of the whole."[73] On one of my visits back to the city, I recall hearing that officials from the *Office Québécoise de la langue française* had just voiced concern about the fact that Montreal shopkeepers were increasingly greeting their customers with a bilingual "Bonjour, Hi"—a greeting that, to some politicians, signaled an undesirable openness to conducting the transaction in English. Predictably, the censure of the bilingual greeting caused some irritation among Anglophones. In the cab from the airport, I listened to a call-in radio program on a local English-speaking station in which one caller sarcastically remarked that perhaps the OQLF would legislate that shopkeepers utter the "hi" portion of the greeting no louder than at a whisper—an obvious reference to the signage laws, which stipulate that French text be more visually prominent than English.

But then I stepped into a car rental office. The man behind the desk chirped "Bonjour" and I happily continued the exchange in French. But when I handed over my Alberta driver's license he switched to English—which was, like my French, discernibly accented, but fluent and comfortable. I appreciated the courtesy but persisted in French; he continued in English. Finally, I said to him (in French): "Please allow me the pleasure of speaking in French. I rarely get to use it now that I live out West, and it does me a lot of good." He smiled and we traded small talk about where I used to live as a child in Montreal, and how things had changed in the local landscape. He relaxed, and so did his diphthongs, sliding away from the stiffer French used between strangers into the warmer, looser sounds Quebecers utter at home. And when he handed over the keys, I felt more than welcome.

Together with my mother and several of my siblings, I *(far left)* enjoy the Moravian wine made by my uncle *(third from right)* in his wine cellar on our family's property in Moravská Nová Ves.

Chapter 5

Revival

Several years after my father's death, with kids graduated and fledged, work obligations assuaged, and no major crises in view, I was finally able to make the extended visit to my native land that my father had hoped to share with me. I packed up my laptop and a large suitcase, half of its space taken up by gifts for my Czech relatives, and flew to Vienna, which has the nearest major airport to my father's village of Moravská Nová Ves. My uncle, who bears a startling resemblance to my father, met me at the airport to drive me home, an hour and a half away. My Czech language was in tatters. Our attempts at conversation in the car kept lurching into speed bumps as I stopped to ask the meaning of unfamiliar words, and not infrequently, it smacked into walls of bewildered silence. The whole exchange was made worse by the fact that I had ill-advisedly flown with a terrible head cold and my ears were badly plugged from the plane's descent, fermenting what would develop into a furious middle ear infection. Between the mucus barrier in my ears and my brain's sluggishness at connecting my uncle's muffled speech to some spark of meaning, it felt as if we were conducting the entire conversation underwater. Guesswork filled in for competence at my end—I guessed at the meanings of the questions he was asking and guessed at the shapes of the words that would answer them. I suspect that to him, I sounded somewhere between stupid and insane.

There was no reprieve to be had when we arrived at the village. Aside from snippets of lyrics of English pop sounds mouthed by my younger Czech relatives, English was almost entirely absent. It was true that the children studied English in school from a young age, but as far as I could tell, they studied it as they studied algebra, as a series of grammatical word problems that had a single correct answer, rather than as a viable means of communication; as a result, they were about as fluent in spoken English as they were in spoken algebra. One sixteen-year-old cousin sported a T-shirt with a suggestive English phrase on it, of whose meaning both she and her parents appeared happily oblivious. There was no one to translate, no one to recognize my English words jammed unconvincingly into a vaguely Czech sentence. My Czech language and I were on our own. I had to shed English like a useless skin.

My memory of that time is that of an altered reality—or rather, it was as if *I* were being altered in some way, but not so much transformed into something new as restored to a plausible version of myself, perhaps even into the original version of myself that would have existed had my parents not flung themselves and their offspring across the ocean so many years ago. My Czech relatives lived a life that was astoundingly continuous with the lives of their ancestors: My uncle and two of his children, along with their families, occupied the same compound on which the Sedivy clan has lived for hundreds of years. During Soviet times, the property was seized, but my father's family was permitted to live on a portion of it, provided they paid rent to the government. The compound consists of a large, L-shaped stone building wrapped around a courtyard. The building contains several apartments, a small grocery store, a pharmacy, and a doctor's office. After my family was allowed to reclaim the property, a new house was built at the back for one of my cousins and her family, and the outbuildings and pens that had once housed livestock now contain a swimming pool and a games room. Several decades ago, my uncle had built an elaborate wine cellar to store the many varieties of wines he made from grapes he grew in a small vineyard nearby. Aside from these changes (and the open border with Austria, which allowed one of my uncles to commute there for work), the daily rhythms of life were much the same as they had been for many years. There was work, church, the growing of food, the preserving of fruits and vegetables, the making of *slivovice* (a strong and fragrant brandy made from the plums or apricots that grew in local profusion), and the preparation of dishes I remembered from my childhood, before my mother's culinary habits veered off in all sorts of internationally influenced directions.

I found myself quickly absorbed into this stream of continuity. I stayed in a small apartment in the family compound, sleeping in the very same bed on which my father and his three brothers had been born. My window was right next to the village church, and I would wake each morning to the sound of church bells and mourning doves, sounds that stirred some of my earliest auditory memories, provoking a strange sense of *déjà entendu*.

Language stirred in me also—and at times roiled more than stirred. On the day I arrived, I found myself struggling to excavate common Czech words, like the words for "stamp" and "fork," and I made grammar mistakes that prompted a four-year-old to snicker in disbelief. Short, simple phrases or sentences were at the apex of my linguistic ambitions. But my verbal mind felt in constant motion. I found myself waking often in the nights, aware of having dreams, not of images or movement or people or events, but of Czech words and phrases that frothed and bubbled into consciousness. Within weeks, a measure of fluency began to unspool during my waking hours. Words that I'm sure I hadn't used in decades leapt out of my mouth, astounding me. Longer words, which began as a vague mental blur of sound, were coming into sharper focus, and I bravely attempted to utter them. (Sometimes they were correct. Sometimes not: when a man asked what I did for a living, I startled him by claiming to be a savior—*spasitelka*. Sadly, I am a mere writer—*spisovatelka*.) The complicated inflections of Czech nouns, with their ostentatious markings for grammatical gender and case, began to assemble themselves into somewhat orderly rows in my mind, and I quickly ventured onto more and more adventurous grammatical terrain. My inner thoughts began to sometimes assert themselves in Czech. And about a month into my visit, I very briefly passed as a native Czech speaker in conversation with a stranger.

Relearning Czech so quickly felt like discovering unexpected linguistic superpowers. I would open my mouth to give shape to a thought, and, to my astonishment, an adequate sentence would often roll out—it was like discovering that I could move a book across the room with my thoughts alone. My expressive powers seemed to ripple like new muscles. It became clear that so much of the language that I believed I had forgotten was not truly forgotten. Much of what I had thought I had lost was not lost, but simply long-buried under the dust and debris of other languages.

Surprised by the speed of my progress, I began to look for studies of people relearning their childhood languages after they had fallen into disuse. I discovered that perhaps it is not so easy to forget a language after all—that is, if forgetting implies that language is erased rather than merely misplaced or submerged. I found a number of scientific papers that reported having unearthed living remnants of "forgotten" languages, showing how these could float to the surface under the right conditions.

Perhaps the most dramatic were the reports by psychologists who described how some of their clients, upon being taken back to their childhoods under hypnosis, were able to fluently speak a language they claimed to have lost. One of these involved a twenty-six-year-old Japanese-American student who, from the ages of one to four, had lived in a relocation camp during World War II. He claimed that he couldn't speak Japanese, but once hypnotized and immersed in his memories of being a three-year old, he produced a steady flow of Japanese speech, much to the astonishment of his therapist. Later, when he heard a recording of the session, he said he was only able to understand a few words here and there, and was unable to reconstruct the meaning of his ten-minute Japanese monologue.[1]

In another more recent and more systematic investigation, researchers set out to study the hidden language abilities of a young French student who had lived in Togo between the ages of two and five, where he learned Mina (a variant of the Ewe language).[2] When the family returned to France after that, they stopped speaking Mina at home, heeding the advice of the boy's school that continuing to speak this language would be a drag on his development and academic performance. When the student's ability to speak and understand Mina was tested outside of hypnosis, it appeared that he could understand only a few isolated words. However, he was able to recover more and more of his Mina language over a series of six hypnosis sessions. Unlike the Japanese student, who spontaneously burst into his childhood language, this student needed to have the language cajoled out of him. When he resisted speaking Mina under hypnosis, the therapist conducting the session asked him to report the words uttered by *other* Mina speakers—which he was able to do—and eventually convinced him to utter his own thoughts in Mina by assuring him that he knew how to speak the language and that it was all right to speak it.

Initially, the researchers had planned to scan this speaker's brain both during hypnosis and outside of it, to see if this would show different responses to the Mina language depending on his state of consciousness. And indeed, at first, the student reported understanding very little of what he had uttered in Mina while hypnotized and was astounded—and delighted—to hear recordings of himself speaking Mina under hypnosis. But as the sessions progressed over the course of a month, his Mina abilities soon leaked from his hypnotized state to his aware state; after a few sessions, he was able to understand a great deal more, and could produce grammatical sentences in Mina even when he was not hypnotized. It was clear that the barrier between his two states of consciousness was highly permeable.

Reading these studies fascinated me, and it occurred to me that my stay in the Sedivy compound was about as close as I could possibly get to being plunged back into my childhood consciousness without the help of hypnosis. Everything that came in through my senses nudged my early memories awake—the sounds of the village and the songs of birds not heard in North America; the folk songs performed by young musicians at a local music competition; the smells and flavors of foods I hadn't eaten in decades; even my uncle's resemblance to my father, not just in his features, but also in his mannerisms, habits, and wry sense of humor. Sitting at his kitchen table, I had the eerie sensation that I was conversing with my father's proxy in the language my dad had always spoken to me. Perhaps it should come as no surprise that the language came flooding back.

As fascinating as they are, the case studies of languages recovered under hypnosis are not enough to convince most researchers of the secret resilience of neglected childhood languages. And indeed, some studies appear to show that a long-lost language truly has been wiped from memory. In one of these, researchers used the hallowed tool of brain imaging to probe for any remnants of a childhood language among young adults of Korean origin who were between the ages of three and nine when they were adopted by French families and taken out of their home country.[3] Once in France, they were abruptly severed from the Korean language. By the time they participated in the study, they could no longer reliably discern whether a spoken sentence was in Korean or in Japanese, and when asked to choose which of two Korean words was the correct translation of a French word, their guesses were completely random. In fact, their performance did not differ from French speakers who had spent their entire lives in France and who had never had any meaningful exposure to the

Korean language. What's more, the adoptees' brain scans showed no sparks of neural recognition upon hearing their native language—just like the French-born participants, the patterns of activity in their brains when they heard Korean were exactly as if they were hearing another foreign language, like Japanese or Polish. The authors of this study concluded that their learning of French had entirely displaced Korean; indeed, they suggested that losing all trace of their first language may well have been necessary in order for them to attain native-like proficiency in their second.

But other researchers have objected to these conclusions, pointing to influential studies of memory showing that material that appears to have been forgotten is surprisingly long-lived.[4] These studies reveal that even though people may perform as if they have entirely forgotten some previously learned material (think about how you might fare if tested on the contents of your high school biology or history class, for example), their previous mastery comes to light once they begin *relearning* the material. Their progress outpaces that of people who had never learned it in the first place. Such results have prompted researchers to argue that a great deal of what we believe to have fled our minds is in fact still there—it has simply become hard for us to retrieve. Once we begin to unearth that store of knowledge, all of its contents become more accessible.

Based on this logic, several scientists argued that the French study could easily have missed trace remnants of the adoptees' native language, despite its sophisticated scientific tools. If the adoptees' Korean language had really gone dormant, one wouldn't necessarily expect to see these traces on an initial test, they suggested; it's only after the language is prodded awake that one would truly expect the adoptees to outperform their French-born peers. And indeed, this prediction has been borne out by a number of subsequent studies of international adoptees.

In one case, the relearning advantage for adoptees was even used as a way to sleuth out the origins of a thirty-three-year-old adopted woman who did not know who her birth parents were or even what country she had lived in as a child, though she did know that she had been brought to the United States from elsewhere soon after the age of three years.[5] She was able to produce a few words that sounded Slavic, most plausibly Russian (or Ukrainian, which is very similar to Russian), but she had no idea what they meant. To determine whether she had indeed known one of these languages as a child, researchers Ludmila Isurin and Christy Seidel devised a series of word-learning lessons. In these lessons, the adopted woman was to learn a set of Russian vocabulary items (focusing on words that were identical or very similar to their Ukrainian counterparts). Some of these words were ones that Russian children typically learn by the age of three whereas others were ones that only an older child would be likely to know. Like detectives testing a favorite theory, the researchers laid out the following logic: if in fact this woman had known Russian (or Ukrainian) as a toddler, there should be some embers of familiarity for the words that are typically known by children. Hence, she should be able to re-learn these words more quickly than the Russian words that were unlikely to be in her vocabulary before arriving in the United States. This is exactly what happened over the course of the language lessons. In contrast, a group of participants who had never been exposed to Russian showed no advantage at all for learning words that are familiar to Russian toddlers over words that children acquire at an older age, and they took longer than the woman did to learn these particular words. This suggests that the woman's selective aptitude for Russian / Ukrainian words that are known by very small Russian or Ukrainian children sprang from familiarity and not simply because these words are easier for newcomers to the language. The researchers concluded from this that her life likely did begin in Russia or Ukraine.

Studies of adoptees have found accelerated learning of native language grammar in addition to vocabulary.[6] However, children who are adopted at a very young age may not have a chance to learn much grammar before they are whisked off into a completely new language milieu. To find the earliest remnants of a native language, researchers have to test for knowledge of a native language's sound patterns. These sound patterns are among the earliest aspects of the native language we learn as children. For this reason, the adoptee studies tend to focus on certain skills of speech perception that very young children would have had a chance to master before moving to their adoptive countries.

One of these skills is the ability to discern which variations in sound are especially meaningful in the native language. We tend to think of our language as having a fairly small and fixed set of distinct vowels and consonants, but this is an auditory illusion. In fact, speech sounds vary along a continuum, much like color does. Just as we might agree that two color swatches are both blue but represent different shades of blue, two instances of a sound like *t* may actually not be identical at all. For example, the *t* sounds in the words *top* and *stop* are really quite different from each other. In *stop,* the vowel begins almost immediately after the release of the *t,* but in *top,* there is a bit of a delay between the release of the *t* and the onset of the vowel. We tend to hear this as a very subtle puff between the *t* and the following vowel, and we can see visible evidence of the puff by holding a lit match near the lips. If held at the right distance, the match will be snuffed out when the word *top* (but not *stop*) is uttered. To most English speakers, the difference between these sounds is so subtle that it is hard to discern by ear alone. But to speakers of a language like Thai, the difference between the sounds is glaringly obvious, and uttering one in place of the other results in different words, just as the very similar sounds *t* and *d* signal different words (*tip* versus *dip*) in English. That is, in English, different variants of *t* belong to one category and *d* to a different category, while in Thai, the *t* variants fall into separate categories, both of them distinct from the *d* category. Each language has its own unique way of carving up speech sounds into categories. In Japanese and Korean, for example, *r* and *l* sounds fall into a single category, so that native speakers of these languages have a hard time discerning the difference between them. As a result, Korean and Japanese speakers may swap one for the other when speaking English. One of an infant's first linguistic tasks is to learn which subtle differences in sound mark a boundary between categories of speech sounds.

In some ways, very small babies are much more sensitive to differences in speech sounds than adults are. Before six months of age, they can easily distinguish most subtle differences in speech sounds, whether their language makes use of those distinctions or not. That is, a baby born into an English family will easily distinguish the variants of *t* in the words *top* and *stop,* and a baby born into a Japanese family will have no trouble hearing the difference between *r* and *l* sounds. This sensitivity springs from an ignorance of how the language carves sound into categories. But over the second half of the first year, they gradually tune their perception to the sounds of the language they hear around them, as they learn which sound distinctions are meaningful and which ones are not. Children who hear English lose the ability to notice the difference between the *t* variants, and children learning Japanese begin to hear *r* and *l* sounds as variants of the same sound. Pat Kuhl, a linguist who has studied this phenomenon for decades, describes the process as one of perceptual narrowing.[7] As the brain becomes more and more committed to the sounds of the native language, it becomes harder to perceive other languages in the way their native speakers do. It is like the closing of a perceptual window, a closure that privileges the native language at the expense of others. To me, this focus on the native tongue is reminiscent of a famous poem by Emily Dickinson:

> The Soul selects her own Society—
> Then—shuts the Door—
> To her divine Majority—
> Present no more—
>
> Unmoved—she notes the Chariots—pausing—
> At her low Gate—

Unmoved—an Emperor be kneeling
Upon her Mat—

I've known her—from an ample nation—
Choose One—
Then—close the Valves of her attention—
Like Stone—[8]

Some researchers, like the authors of the French adoptee study, are of the opinion that the brain can only achieve nativelike abilities in a second language if neural commitments to the first are loosened. They suggest that only then can the valves of attention open to truly admit another language. But more recent research has shown that the commitments made in early childhood are remarkably resilient, even after they seem to have been overwritten by other perfectly learned languages.

An example of such remarkable language reawakening can be found in a paper led by psychologist Leher Singh, who tells me that she was inspired to design the study when she reimmersed herself in her childhood language of Punjabi and was struck by the easy familiarity of its sounds. Singh and her colleagues compared American-born native English speakers with a group of Indian adoptees who had been raised in the United States from a young age (between six months and five years old) by English-speaking families, with no contact with their language of origin.[9] The children were between the ages of eight and sixteen years old at the time of testing, and initially, neither the adoptees nor the American-born participants could hear the difference between dental and retroflex consonants, a distinction that's exploited by many Indian languages. (To an English speaker, they all sound like *t* or *d* sounds, but the dental sounds are made by touching the tip of the tongue to the back of the teeth, while retroflex sounds are made by curling the tongue back slightly towards the back of the mouth, resulting in a slight difference in sound that

Punjabi speakers can easily discern.) But after listening to the contrasting sounds over a period of mere minutes, the adoptees, but not the American-born children, were able to discriminate between the two classes of consonants.

Similar results have been reported elsewhere. In a Dutch study, Korean-born adoptees who had no memory of their first language were quicker to learn to pronounce Korean sounds than Dutch-born participants with no exposure at all to Korean.[10] Astoundingly, this advantage was found even among those who had been adopted and brought to the Netherlands before the age of six months, well before they began to speak Korean. This suggests that simply hearing Korean in infancy helped them to organize its sounds in a way that proved useful much later when the adoptees were learning to speak Korean for the first time.

Another striking example of the brain's attunement to native sounds is apparent in languages such as Mandarin, where varying the tone of an utterance can produce entirely different words. (For instance, the syllable *ma* can mean "mother," "hemp," "horse," or "scold," depending on the pitch contour you lay over it.) When Mandarin speakers hear nonsense syllables that are identical except for their tones, they show heightened activity in the left hemisphere of the brain, where people normally process sounds that signal differences in meaning—like the difference between the syllables *pa* and *ba*. But speakers of nontonal languages like English or French have more activity in the *right* hemisphere, showing that their brains don't treat tone as relevant for distinguishing words. Researchers found that Chinese-born babies adopted into French homes showed brain activity that matched that of Chinese speakers and was clearly distinct from monolingual French speakers—even after being separated from their birth language for more than twelve years.[11] Though they may not have recognized any Chinese words at all, unconscious knowledge of *how* to listen to the sounds of their first language remained with them.

These studies are especially revealing because a language's phonology, or sound structure, is one of the greatest challenges for people who start learning a language in adulthood. Long after they've mastered its syntax and vocabulary, a lifelong accent may mark them as latecomers to the language. Arnold Schwarzenegger was the star of many American movies and the governor of the country's biggest state, but his Austrian accent is a constant reminder that he can never run for president of the United States. Because a language's phonology congeals so early in life, many people who have only partial knowledge of their childhood language end up sounding oddly like natives, despite their limited vocabulary or flawed grammar. More than anything, accent offers a glimpse of a person's origins.

This glimpse is apparent in my own family. One of the most notoriously difficult sounds in the Czech language is the ř sound—as in the name of the composer Dvořák—pronounced as something of a combination between a Spanish rolled r and the first sound in the word *genre*. As far as I know, no other language makes use of it, and for good reason: it is so fiendishly hard to pronounce that it is easily the last sound Czech children master, and not even the sensible Slovaks, whose language is exceedingly close to Czech, embrace it as one of their own. It is a reliable shibboleth that can be used to identify native Czech speakers. The many Slovaks who have come to live and work in the Czech Republic invariably replace the ř with a simple r sound, even if their Czech language is otherwise indistinguishable from the natives. At some point in my childhood, I did master this sound, and can pronounce it to this day. But my brother, born three years after me in Vienna, cannot. I find myself greatly comforted by the fact that language attrition has spared my attunement to the sounds of Czech, even if my grammar remains shaky. To me, it is an audible emblem of the language as my birthright. It reveals that, wherever else I have lived and traveled, Czech has been admitted into my soul's select society, that this language entered my life and memory before the valves of my attention closed.

THE BRAIN DOES not accord equal privileges to all the languages it harbors. Childhood languages enjoy certain favors. Admittedly, even languages learned by adults are more resilient than we might believe. Regardless of how little we think we've retained from those foreign language classes in college, researchers have found that if a later-learned second language is set aside for some time, it too can be prodded awake, such that relearners show faster progress than those struggling with the language for the first time.[12] But memories that are laid down early in life, whether linguistic or not, tend to be stronger than later arrivals.

This is apparent in many ways. For example, patients with Alzheimer's disease often lose their recent memories well before they lose memories of their childhood days. Their early memories can remain crisp even after most memories of adult life, including all recollection of marriage or children, have disintegrated like wet cardboard.[13] In old age, early-learned languages can assert themselves particularly forcefully: there are reports of elderly immigrants in whom a first language surges to the fore after decades of being subjugated by the dominant language of their adopted country. In one study of German émigrés, researchers assessed the language attrition of middle-aged and elderly participants and found that decay of their native German peaked between the ages of sixty-eight and seventy-one. Participants who were even older showed no greater signs of language erosion than the youngest group, between the ages of fifty-seven and sixty-four, even though the oldest group had lived the longest in their adopted country.[14] After the study participants had retired from their jobs, they lacked the constant, daily reinforcement of their adopted language in the workplace, and so the newer language proved too weak to withstand the resurgence of their native tongue.

Even among young, healthy people who know a single language, the strength of very early linguistic knowledge can be detected: university students are faster to read or produce words that they learned early in childhood compared to words learned late, even if the latter are very commonly used.[15] In fact, some researchers have reported that retrieving words learned early involves quite different patterns of brain activation than accessing words learned late.[16]

And then there is the apparent effortlessness with which children sop up a language. While adults sweat their way through conjugation drills, commit sections of grammar texts to memory, diagram sentences, and fill in worksheets on how to build a subordinate clause, their children seem to take the language in through their pores without any sign of mental exertion. And they are ultimately more successful. Not only do children eventually master the sounds of a new language in a way their parents generally cannot, they also exceed their parents' ability to learn the intricacies of its grammar. A massive study of more than 600,000 English learners of various ages concluded that those who began learning English after the age of ten to twelve were unlikely to attain native-like grammatical proficiency, regardless of how long they continued to speak the language.[17]

Researchers still don't agree on why it is that children are such superior language learners. Given that the process involves learning many different facets of a language (vocabulary, sound patterns, the structure of words and sentences, subtleties of usage, and so on), each of which recruits different brain networks, there is unlikely to be a single, simple explanation for this advantage. And there is probably no single optimal age for learning all the various components of a language—for example, the speech perception system starts to close down to new language sounds much earlier than the ability to master a new grammatical system. But a number of language scientists have argued that early languages are privileged in part because children and adults learn language in deeply different ways, using different learning strategies and different networks of the brain. Paradoxically, the ease with which children master languages may be rooted in the fact that their brains are too immature to learn the kinds of things that adults excel at learning—things like calculus, the rules of bridge, or how to spot a logical fallacy. Very small children have no recourse to the deliberate, reflective tools that adults bring to these tasks. Unlike adults, they do not rely on them to learn a language—it does no good to tell three-year-olds where to place the verb in a sentence or present them with tables of endings for the imperfect past tense or a list of rules for when to use the past conditional form. Children have no choice but to learn language the way they learn to ride a bike—without the benefit of diagrams about muscle physiology or the physics of motion, but relying on raw intuition and repeated trial and error. You get on the bike, do your best to keep from falling over, and instinctively do more of that, over and over, until the motion is dialed in.

The explicit, reflective kind of learning that adults excel at is good for many things, including playing bridge and testing scientific theories, but it is less useful for learning to ride a bike—most of us could hardly describe *what* it is that our bodies do on a bicycle, even if we are experts at knowing *how* to do it. Psychologists draw a sharp distinction between these two kinds of knowledge, the "knowing what" and "knowing how." The former includes memories of facts and events (whether real or fictional), as well as consciously learned formulas, like the formula for calculating the circumference of a circle, or the rule for forming that pluperfect tense in French. The "how" system of knowledge includes much of what we think of as "muscle memory," or instinctive memory for actions—the sequence of movements involved in driving a stick shift car, playing a favorite piano piece, or reciting a deeply familiar nursery rhyme. We use both systems in daily life, and they may feel more intertwined than they really are. Most people don't realize that their ability to recognize a comb (that is, *what* the object is) is not married to their knowledge of *how* to use it; the split becomes apparent in some patients with brain damage, who may be unable to name the comb or describe its purpose, but who nonetheless intuitively know to pick it up and run it through their hair. If you've ever forgotten a familiar phone number or password, only to be able to produce it from muscle memory on a keypad, then you've experienced the disconnect between the two types of memory.

Like languages that compete with each other for dominance in the mind of a bilingual person, these two systems vie with each other for control. In childhood, the more intuitive "how" system is dominant, as the more deliberate and reflective "what" system takes longer to mature. As children grow into adulthood, the more mature reflective system can handle greater complexity and it is called on to learn material that had previously been left to the more intuitive system. Adults, but not small children, are able to confront the syntax of a language armed with explicit grammatical rules like: *In French, make sure that an adjective is assigned the same gender as the noun it describes.*

But just as with cycling, the more deliberate system may not be the optimal tool for learning certain aspects of language, as revealed by studies that pit the two systems against each other. In one of these studies, researchers invented a language with abstract grammatical categories, which, like nouns, verbs, and adjectives in real languages, were each subject to particular patterns and structures. Half of the participants were instructed to consciously try to identify the patterns, and the rest were told to simply listen to the language while coloring. The exertions of the first group appeared to be for naught; despite their efforts, they were less adept at picking up the patterns of the language than those who colored while passively listening to the language.[18] Another study found that encouraging English speakers to rely on deliberate rather than intuitive learning thwarted their ability to categorize tones in Mandarin—a skill that is crucial for distinguishing Mandarin words, and one that many English speakers struggle with when learning the language.[19]

It would be natural to assume that when grammatical patterns get very complex, this is where the analytical adult would outshine the intuitive child learner. But paradoxically, it is precisely the most complex information that is better suited to the intuitive system, for the simple reason that the most complicated language patterns are not easily pinned down by explicit rules. Grammar's logic is a mere approximation—language *is* patterned, but the patterns are slippery. Rules have a mirage-like quality, often evaporating just when you think you've found the formula that correctly captures the patterns, as sub-patterns and maddeningly illogical exceptions emerge. A shining example is the English definite article *the,* whose proper use bedevils even very fluent nonnative speakers of English. This small word seems to insert itself or alternatively vanish for entirely capricious reasons. The following sentences offer a small glimpse of the problem:

> *Shaheen took **the** bus to Baltimore.*
> *Shaheen arrived from Baltimore by bus.*
> *Rory walked to school every day.*
> *Rory walked to **the** store every day.*

Speakers who learned English in childhood may have no clue why definite articles should be inserted in some cases but not in others, but they know it sounds jarring when someone gets it wrong. The poor souls who learned English as adults may be left searching in vain for an explanation or useful rule to follow.

A Belgian study, focused on learning visual patterns rather than linguistic ones, offers a humbling demonstration of how raw intuition can sometimes outshine analysis.[20] In this study, researchers devised a task that involved learning to sort stripe-filled images into categories. In the simpler version of this task, the categories were each based on a single characteristic. (For example, one category might consist of images in which stripes were angled slightly off the vertical axis, while another category might include only images with thick stripes rather than fine ones.) In the more complicated version, the categories were based on both stripe thickness and orientation; as no single rule defined each category, the optimal way to approach the task was to rely on a gut feeling of overall similarity between the items that fell into each category.

Adult participants, who may have done their best to consciously identify the rules underlying the different categories, performed poorly on the more complicated version compared to the simpler one. But that wasn't the worst of it—they were outperformed *by rats* on the more complex version of the task, which proved no more difficult for the animals than the version that could be captured by a straightforward rule. Presumably the lab rats, not being tempted to form explicit rules at all, relied solely on instinctive judgments, which turned out to be the winning strategy—much as it might be in learning the dastardly definite articles of English.

Based on this handful of studies alone, it might be tempting to conclude that adult learners have been led badly astray by misguided pedagogical practices—that if only they could be convinced to abandon their grammar books and learn language on the fly, like children do, all would be well. But that seems unlikely. First of all, the researchers who assessed the grammatical proficiency of 600,000 English learners compared adults whose first exposure to English was in a school environment against those who learned it by being thrown into an English-speaking environment, without any formal instruction. Both groups of adult learners hit a ceiling beyond which they no longer progressed.

Second, relying on explicit learning strategies may not be a bad approach for adults, even if it's not the best way to learn many aspects of language. Adults may *need* to resort to deliberate learning of a language in order to compensate for the fact that the more intuitive stream of learning has become less efficient with age. Another Belgian study, led by Eleonore Smalle, offers a glimpse of the divergent learning abilities of children and adults; the details are a bit complicated, but they reveal some fascinating and important age-related differences.[21] In this study, Smalle and her colleagues tasked adults and eight- and nine-year-old children with repeating a series of nine-syllable sequences—for example, they would hear (and see onscreen as text) a serpentine "word" such as *furawomuzuvozakuwu* or *garozuhi-*

wigufimoza. This task was somewhat daunting because of the length of the sequences, but it captures an important skill involved in learning new words—the ability to remember and reproduce sequences of sounds. The participants were told that one of these sequences would be repeated over and over again, preceded by a beeping tone. The beep allowed the participants to focus their attention, if they chose, and to devote extra effort to committing this particular sequence to memory so they would remember it better the next time they heard it. The researchers also planted a second recurring pattern but did not tell the participants about its existence, and nothing was done to set this sequence off from the others that appeared only once during the session. The researchers wanted to compare how well children and adults could parrot the sequences right after hearing them. But they also wanted to see how well they would retain memories for the recurring sequences, so they tested their ability to accurately repeat the recurring sequences four hours after the initial session, then again a week later, and finally, a full year later. An important goal was to see whether the children and adults would differ in how they learned and remembered the explicitly marked recurring sequence and the secretly recurring one—that is, whether applying deliberate effort helped or hindered their learning.

Adults generally have a more spacious working memory than children—they can hold more information in mind at once, which gives them an edge in performing mental arithmetic and the like. In this "word learning" task, this advantage was apparent in the fact that adults outperformed children in correctly repeating the long strings of syllables immediately after hearing them. Despite this, the children were just as good as the adults at learning the recurring sequences over the course of the first session, whether or not they were accompanied by the telltale beep. And they were even better than the adults when it came to *retaining* the recurring sequences for some time after the initial session, whether the time lag was as short as four hours or as long as a year. And the children's advantage over adults was especially strong for the secretly recurring sequences that were not cued by a beep, suggesting that they easily remembered these sequences whether or not they deliberately tried to learn them.

There were some hints that adults were leaning on deliberate and effortful strategies to remember the long "words," and that these strategies were serving a useful purpose. First, they remembered the recurring sequences marked by a beep more easily than the secretly recurring sequences; this suggests that they benefited from the explicit signal and modulated their attention in some way that helped them remember these sequences. Second, they were quicker than the children to notice that some sequences recurred even though they were not signaled by a beep. More important, a conscious awareness that these sequences were repeated led to better retention for adults but not for children—the children's performance was the same whether or not they noticed the repetition. It would seem, then, that for adults, just going with the flow in this task, without exerting any special effort to notice and remember recurring patterns, was not enough to allow them to retain the sounds as well as children were able to. They appeared to be compensating for a weaker system of implicit learning by leaning on other cognitive skills. The children, on the other hand, were enviably efficient at learning without trying to learn.

This particular study focused on just one kind of linguistic ability and assessed this skill over a very narrow window of time in childhood, so it can't tell us how well it captures other aspects of learning, or what strengths and limitations children bring to the task of language learning at other ages. But it reminds us that learning a language is a different undertaking at different points in our lives. A person who easily soaks up a language as a child may not necessarily be linguistically gifted as an adult. This bittersweet point is driven home by a study of English proficiency among a group of Hungarian immigrants to the United States; the proficiency of those who arrived as adults proved to be closely linked to their scores on tests of verbal analytical ability, but these test scores were not relevant for successful learning by the child immigrants, who easily outperformed all but the most talented of the adults.[22]

They say you never forget how to ride a bike. If children learn language much as they learn to cycle, perhaps this is why their childhood language has a way of embedding itself deep in their memory. There is no doubt that my learning of Czech was mostly of the muscle memory variety. Czech schools do teach children about the grammatical structure of Czech, but these were not lessons I ever received. It wasn't until I began to study linguistics in university that I even became aware of the notion of case marking. Until then, I don't remember ever noticing that Czech nouns transformed themselves depending on whether they played the role of subject or object. And yet, back in my father's Moravian village, when I had no choice but to climb back onto the bicycle of a language I'd learned as a tot, the intricate, organic, illogical patterning of Czech nouns emerged from somewhere in my brain, asserting itself in shape-shifting forms that I didn't know I knew, ones I had learned long ago without ever trying to learn.

The term *heritage language learner* applies to people like me, whose childhood learning of a native language later becomes swamped by the language spoken by most of the people around them. Some educators and language researchers also use the phrase to refer to people who learned little or none of their ancestral language early in their lives, but who want to learn it later in life, wishing to claim it as a birthright. In both of these circumstances, these late language learners feel they belong to a particular language by birth whether or not it is lodged in their childhood memory. They have a relationship with their language that is fraught with ambiguity: They are inside the language, but also outside it. Their earliest, most intimate memories may be suffused in the language, yet they may speak it haltingly. They may not be recognized as belonging to a community of its speakers even though they feel like aliens within any other community. Whatever their level of proficiency, they are subject to misunderstandings that challenge their linguistic identity.

Many people who learned their heritage language as children but have lost much of it decide to relearn it through study at college or university. They arrive in the classroom, bringing their buried fragments of language with them, slide behind a desk, and join a group of students for whom this language truly is foreign. And when they encounter vocabulary lists of words they may never have seen in written form, and the charts and diagrams that attempt to distill their wild, unruly language into small, tidy packages, this most intimate of languages may well begin to seem foreign to them too. In the classroom, it is severed from the rhythms of the life in which it was originally learned. It is uttered by complete strangers. The gestures, the movements of eyebrows, the odd catchphrases, the swoops of intonation, and the social dance steps that were braided into the language of their childhood—everything about the language that feels familiar—are nowhere to be seen on the curriculum. In the classroom, they must enter the language through its periphery, as outsiders.

Classroom methods for teaching foreign languages can be reasonably efficient for those who approach the language as adult newcomers. While children can easily learn to swim in a language into which they are tossed, the adult brain may not be so adept. And learning a language through immersion requires being, well, *immersed* in it—for many hours in a day, ideally in interactions with many different speakers of the language and in many different settings. Children can soak up the patterns of a language without being taught what they are, but even they need to hear thousands upon thousands of hours of the language. A foreign language classroom offers the efficiency of compression for those adult brains that are able to take advantage of its explicit, guided instruction. Language learning in adulthood is not without its advantages; while adults almost never attain native-like fluency in a new language, their early steps often proceed at a faster pace than is typical for children, possibly because they *are* noticing patterns and using deliberate strategies to remember what they hear. This advantage becomes especially apparent in studies that compare how well adults and children learn language in a classroom setting—adults are better able to make good use of the shortcuts that are offered by formal instruction.[23]

However, while structured language courses offer some benefits to adults who are learning a language for the first time, it's not obvious that they are the best fit for people who are relearning a heritage language. Their language may appear to be lost, but these relearners are not starting from nothing. They have already logged many hours, often thousands upon thousands of them, immersed in the language. What they have learned about their language they have learned in the intuitive, resilient style in which children learn language. It's unlikely that their language memories will be best sparked to life by classroom lessons that are nothing like the environments in which they heard the language in the first place. It is as if we required someone who learned to ride a bike as a child—but hasn't been on one in many years—to attend a lecture on the mechanics involved before letting them get back onto a bike. At the very least, it seems an immense waste of their previous experiences and learning. And, because the design of the course draws on a different set of cognitive skills than the ones that allowed them to learn their language in the first place, I imagine that in many cases, heritage learners find themselves outperformed by linguistically talented students who are entirely new to the language. They may well come to feel that their native tongue is even less accessible to themselves than it is to people who come to it as utter strangers.

Although heritage language learners are usually shoehorned into classes for rank beginners, language researchers are beginning to draw attention to the ways in which such classes are a poor fit, especially for those who had some meaningful exposure to their ancestral language in childhood.[24] Foreign language classes, particularly for teenagers or adults, are tailored for complete newcomers. Students who encounter a language for the first time in the classroom are marched in lockstep through the full range of linguistic skills—they learn to speak and to read simple sentences as soon as they learn to understand them. But learning language as a child proceeds through a very different set of stages: children can understand complex language long before they are able to produce it, and literacy lags far behind verbal fluency. A person whose progress in their native language was arrested at a certain point in childhood will inevitably have a very uneven portfolio of skills as an adult. Many are able to carry on those asymmetrical conversations that are so common among immigrants who arrived as children: they understand the heritage language well enough, but they always reply in English. And they may have little to no exposure to the written word in their language. But language placement tests presume an even—if somewhat artificial—progression through comprehension, speaking, and literacy skills. Failing to capture the peaks and valleys of competence among heritage language learners, these tests sort them into classes that are too easy in some ways and too difficult in others.

Unlike many of their classmates, heritage learners drag a certain amount of emotional luggage with them into the classroom. The language is not just an appealing foreign language that they are trying out, like an outfit. The language is something that is supposedly already a piece of them, or a piece of their forebears, or a linguistic legacy that they now wish to claim for themselves. Perhaps they have traumatic memories coded in that language. Perhaps they felt embarrassed to speak it in front of their childhood friends. Perhaps they were instructed not to speak it or were even punished for speaking it at school. Perhaps they were mocked by a relative for not speaking it well enough. Perhaps they are saddened and demoralized at the extent to which they feel they have lost a language that once came naturally to them. Perhaps they are trying to revive, along with the language, their connections to family, place, historical events—

even their own life story. Whatever their relationship with the language, it is almost certain to be more complicated and loaded than the feelings one has about sidling up to a shiny new foreign language. These complicated feelings find little place in a classroom that treats their language like a grammatical object.

And heritage language learners almost certainly have different goals than foreign language learners. For them, the ability to get around as a tourist or function as a professional is probably much less important than being able to feel that they belong to their ancestral culture. Language classes tend to focus on a style of language appropriate with strangers or acquaintances, but heritage speakers may need to learn the language spoken between insiders, or language that is highly socially nuanced and not just grammatically proficient. Moreover, their language instructor likely teaches whatever version of their language is considered to be the standard, but this may not be the dialect of their immediate and most important language community, and they may find themselves being corrected for speaking just as their parents did, inadvertently becoming further alienated from their own history.

Misunderstanding is not limited to the classroom. I have never taken a Czech language course, but I did encounter some startling assumptions and attitudes among the Czechs with whom I interacted in my birth country. It dawned on me that English speakers are quite accustomed to hearing their language spoken by people who learned it late in life, but this is not the case for many Czechs. Despite the centuries-long cosmopolitan standing of Prague, its capital city, very few expats from abroad make their way into the many small towns and villages that hold much of the country's population. On a global scale, Czech is a relatively small language. For the most part, those who can speak it were born into it. As a result, the experience of hearing an adult speak it badly is a very unfamiliar one for many Czechs. It is so unfamiliar, in fact, that several years ago, the Czech government issued an ad campaign with the tagline "Czechs, help us out, we're learning," intended to teach Czechs how to interact with foreigners who make the brave attempt to speak their language. In one of these ads, a young French tourist tries to buy a train ticket to Brno. The clerk at the ticket counter asks, "Jednoduchý nebo zpáteční?" *("One-way or round-trip?"),* a phrase the tourist fails to comprehend. The clerk's strategy is to repeat exactly the same phrase, but louder and louder each time. When this fails to achieve results, a colleague comes to the rescue. "Tam?" *("There?")* he asks, pointing in the direction of Brno, and then "Zpátky?" *("Back"?)* pointing in the reverse direction. Relieved, the tourist nods with understanding. "Tam." Evidently, the government believes that many Czechs need to be taught to use gestures and simpler language—rather than brute volume—to make themselves understood to a new learner of Czech.

I had my share of baffling encounters due to lapses in my Czech. On numerous occasions, upon committing a grammatical error (and oh, what an infinite selection of possible errors there is!), a relative would point out, "But you made exactly the same mistake last week, and I corrected you—don't you remember?" It was clear that my intelligence was in question. I would shake my head, thinking of an Iranian-born friend back in Canada, who still occasionally mashes together her personal pronouns, replacing *he* with *she* after more than a decade of speaking English every day at her highly paid office job. (In her native language of Farsi, all pronouns are gender-neutral.) Cut me some slack, will you, I would think to myself.

At least I fared better than my younger brother, with whom I traveled in the Czech Republic for a couple of weeks. Because of my lengthier immersion in the language as a child, I sound more like a native than he does. To my ear, he has a fairly subtle accent. For example, he struggles with the palatalized *t'* and *d'* consonants of Czech, which do not exist in English; he produces the next best thing, which are the first sounds in the English words *chin* and *gin*. Phonetically, these sounds are very similar, but to some Czechs, the substitutions seem to render his speech utterly incomprehensible. (And to be fair, there is good psychological evidence that people who are exposed to a narrow range of pronunciations in a language develop a fairly rigid perception of speech in that language, whereas hearing multiple accents—as many of us do with English—cultivates a greater auditory elasticity.)[25] One store clerk in particular appeared to have great difficulty understanding him. She informed him, as if she were instructing a child, that he was not pronouncing certain words correctly—as though being informed of this fact would somehow remedy the accent. "I'm sorry," said my brother, "My Czech is not very good." "Yes, I can hear that," said the clerk, without the slightest hint of a smile or note of encouragement.

Needless to say, encounters like these feel like barriers. I could not fault the Czechs with whom I interacted—their reactions seemed perfectly understandable given that Czech is, at least in the twenty-first century, not exactly a cosmopolitan language. But the lack of gradation in their minds between a speaker and a nonspeaker of the language often felt like an invisible wall between me and the language, undermining my claim to it—a claim that to me, at least, felt wholly legitimate. It seemed, at times, that my errors were perceived as a casual disregard for the language, when nothing could have been further from the truth.

On more than one occasion, I stifled the urge to slap on my expert's cap and launch into a brief lecture on the nature of language learning and the effects of attrition and age of linguistic exposure. Surely, it would have done little good in those particular situations. But I found myself bristling at such interactions. They were a visceral reminder of the many obstacles faced by someone who is trying to reclaim their native language—obstacles that arise out of a lack of understanding of the convoluted linguistic journey of a person who is born into a language but then kept at a distance from it.

The story of my linguistic journey is a common thread in the tapestry of immigrant stories: complete immersion quickly giving way to less and less contact. In my case, Czech remains stunted, never having grown into its proper, flourishing adult state. Still, the language is within me. If it is properly nurtured and coaxed back to life, I can be easily distinguished from a true outsider to the language. It is, in a literal sense, my *mother tongue*—the language that danced on the tongue of my mother, as well as my father.

But this narrative is far less common among many heritage learners of Indigenous languages. For them, pages have been ripped out of their language story—the pages leading up to their birth. Many Indigenous people do not know their heritage language as a mother tongue because their mothers and grandmothers (and fathers and grandfathers) were sent away to a residential school in order to forget it, and where they were punished or shamed for speaking it. Their languages have lost generations of speakers—a seventy-year-old who can speak the language with native-like fluency may be considered young among his or her linguistic peers, with later generations unable to pass the language on to their own children. This creates a terrible rupture in the chain of transmission.

In Canada, for example, data from the 2016 census revealed that only 13 percent of Indigenous people spoke their ancestral language at home at all, with a mere 3 percent using it as the only language spoken at home. English, on the other hand, was the sole language spoken at home for 75 percent of Indigenous people—an impressive monopoly given that this figure includes respondents in Quebec—and it had a seat at the dinner table for 89 percent of them.[26]

These are conditions for widespread, imminent language death. There's a consensus among language researchers that one of the clearest signs that a language is in danger is when it is no longer spoken in the home.[27] Once children arrive at school, it is hard enough to sustain a childhood language that has already taken root, especially if it is not richly woven into the fabric of public life. To teach it to children from scratch is an enormous burden to place on a school. No child can possibly come to be at ease in a language that is taught a few hours a week. In order to achieve true proficiency through schooling, children need an intensive program in which the language is not squeezed into a corner of the curriculum the way a foreign language might be, but used front and center, perhaps as a medium for teaching subjects like math and science—and for this, there would need to be books and teaching materials available in that language, a situation that is very hard to come by. The longer such learning is postponed, the harder it becomes to master the language as adulthood looms.

For Indigenous people who want to breathe life back into their vulnerable languages, one of the critical tasks, then, is to find a way to replace the linguistic legacy of those lost generations of native-speaking parents. One way to do this is by establishing "language nests"—a concept and term that originates from efforts in the 1980s to revitalize the Māori language in New Zealand (also known simply as *te reo*—"the language"). A language nest is a program whose specific purpose is to create an environment where children can interact with speakers of their heritage language from a very early age. Some language nests take in children beginning at a few months of age, while others begin with children who are out of diapers, depending on the logistics and available resources. Native speakers of endangered languages are usually quite old, so in order to staff the language nest, it may be necessary to bring elders out of retirement to play with and talk to children all day—often with the support of staff members who do not speak the language well, but who can help by preparing meals, cleaning the facility, changing diapers, and so on.

A well-run language nest would likely draw nods of approval from any researcher who is familiar with how children learn language. It takes advantage of those early, receptive stages in which a child's perceptual window is wide open to the nuances of sound in different languages. It allows the child to learn the patterns of their language intuitively, by sinking into the language and laying down deep memories of how to speak it, using the networks of the brain that seem optimal for learning and retaining language. And the language nest also honors the fact that in order to learn language this way, the child must be steeped in it for many hours a week, hearing and producing hundreds of thousands of sentences. (Linguists William O'Grady and Ryoko Hattori suggest that, in order to learn enough of a language to be able to speak it fluently, a child would need to be immersed in it for a bare minimum of four hours a day, five days a week.[28])

Language nests have sparked new life into the Māori language. Within six years of the opening of the first language nest in 1982, 400 new ones had sprung up.[29] Full-immersion primary schools opened in 1985, to be followed by secondary schools. Before this groundswell of linguistic revitalization, only about one in five Māori people reported that they were able to have a conversation in their ancestral language; by 2006, half of the Māori population claimed to be able to converse in their language.[30] Today, it's possible to study in the Māori language from preschool to graduate school, and the language has become more and more present in public life, having achieved status as an official language in 1987, right next to English and New Zealand Sign Language. Television programs, news reports, and movies are all available in the Māori language, and there is a demand for Māori-speaking lawyers, teachers, writers, translators, and media specialists. When Prime Minister Jacinda Ardern gave birth to her daughter in 2018, she announced that the child would be learning Māori alongside English, even though this is not her ancestral language.

The success of the Māori language nests has inspired many groups who are trying to revive their Indigenous languages, and there is now a global network of educators, researchers, and parents who share experiences and results with each other, whether it involves the renewal of Saami (a language group spoken in Finland, Sweden, Norway, and Russia), Hawai'ian, Mohawk (spoken in Ontario, Quebec, and New York State), Alutiq (spoken in Alaska), or Ainu (spoken in Japan). In reading about these efforts, I was struck by the words of various language workers who visited an established language nest and observed tiny children there speaking their ancestral languages with casual ease, as if it involved no effort at all. A common refrain was how startling it was for them to see these languages being learned with no teaching involved—the children simply absorbed the language in their daily interactions with elders, by hearing stories, sharing food, going for walks, and exploring the natural world outdoors.[31] It struck me, because this seemed to be precisely opposite to the reaction of the Czechs with whom I interacted in my attempts to relearn my native tongue. Czechs have little experience of anyone learning to speak their language *other* than as a child, which can obviously be done with little fuss or apparent effort, making me and my siblings seem a bit obtuse by comparison. Many Indigenous adults, on the other hand, have no direct experience of their heritage language being learned in this way—if they have reclaimed their language as adults, it has cost them a great deal of strenuous effort, and they are aware that they are less fluent than they would wish to be. To hear the language come spilling casually out of the mouths of babes must have been very moving.

For many advocates, however, language nests are more than just the most effective way of transmitting a language—just as important is braiding the ancestral language with early memories of being cared for and of *being* in the language in a way that is culturally true. The Māori language nests are not just about passing the language to a new generation—they are equally about soaking up the Māori culture. Children learn about the history and spiritual practices of their people. They learn traditional chants and prayers. They go outside and pick fruit from trees and talk about the local wildlife. Because all these things occur in the Māori language, the language itself becomes linked with the Māori way of being—just as my own Czech-language memories are intimately linked to the music, food, celebrations, relationships, values, and social habits of a childhood lived in Czech. It's only under these conditions that the language can exercise its Proustian powers.

Involving elders is important not just because they happen to be among the last native speakers of their language, but also because their memories are the storehouses of the ancestral culture—its collective knowledge of the natural world, spiritual ceremonies, ethical systems, art forms, social values, and so on. It is not just language that has suffered a rupture in historical continuity; everything that was ever done in the language has been disrupted as well. By creating an environment that is as similar as possible to how small children around the world learn their mother tongue—in the heart of their families and communities, rather than in a classroom with a structured curriculum that relies on the pedagogical template of an outsider culture—these language nests offer a place where language can be reunited with its culture.

The concept of the language nest seems so natural and so simple, but in practice, it is no trivial matter to start one and keep it running, especially in a small community with very few remaining speakers. The challenges are documented in detail in a doctoral dissertation by Natalie Chambers, a woman who married into an Okanagan community in British Columbia, and whose own children attended language nests.[32] Recruiting speakers of the language is one of the biggest hurdles; the few who speak it are no longer young, and they may not be prepared to spend all day, every day with small children—after all, visits from small children may be delightful, but even the most dedicated of grandparents might balk at caring for their own grandchildren day in and day out, let alone other people's children. The elders may have very real health concerns, limited mobility, dwindling energy, or hearing problems. It is a hefty weight indeed to place on the shoulders of an elderly population. Ideally, the language nests would be fully staffed by native speakers of the language, but in the real world, many of these schools rely quite heavily on younger staff who are learning the language alongside the children, or who learned it to some degree of proficiency as adults. At the very least, the elders usually need other adults present to help with some of the more physically taxing aspects of childcare. Keeping even one small language nest afloat is an undertaking that requires passionate commitment, along with constant fundraising efforts—a study of language nests around the world reports that it takes a minimum of about $100,000 USD per year to run even the smallest nest of five or six children.[33] Even with funding from the state, as with the Māori nests, the programs rely very heavily on unpaid labor or free access to space donated by dedicated parents and volunteers.[34]

As intensive as it is, the language nest alone is not enough. Given that four hours a day is the *minimum* amount of exposure that is needed for a child to become proficient in a language—though still not to the level of a child who hears a single language in and outside of the home—the language nests have the greatest chance of producing strong speakers of the language if the children can also speak it at home, as noted by many of the staff interviewed by researchers. So, as if raising children weren't enough of a job for elders to undertake, in some communities, they take on the additional responsibility of helping the children's parents learn the language. Especially urgent is the task of helping other, younger adults become proficient enough to step into their shoes as keepers of the language. After all, it will be a long time before the children themselves are old enough to pass the language on to the next generation of language nesters.

Even if a five-year-old emerges from a language nest with perfect fluency, then what? At this point, the language nest will have achieved what many immigrant households have produced: a child with an excellent foundation in their heritage tongue. But as can be gleaned from countless language stories of immigrants, this is not enough to sustain a linguistic legacy from one generation to the next. Many such children will speak the heritage language less and less as their lives hurtle forward, even if their parents continue to speak the heritage language at home. And if language exposure comes to an abrupt end, their ability to speak and understand the language may drop off a cliff. Researchers agree that the risk of disastrous language attrition is greatest for those who have not been able to continue learning their language beyond childhood. And the loss begins shockingly soon after the child is whisked from one language environment to another. For example, a detailed case study of a six-year-old child immigrant from Korea showed that her active vocabulary began to unravel within the first month of her departure from her home country, and after two months in the United States, she was able to produce only half of the words she had previously known.[35] In another study, a three-and-a-half-year-old child lost her ability to speak and understand Hebrew just a few months after her arrival in North America.[36] True, reimmersion in a language that was learned in childhood may awaken much of it. But although I can travel to the Czech Republic and have instant access to a nation full of fluent speakers of my mother tongue—largely monolingual ones at that—this is hardly an option for many Indigenous people.

Planting children in the soil of their heritage language is the best way to grow new native speakers. But they can't then be yanked out of that soil as soon as they reach school age if we expect their heritage language to continue to thrive and grow. There is no doubt that the Māori language nests would not have had the impact they did if the first nests were not quickly followed by Māori-language primary schools, and then high schools and university programs. While a child's brain is uniquely equipped to soak up the intricate patterns of a language, learning a language does not stop in childhood—as older children are exposed to more complex ideas, situations, and works of literature (whether written or oral), they are also exposed to more complex language. In fact, a person's vocabulary continues to expand well into old age. To grow native speakers who have a full *adult* language, with the expressive range of an *adult* native speaker, they need to be able to use that language at all stages of their development. This means they need to have access to their heritage language that goes beyond the language nest (or beyond their own home).

The importance of a rich linguistic environment outside of the nest or home is about more than sheer exposure, or simply having enough time to practice the language. In order to maintain proficiency, it's also important to have access to a variety of speakers. In one study, researchers studied both children and university students and found that those who were strongest in their heritage languages—whether Spanish, Chinese, or Hebrew—had the opportunity to speak the language with many different speakers.[37] The number of people they spoke their language with turned out to be even more important that the number of hours logged in that language. This may be because every person has their own unique style of using a language—a different vocabulary, a slightly different way of pronouncing words, and a different set of grammatical structures they tend to use most often. Learning a language involves learning a very wide range of skills—so sampling widely from among various individual styles is the linguistic equivalent of eating a varied diet, guaranteed to provide all of the nutrients that one needs. Moreover, being part of wider community of speakers is the strongest affirmation there is that this is a language in which important and interesting things take place.

Aware of the importance of creating such a community, a group of language advocates for Aanaar Saami (a language spoken in Finland by about 350 people) set out to do just that.[38] Before the first language nest opened in 1997, there were only four native speakers younger than nineteen years of age, so the task was urgent. Language nests succeeded in churning out children who could easily chatter in Aanaar Saami. But the community recognized an equally urgent need for speakers in the middle generations—those "lost" generations of speakers—who could bring the language into their professional lives as teachers, journalists, artists, writers, and so on. These were the people who would be able to build an environment in which the young graduates of language nests could continue to grow in their heritage language. The language workers established an intensive one-year immersion program for adults, with elders assisting in the language teaching. It was not expected that these students would become native speakers of the language after a year of study; rather, the hope was that they would become proficient enough in the language to use it in a variety of professional settings (including in schools, where they could teach the language to older children), and that they would be able to promote its use in the community.

The program achieved many of its goals. Its graduates started up community clubs and activities focused on the Aanaar Saami language: people could now gather to speak the language together while playing games, fishing, birdwatching, mushroom picking, and so on. One graduate began a conversation club attended largely by elders, giving them the opportunity to rejuvenate their own mother tongue. "We were totally forgotten and lost," remarked one of these participants. "She [the teacher] taught us who we are. She has given our lost language and our identity back to us. We are so happy now."[39] The language began to be more commonly heard on playgrounds, in supermarkets, and in church services. One mother noted that before the adult immersion program, her child almost never spoke Aanaar Saami outside of the language nest. But as a result of the program, her child gained a whole new group of adults with whom to speak the language. In fact, the language nest children became so accustomed to hearing Aanaar Saami as an "outside" language, they began to automatically use that language rather than Finnish when starting conversations with adults in their social circle.

To people lucky enough to inherit an unbroken cultural and linguistic legacy, especially one that is shared by the majority where they live, it is hard to imagine the heroic efforts and endless resources it takes to restore a legacy that has suffered a serious breach. These fortunate heirs are born into their language, are loved and cared for by people who speak it with ease. Their shelves are filled with books in the language, written by people who have honed their mastery of it. Their teachers skillfully use the language as scaffolding to expand their knowledge, relying on texts and teaching materials carefully designed by experts, who also happen to be professional practitioners of the language. They are moved by songs that amplify the beauty of their language; they see evidence of its value announced on street signs and storefronts, its authority is blared by radio and television programs, engraved in newsprint. All these cultural labors, and everything that it took to make them possible, can recede into invisibility. It is so easy to take them for granted; when our culture and language simply feel like the air we breathe, it is hard to keep in mind the countless generations' worth of human work and creativity that have built and sustained them.

Several years ago, I came across an article written by a regular columnist of the *Calgary Herald*, one of the daily papers where I live. The author, Naomi Lakritz, questioned the need for further investment into revitalizing Canada's Indigenous languages. She listed some of the various programs and organizations that already existed in Canada for the purpose of preserving and revitalizing these languages "How can all this not be enough?" she wrote.

"If languages are dying out and remaining unlearned despite the millions of dollars spent annually on teaching and preserving them, the problem is not a lack of multimillion dollar initiatives. At some point, people have to take advantage of the opportunities offered them. If they won't, that's not something more money and more programs can fix."[40]

Had the author delved into the arithmetic, she would surely have been struck by the cavernous gap between the funds available for certain programs and the resources actually needed to run them. For example, in 2011, the Canadian government allotted eight million dollars to its Aboriginal Language Initiative, a program that supports, among other initiatives, the launch of language nests. But in the province of British Columbia, which is home to about two-thirds of Canada's more than sixty Indigenous languages, the annual allotment per Indigenous person from this fund amounted to a mere $3.48—a sum that is utterly negligible next to what is needed to run a language nest for a year. [41] A Canadian report on the costs of preserving Indigenous languages estimates that, over a fifteen-year period, it would take about five million dollars per year to maintain just *one* language that was reasonably widely spoken in the community; to revitalize a language that had slipped into greater peril, an estimated six million per year would be required.[42]

But the question of what it truly takes to renew a vulnerable language—let alone more than sixty of them—did not come up in the article. In this, the columnist struck me as being somewhat similar to the Czech relative who complained that I continued to make grammatical mistakes despite having been corrected the previous week. When one has everything needed to learn a language as a child without ever breaking a sweat, it is hard to appreciate the extraordinary accomplishment that it is to learn (or even relearn) it. In the same way, when the ambient culture makes learning your language not just easy but *inevitable,* it is, apparently, hard to see all of the cultural and institutional supports that make it so. How easy it is to suppose that when a language fails to thrive, this is evidence of a casual disregard of the language, or a lack of interest in it by its community, when nothing could possibly be further from the truth.

While I was visiting my family in the Czech Republic, I came under the spell of objects and places that represented continuity. Sleeping on the bed on which my father was born, I found my dreams infiltrated by ancestors. In them, I was sometimes visited by my grandmother, a tiny, indestructible woman who bore four sons and grew them into men despite the many pressures of the Communist regime; shortly after my family's property was seized, my grandfather suffered a paralyzing stroke and eventually died, but my grandmother—whose first name I've inherited—soldiered on for another half-century as the staunch head of the household that she was. I moved through rooms where various family members had lived, through successive generations soothing babies, preparing *koláče* (delicious pastries stuffed with cheese or fruit), pouring wine for friends who came visiting. I envisioned how the apricot tree in the courtyard had been tended by many hands over the years, how countless harvests of cabbage, beans, and strawberries had steadfastly grown in the same soil through all the various wars, upheavals, and occupations of the past few centuries.

North American culture, with the brashness of its youth and its historical estrangements from its own ancestry, tends to devalue the past to the point of amnesia. Disruption and innovation are seen as more precious than continuity. Inculcated as I have become in this culture, I was surprised at how much emotion rose up in me at finding myself in the same physical space as my ancestors. I felt anchored in a way I had not felt before. Like the elder Aanaar Saami speakers who gathered together to speak their mother tongue, I felt, in some profound way, restored to myself. I could not have imagined or predicted feeling this way, and when in the middle of feeling it, I could not readily explain it. But the effects of that restoration have been life-changing for me. My sense of myself has acquired a deeper sense of time, less strictly bounded by the edges of my own lifetime.

For many people, language is the thread that links them to their history and provides a sense of continuity, a bulwark against chaos and uncertainty. This is especially true of many speakers of endangered languages, who have already been dispossessed of land and traditional ways of life. But languages, like physical objects or places, can change over time—in fact, linguists argue that language change is natural and inevitable, much like mutations and changes within a species. But if languages change drastically over a very short period of time, can they still provide the same sense of continuity and restoration? This is a vital question because endangered languages may be acutely susceptible to sweeping changes precisely as a result of the interruptions in their passage from one generation to the next.

Small Indigenous languages face change-inducing pressures from multiple sides. First, it's well known that contact with other languages tends to accelerate change within a language, much as the presence of a competing species within the same ecosystem often spurs biological changes. Some of this change can be traced to bilingualism.

We know that languages compete within the minds of bilingual speakers, mutually influencing each other. If there are enough bilingual speakers, features from one language may seed themselves in the other language and take root. A great many speakers of Indigenous languages are by necessity bilingual, since those who don't speak the dominant language are shut out of many aspects of public life. This heightens the odds of cross-fertilization.

Second, in many Indigenous communities, the native language has been actively suppressed by the dominant culture and its policies. Many people have been dissuaded or prevented from speaking it, and the breadth of contexts in which it is spoken has shrunk. As a result, the language has suffered widespread attrition—and attrition often brings with it a simplification of the grammar or a loss of certain distinctions and features. At the very least, there is a narrowing of its range of registers as it retreats to smaller and smaller spaces.

A third source of instability might be introduced in the process of trying to bring the language back to life. As with the Aanaar Saami language, in order to create a linguistic village in which children can grow up to be full-throated native speakers, it may be necessary to replace lost generations of speakers. Adults can be trained to become proficient speakers of the language—certainly they can become proficient enough to help support the language in the community. But they rarely, if ever, learn a language as children do, as native speakers who command all aspects of its sound and grammar. If these adults, who learned the language late in life, make up a large proportion of the language's speakers, will they drive the language toward change? That is, if much of the language that children hear comes from adults who haven't perfectly mastered all of its subtleties, will they be able to replicate the original language?

Several linguists have suggested that when a language becomes flooded with adult learners, their presence in the linguistic community can permanently alter its course. Among them is John McWhorter, who argues that this is exactly what happened to English.[43]

In some respects, English is much simpler than many of its linguistic relatives, namely, other Germanic languages. Among various grammatical trappings, present-day speakers of German have to remember which gender—masculine, feminine, or neuter—is assigned to each and every common noun in the language. These assignments often seem arbitrary, or even nonsensical, so they must be committed to memory; das Mädchen ("the girl"), for example, is assigned neuter gender, while der Kohl ("the cabbage") is elevated to masculine status and die Karotte ("the carrot") to feminine. German also uses case markers to signal the role that nouns play in the sentence (though not as elaborately as the Slavic languages), and it allows much more fluid rearrangements of word order. Compared to German—let alone even more complicated Germanic languages like Icelandic or Faroese—English seems much easier for an outsider to learn, and McWhorter argues that it is. Its simplicity, he claims, is the result of waves of Scandinavian Vikings invading northern England beginning in the eighth century, which also meant that the English *language* was invaded by hordes of new language learners who failed to learn all of its complicated flourishes at the time. Thus, English was permanently shorn of some of its grammatical features. McWhorter makes similar arguments for the streamlined character of several other languages, including Persian, Mandarin Chinese, and Malay. "Polish has developed unimpeded," he writes, but "someone put their foot out and tripped English. The human grammar is a fecund weed, like grass. Languages like English, Persian, and Mandarin Chinese are mowed lawns."[44]

If English has been trimmed back by newcomers to the language long ago, then many of the world's Indigenous languages have lush, overgrown grammars that have sprouted vines and shoots over time that would boggle the mind of the average monolingual English speaker. In fact, if they are small languages that have been spoken by a close-knit group of people with relatively little infiltration from outsiders, their grammars may be extremely intricate. A number of researchers have pointed out that such small, encapsulated languages tend to have a cluster of features in common.[45] They often express information that other languages might leave at the mercy of guesswork, to be gleaned from the context if at all. For example, some languages have an obligatory grammatical tag in the sentence that specifies whether an assertion is based on direct observation or is reported as secondhand information. Encapsulated languages also tend to embrace linguistic redundancy; in Czech, for example, case must be marked not just on every noun in the sentence but also on any adjective, numeral, *and* article that accompanies the noun. And they tend to be riddled with grammatical exceptions, forms that can't be logically deduced from a tidy rule but that you just have to *know,* based on an intimate familiarity with the language and its own special quirks. It's not hard to imagine that all of this would make a language as easy for a newcomer to approach as a thicket full of brambles, especially for an adult who is relying on deliberate, rule-formulating mental machinery rather than learning the language through some version of muscle memory.

These theories about the link between a society's history and the structure of its language are quite new, and some pieces of evidence are still missing. For example, although we know that children and adults learn language differently, and it seems quite plausible that grammatically lusher languages would be especially hard for adults to learn, this has not been clearly established. No one has closely compared the learning trajectory of adults versus children with respect to English and Icelandic, for example, and demonstrated that adults make more of a hash of Icelandic while managing better with English—and more specifically, that adults but not children mangle exactly the kinds of features that Icelandic has but that English has long since abandoned. But if these ideas turn out to be true, then the loss of generations of speakers and their replacement by new adult learners would make it that much harder to maintain continuity in languages that are lushly complex. It would be a sad irony if the features of a language that naturally emerged within a tightly woven community now serve as barriers to many of the community's own, who in adulthood are eager to learn the language they were deprived of as children.

Regardless of the inevitability of language change, which sometimes proceeds slowly and sometimes quickly, a feeling of existential threat rises up in the throat when people are confronted with change in their own language. Bill Labov, a linguist who has spent his long life studying the various pressures and circumstances that have provoked changes within the English language, once wryly remarked: "Some older citizens welcome the new music and dances, the new electronic devices and computers. But no one has ever been heard to say, '*It's wonderful the way young people talk today. It's so much better than the way we talked when I was a kid.*'"[46] If anything, this feeling of threat is heightened among those who love language and are hyperaware of it; I have a number of writer friends who fervently excise the signs of language rot they see everywhere, whether it's the use of "less than three" when it *should* be "fewer than three" or the appearance of the word "whomever" in aesthetically offensive contexts.

If people can have such a protective response toward English—a language that has been pinched and pulled into so many different shapes over time, and that has happily devoured foreign words and accommodated countless regional varieties—I imagine it must be that much more disorienting to witness massive upheavals within a language that has been fairly sheltered from the winds of change. The feeling of continuity with the past is lost. It's like returning to a beloved childhood home only to find that the cozy country kitchen has been "upgraded" with sleek appliances, walls have been knocked down, and a new wing is now growing like a tumor from the side of the house.

For some Indigenous groups, it is a priority to maintain as much continuity in the language as possible, and this includes resisting incursion from the dominant language. Aversion to borrowing or adapting words from English is common, unlike in languages like Japanese, which is content to squeeze an English word into Japanese sound structure and call it a day (for example, *business hotel* becomes *bijinesu hoteru*). Marie Rose Blackduck, a radio broadcaster in the Tłįchǫ language spoken in the Canadian Northwest Territories, has described to me how important it is in her community that elders not feel alienated from their language; as a result, they are consulted whenever a word is needed for a concept that does not have a traditional name. For example, the Tłįchǫ word for AIDS, a disease that only became widely known in the 1980s, was concocted entirely of native ingredients and is a rough translation of the English phrase "disease with no cure." I must admit that it would not cross the mind of any English (or Czech) speaker to seek approval from their grandparents before coining a new word. Our elders are callously left to grumble about their alienation from their own language.

It is not that difficult, especially in a small community, to create a border patrol of sorts to decide which new words can enter the language. But it is much more difficult to monitor and control other aspects of language that may be more subtle, such as the exact use (or omission) of certain grammatical tags or the precise pronunciation of words. And it is nearly impossible for a community to enforce strict linguistic norms if many of its speakers have learned the language as adults, to varying degrees of proficiency. This may cause elders to question the value of pouring energy into preserving a form of the language that to them looks like a flimsy renovation of the language they learned from their own parents—or worse, perhaps even a desecration of words that are considered sacred.

All of this means that the keepers of endangered languages are faced with profound questions about the form their language will take if they do manage to save it, and to what extent a much-altered language can offer a sense of continuity. This is something that each community will have to decide for itself. But it is clear that for some, reviving a language has provided powerful connections to the past, even when that language is revived into something that is very different from its previous state.

THE POSTER CHILD for language "resurrection" is, of course, Hebrew, a language in which the Judean people had conversed for about 1,300 years when they stopped speaking it to their children by the second century, under pressure of the dominant languages of the time, Aramaic and Greek. (Jesus, for example, spoke Aramaic, not Hebrew.) Hebrew was preserved, however, in two separate sacred literatures, which together encompassed a range of styles from the poetic and epic to the prosaic and legalistic. These texts did not simply sit in an archive somewhere; they continued to be studied by Jewish people all over the world. These people spoke to their children in a variety of local languages, but they read religious texts in Hebrew, prayed in Hebrew, and occasionally used the language in personal letters and business or legal documents; in many Jewish communities, Hebrew was the only language that people knew how to read and write.[47] (It may seem odd to us today that people would speak one language but write in another, but in fact this was the case throughout much of the world during the Middle Ages. People grew up speaking their various local languages, but if they were literate, they were educated in Latin, Classical Arabic, Sanskrit, or Old Church Slavonic.) Nor was Hebrew entirely confined to the page—some people spoke it as a common Jewish language in conversations with visitors from different countries, and visiting rabbis delivered their sermons in Hebrew when they did not speak the local language. Still, nowhere was it the language of daily life, and for more than 1,700 years, no children learned it as their mother tongue. In 1881, Elezier Ben-Yehuda, out of a fierce belief that the Jewish people needed a national language, decided to speak Hebrew to fellow Jewish people when he moved from Paris to Jerusalem, and when his son was born in 1882, the child became the first native speaker of what has come to be called Modern Hebrew.

This language is quite different from the one that is inscribed in the sacred Hebrew texts—not just because many new words came into being to fill gaps, but also because Ben-Yehuda was not a native speaker of the language, nor were many in the first generations who adopted Hebrew as the language they spoke in the home. Linguist Ghil'ad Zuckermann has even argued that it is somewhat misleading to call this new language "Hebrew" or "Modern Hebrew"; he himself insists on calling it "Israeli." The Israeli language, he argues, really has two parents: Hebrew and Yiddish, the latter being Ben-Yehuda's own mother tongue, and whose influences upon the Israeli language Zuckermann has documented in his research. He suggests that any time a language is lifted from the page and brought into the home and the street, it will inevitably be tinged by the mother tongue already lodged in the minds of its new speakers—and since the language has no native speakers who can correct or contradict, the speech habits of these early speakers will give the language its new shape.

For example, related languages of the Middle East (such as Arabic) make heavy use of a sound called the glottal stop, a consonant that is essentially a gulp in the throat. And though Hebrew texts unambiguously mark this sound—in fact, it appears as the diacritic mark in the English version of Ghil'ad Zuckermann's first name—the sound is not found in European languages. As a result, it is absent from the speech of most Israelis. Moreover, while some elements of a language are fairly well preserved in text, other aspects elude written language altogether. The intonational melodies that float above a sentence, the connotations of a word, the typical tone or gesture that accompanies it, the verbal dance between conversational partners—these are all invisible in the written record of a language and could therefore not be recovered from the Hebrew of long ago. As a result, Hebrew forms may sit on the surface of Yiddish patterns of usage. For example, the Israeli greeting *má nishmà* uses *words* that were taken from ancient Hebrew texts (literally, "What is heard?"), but the *manner* of greeting can be traced to Yiddish, where one would say *vos hert zikh* (What does one hear?").

Despite the changes that were injected into the Israeli language when it moved from text to tongue, and his reluctance to call the language "Hebrew," Zuckermann does not deny that its historical connection to Hebrew has been profoundly meaningful for the Israeli nation. Had it not been for the "zealous, obsessive, enthusiastic efforts" of Ben-Yehuda and the early Hebrew revivalists, he writes, "Israelis would have spoken a language (such as English, German, Arabic, or Yiddish) that could hardly be considered Hebrew. To call such a hypothetical language 'Hebrew' would have been not only misleading but wrong. To call today's Israeli 'Hebrew' may be misleading, but not wrong."[48] In the act of reclaiming Hebrew as their national language, its early speakers cordoned off a space apart from the national cultures of the lands into which they had been dispersed. Their reclamation of language was an affirmation of what distinguished them as a people as much as it was a resurrection of an ancient language, and I suspect that this affirmation, perhaps more than the language itself, was what held their community together as they built a new nation. The deliberate act of reclaiming the language was not the *method* by which Israeli / Hebrew came to life—it *was* the breath of life itself; it *was* the meaning that imbued the language and animated it from sacred script to mother tongue.

The path of language revival will be different for each language, but each will be marked by scars of discontinuity and the imprints of its own particular history—and perhaps it will even twine together multiple influences and identities. Some communities have complicated relationships with the language that most of its members now speak as their dominant language, and they may choose to erect barriers to limit its reach. Whether these influences manage to sneak into the language regardless, in the cadences of its words or the bones of its syntax, may be beside the point. The communal discussions and decisions are perhaps the main point, as it is through this process that the community will search its soul and define itself. In the end, it may be less important whether the new speakers of the language can move through the rooms of their ancestors exactly as they were for many years before. It will be the process of rebuilding the language that will reveal who they are as a people.

It occurs to me that cultural memory is much like an individual's memory of her own life. Psychologists have long known that our memories of our experiences are nothing like recordings, in which details of events as they actually happened are preserved. Instead, they are like visitations. Every time we visit a memory, we subtly rearrange it. We may leave behind a new knick-knack, lose a few that were there on a previous visit, color the walls in a different hue, shuffle the furniture slightly. The outcome reflects our own mental realities and psychological needs, often unconscious. In the same way, cultural practices— including language—are not like heirlooms that are passed intact from one generation to the next. They too have the character of visitations, and they too involve repeated subtle alterations that reflect a society's realities and psychological needs. I'm reminded of the words of the nineteenth-century psychologist, William James: "There is no such thing as mental retention, the persistence of an idea from month to month or year to year in some mental pigeon-hole from which it can be drawn when wanted. What persists is a tendency to connection."[49]

To reclaim a language is to reclaim the tendency to connection. It is to assert the right to cultural memory and to retell the story of your life—and not just the part of your life that is contained within your own life span, but also what spills outside of it. Suvi Kivelä was one of the students involved in the Aanaar Saami language immersion program. Though she herself does not have Saami roots, she saw firsthand the impact of the program on those who did. Of these observations, she wrote: "I don't think I have ever seen anything as inspiring, healing, and moving as someone who reclaims his or her mother tongue. And when you see people becoming whole again, when they are reconnecting with their ancestors, history, and long-lost heritage, you cannot but think that it must be right."[50]

So it was for me. As I came to be more at home in the Czech language, I was able to have the conversations I needed to have. I spent many evenings in my uncle's kitchen, sharing a meal that one of us had cooked, drinking his wine, and listening to him talk about his life, which was also, to some extent, my father's life. "What do you find to talk about?" asked my uncle's daughter, who lived a few steps away from her father. "I don't think he and I could fill a half hour with conversation." What we found to talk about were all the things she didn't need to talk to her father about, because she had lived them with him. Unlike her, I had never lived in the place my father called home. The daily habits, the rituals and ceremonies, the social expectations, and the landscape of fields and hills and vineyards that had molded my father's soul were familiar to me, but only as a very distant echo. I needed to talk so that all these things could become intelligible to me. So that my father could become intelligible to me. In that kitchen, with my uncle inhabiting my father's language—and even his gestures and his blunt sense of humor and his obsession with flowers—we re-enacted the scenes of a daughter coming to know her father.

We had not yet run out of things to talk about when it came time for my uncle to drive me to the airport in Vienna. Unlike our earlier drive to the village of Moravská Nová Ves, throughout which I had so ineptly fumbled for words, our talk tumbled back and forth like the talk of two people who would soon miss each other deeply. My uncle parked the car and came inside the terminal to extend the conversation for as long as possible. When it was time to say goodbye, he responded to the gathering wetness in my eyes by saying, with a brusque humor that was also my father's, "Thank God you're finally leaving. Now I can get back to a sensible meal schedule." (He had regularly complained about my North American habit of eating my main meal at the end of the day rather than at noontime but had adjusted his own days to align with mine.) And then, worried about a possible misunderstanding, he quickly added, "Don't take that seriously, that's just how we Sedivys talk." "I know," I assured him.

In the suitcase that accompanied me home, the weight of the gifts I'd distributed was replaced by the weight of Czech books I was taking back with me, many of which had been piled into my arms by a cousin who began pulling volumes from her own shelves when I asked for suggestions of what to read. It seemed an apt metaphor for the imbalance of the exchange that had occurred during my visit; the small pleasures and novelties from Canada that I'd brought with me traded for the heft of language and culture.

I brought other things onto the plane with me as well. I brought a sharpened awareness of my own self-contradictions; during my time in the family village, other ways of being and seeing had asserted themselves and clashed with my English-speaking self. Here, I was someone who attended Sunday Mass; back in North America I was not. Back there, I refused to be on the receiving end of Easter whipping rituals; here I acquiesced. Back home, I railed against patriarchs and their claims to privilege; here I saw how a patriarch might willingly shoulder an ox's burden of responsibility. Here, I could feel how a life lived in pursuit of aspiration was an abandonment of sorts. But rather than feeling fragmented by these contradictions, what I experienced was a sense of wholeness. I felt I could more easily acknowledge and accept the inherent twinning of my soul.

It remains one of the greatest regrets of my life that I had not taken this trip while my father was still alive, and I hope I never add another regret that is equal to it. Nonetheless, what did take place, even after his passing, was a healing of some of the deepest wounds inflicted by the discontinuity of his death. Certain misunderstandings between us could be put right; he was no longer there to hear me articulate my own position, but I had acquired new insights into his, and I could imagine what I might have said that would have allowed me to cross the border between us. The crossing, in fact, did take place. And in return, I felt him spilling beyond the edges of his own life span into mine.

I *(left)* enjoy a backpacking trip with my children in Kananaskis, an area in the Rocky Mountains close to our Calgary home.

Chapter 6

Home

The skies were a deep, clear blue on the day I departed from my Czech home back to Calgary. As the airplane rose higher and higher, I was able to watch for a long time the green fields below with their clusters of red tiled roofs. I felt overcome by an immediate pang of nostalgia as the landscape fell further and further away from me. My thoughts lingered on the English word *homeland,* a word that infuses a tract of real estate with a profound and even spiritual feeling of belonging. And indeed, for my Czech relatives, the notions of *home* and *land* were inseparable. Several times during my visit I had seen my uncle or cousins gazing out at the countryside with an expression usually reserved for one's true love—a mix of hunger, pride, and satisfaction. When they tended their gardens and vineyards, their limbs were relaxed and their movements were peaceful, as if contentment rose up from the ground and passed through them in the places where their feet made contact with the earth. My uncle had told me several times over the past two months that the reason he did not flee the country, as did two of his brothers, was that someone had to stay and look after the family home—this despite the fact that the home was at the time owned by the state and the family was forced to pay rent for the privilege of living on a portion of it, having no legal rights to either the buildings or the land, and no promise of passing it down to future generations. Still, it was the Sedivy home, and as far as he was concerned, it could not be abandoned.

I sat with these thoughts for a long time, and as the plane left land behind altogether and carried us over the ocean, I began to wonder how it would feel to approach Calgary from the air. Having renewed my ties to the land of my birth, would Calgary now seem more *strangeland* than *homeland*? Would it be harder to feel a sense of belonging there, now that I had so clearly felt the presence of my ancestors on the family land?

I thought, too, of an event described by the author J. Edward Chamberlin: a meeting takes place between government officials and members of the Gitksan people (an Indigenous community in northwest British Columbia) in which the officials assert the government's rights to the land.[1] The Gitksan are flabbergasted. "If this is your land," they say, "where are your stories?" And then they proceed to tell *their* traditional stories of the land. In one of these stories, they talk about the transformation of one of the river valleys in the area some seven thousand years ago. According to the story, the spirit of the valley, embodied in a grizzly bear, became enraged at the people's misuse of its natural resources, and came roaring from the top of the mountain toward them. On the way down, the bear tumbled and brought down half the mountain with him, burying the entire valley floor, including the village nestled there. Only a few villagers who were out hunting or berry picking survived. It turns out that this story has its counterpart in contemporary geological evidence: sixty feet below the valley floor, there is clay that matches clay from high on the mountain slopes, suggesting that an earthquake at one time triggered a massive landslide. This earthquake is estimated to have occurred about seven thousand years ago.

The Gitksan people offered their traditional story as proof of their long and deep connection to the land. What stronger evidence could there be of their claim to the land than the direct, intimate knowledge they had of it, reaching back thousands of years? As was the case for my uncle, the government's scrap of paper claiming ownership meant very little.

As I mulled this over, I thought of Calgary, the place I now call home. Where were my stories of Calgary? Next to the stories of the Gitksan and other Indigenous peoples, and even beside my uncle's stories of home, they seemed unbearably flimsy and sparse. Far from spanning thousands or hundreds of years, my Calgary stories do not even stretch out to fill a lifetime. Barely a sliver of a lifetime. In fact, the geography of my entire life is carved into thin slices: an infancy here, a childhood there, a coming of age in yet another place, childbirths, marriages, friendships, studies, heartbreaks, jobs—all of these strewn about various cities in various countries. Even my legal citizenship straddles three nations.

Kde domov můj? asks the Czech national anthem: *Where is my home?* It is perhaps an apt title for the anthem of a people who, throughout most of their history, lived under the thumb of foreign rulers. For me, of course, the title is not rhetorical—I am always at a loss whenever someone asks me where I am from. I honestly do not know what to say. But for the Czech people, it has an answer. The anthem continues:

> *Voda hučí po lučinách*
> *bory šumí po skalinách,*
> *v sadě skví se jara květ,*
> *zemský ráj to na pohled!*
> *A to je ta krásná země,*
> *země česká domov můj,*
> *země česká domov můj!*
> Water rushes through the meadows,
> pines rustle by the crags,
> the orchard is abloom with spring.
> The view is an earthly paradise!
> It is that beautiful Czech land,

> that Czech land that is my home,
> that Czech land that is my home.[2]

With this song, Czechs lay claim to their land. This claim is one that comes not from deep knowledge of the land but from the depth of the feeling they have for it. Perhaps it is really an anthem in which Czechs describe the claim the land has on them. It is sung in a minor key to a haunting melody suffused with longing, a feeling that is a close relative of that particular Czech emotion of *litost*—or rather, that universal emotion that has been given a particular Czech name. It's an anthem that rolls into itself both the feeling of what it is to love the land and what it is like to lose it, an anthem for a perennially occupied people. To me, it's a song that recalls how my relatives looked at their land in the way one would gaze at the face of a beloved.

Where is *my* home? This question, unlike the one posed in the Czech national anthem, has no clear answer. But I do know this: that when the plane began its descent near Calgary, circling over the green, grassy prairie rolled out beneath the snow-capped mountains rising in the west, my heart swelled with anticipation. And I thought how good it felt to be home. Over the next days and weeks, I found that, rather than feeling disconnected from the place where I live, a deepened rootedness began to take hold. It was mid-May when I returned to Calgary, a time when spring in Moravia is already leaning hard into summer, but here in Calgary, new growth was just beginning to erupt. There was much to do in my garden, and while I mulched and weeded and pruned, I found my emboldened Czech language bubbling easily to the surface there, along with the memory of the timbre of my father's voice. It's no accident that many of my conversations with him, and more recently with my uncle, have been on the subject of horticulture. My father's family has spent centuries working the land in Moravia's fertile wine and orchard region, and the cultivating instinct runs deep within our family. Throughout my own life, I've given in to the compulsion to fasten myself to whatever patch of land I happened to be living on by growing things on it, an impulse that has often conflicted with the mobile trajectory of my life. Here, in the lee of the Rocky Mountains, I give in to it again; neither grapes nor apricots will thrive in the brittle mountain air, but I raise sour cherries and saskatoons (berries native to western Canada) along with swaths of flowers that would have delighted my father. Gardening in Calgary is not for the weak of spirit, what with the relentless desiccating winds, the bitter winter cold that is punctuated by sudden thaws followed by another round of plunging temperatures, and the hailstorms that can shred a garden in minutes; it takes a detailed knowledge of the needs and habits of plants and a stoic acceptance of the climate to grow a successful garden here.

I've had to leave behind the land of my ancestors. But working in my garden, I realize that there is much of my heritage that I've brought back with me. I've brought back my ancestors' way of relating to land: the desire to know a land deeply, to understand it through patient discovery of what is willing to grow on it, to root myself in its soil through the rhythm of the work I do there and by watching its cycles of flowerings, fruitings, and fadings. And when I sit in my garden and admire the evening light—that golden Western light that is so shatteringly clear it almost makes me cry—I know what it is to give your heart to a land that is yours and not yours.

And I've brought back seeds of language, which is the part of my ancestry that is portable and that I can plant here in the land on which I now walk and sleep. Just as Czechs cast a loving eye on their land, they often listen to their language with a loving ear. Many years ago, I remember catching my breath as I read this passage by the Czech writer Bohumil Hrabal: "when I read, I don't really read; I pop a beautiful sentence into my mouth and suck it like a fruit drop, or I sip it like a liqueur until the thought dissolves in me like alcohol, infusing brain and heart and coursing on through the veins to the root of each blood vessel."[3] This is a passage I can easily imagine my father reading aloud in such a way as to embody it. I remember how he had treated his own language like a lovely object to be turned over, admired, stroked with a fingertip, deserving of deliberate and leisurely attention. Just as my way of relating to land has survived beyond the confines of my homeland, I realize that my way of relating to language has deep roots. It's when I steer my inner monologue toward Czech that I'm most easily reminded of what it feels like to sink into language, to be startled by the aptness of a word or the twist of a phrase, to be delighted by the arrangements of its sounds, and lulled by its rhythms.

It occurs to me that along with *homeland,* there needs to be another word: *homelanguage.*

The feeling I have for my current home is complicated by an inescapable fact: I'm able to call this land my home only because there are many other people who, after making their home here for thousands of years, were dispossessed of it. If I'm truly to belong to this land, it will require more than simply planting pieces of my own heritage in it; I will need to allow pieces of the land's long heritage to become planted in me. At first glance, this seems impossible. The nomadic ways of its first citizens are so different from my ancestors' habits of tethering themselves to the soil that the two cultures seem almost irreconcilable. I have no shared history with the Indigenous peoples whose homeland this is, and little in the way of overlapping customs. But it is becoming clearer to me that there is a great deal I have in common with them: we share the monumental task of remaking ourselves under the shadow of a dominant language and culture while trying to preserve threads of continuity with our own ancestral heritages. It occurs to me that I might have something to learn from individuals and communities who have been forced to shoulder this task on a scale that makes my own immigrant experiences seem trivial in comparison.

For those dispossessed of homeland, it is natural to seek refuge in homelanguage, and for many who are in danger of losing even the latter, the reclaiming of language has an urgency I can only try to imagine. Not long after my return from the Czech Republic, I spent some time in Edmonton, observing a few of the classes offered by the Canadian Indigenous Languages and Literacy Development Institute (CILLDI). This is a program that aims to equip people of Indigenous heritage with skills they can use to learn, document, and teach their ancestral languages. In one of these classes, the instructor, Darin Flynn, taught students the basic tools of linguistic analysis: students learned how to catalogue the various sounds of their language, describe recipes for assembling sentences, and recognize the elements of grammar their language shared with other languages, as well as its own unique means of expression. Shortly before coming to CILLDI, I'd had a conversation with a man who referred to Indigenous languages as "not real languages"—it became clear as we talked that he held the mistaken belief that the native peoples of North America communicated by means of primitive codes that included some basic vocabulary but little in the way of grammar or sophisticated structure. When I asserted otherwise, he remained skeptical, and as I sat in Darin's classroom, I found myself wishing he could witness this group of Indigenous speakers prying open their languages to examine how they were put together. They would have quickly disabused him of his naïve assumption.

When laid beside other languages of the world with their parts exposed, it rapidly becomes apparent how the first languages of North America display just as much enthusiasm for complexity as any other language, drawing on a vast range of techniques to achieve precision and expressive power. Some of the participants' languages used differences in pitch to distinguish between different words, much like Mandarin does. All of the languages had rich systems of prefixes or suffixes (often both) whose complexity was at times dizzyingly elaborate. Some were particular about the ordering of their nouns and verbs, as is English, others less so, as is Czech, relying on different tricks to keep track of the relationships between them. Some showed patterns that were the exact mirror image of English, with adjectives and then articles trailing after nouns rather than preceding them. Grammatical notions of gender, as found in French or German, were largely irrelevant to these languages, but a distinction between animate and inanimate nouns often reverberated throughout the grammatical system. In Stoney Nakoda, for example, a suffix is attached to animate nouns to show that the noun is plural, but not to inanimate ones, which remain bare even when plural. In all of the languages, intricate patterns emerged, and when there were several speakers of the same language, vigorous debates occasionally erupted about the correct way to express a thought, revealing systematic variations in dialect by region or age.

For many of the students, dissecting their mother tongue to inspect and tag its grammatical anatomy was a completely alien way to think about language, and it was not always apparent how these tools could help to keep the flame of their language alive. It was obvious that linguistic analysis was useful for certain purposes—for demonstrating the relationships between languages in the same family, for example, or for making the point that these were fully evolved languages and not primitive codes, or for documenting their languages in the event of catastrophic loss. It was less clear how it could help people *live* in their language and make it their home. Some students felt that all the analysis made it harder to feel connected to their language; one man objected that this was a very "White" way of relating to language, not at all like the way elders described and taught it. I imagined looking out at the Moravian landscape through the eyes of a geologist rather than the eyes of a farmer, and how strange that would feel to me.

What was happening in this classroom was, in many ways, a small demonstration of the enormous adaptation facing many Indigenous peoples: how to absorb the useful tools and practices of Western culture without becoming alienated from their own cultures in the process. Practical concerns could not be stripped of their existential implications. Occasionally, the linguistic analysis itself brought these existential questions to the surface. One day the question arose of the best way to write the phrase that is used as a greeting in Stoney Nakoda. The greeting is used in the same way that one might say "Good day" in English, but rather than representing a *wish* for a good day (as in "Have a nice day"), its literal translation, I was delighted to learn, is an assertion: "It is a good day." To an English speaker, the most transparent way of writing how the phrase sounds is: *amba wathtech*. But speakers of Stoney Nakoda most commonly write it as: *âba wathtech*. The character *â* indicates that the vowel is pronounced with a nasal quality, an important feature in Stoney Nakoda: the presence or absence of nasalization on a vowel can signal different words, much as it does in the French words *paix* and *pain,* which differ only in the nasal nature of the vowel in the second word of this pair. English has nasal vowels too, even though we don't distinguish them from nonnasal vowels in writing. This is because vowel nasality is not important for distinguishing between otherwise identical words, and nasal vowels predictably occur only in very specific phonetic contexts: a vowel inherits a nasal quality when it precedes a nasal consonant such as *m* or *n*. Typically, the orthography of a language will not bother notating sound properties that are completely predictable, so it's no surprise that English uses the same symbol to write the different-sounding vowels in words like *bed* and *bend*. But in Stoney Nakoda, vowel nasalization is not predictable because nasal vowels can occur in a variety of phonetic contexts, with or without a following nasal consonant. What *is* predictable is the presence of the nasal consonant *m* in the word *amba / âba;* a nasal vowel can never occur in front of the consonant *b* without an intervening *m* as a sort of transition between the vowel and the following consonant.

In other words, English and Stoney Nakoda are mirror images of each other when it comes to being able to predict certain properties of sounds: English speakers can predict the nasal property of vowels in English words, whereas Stoney Nakoda speakers can predict the presence of certain nasal consonants in their language. Hence, speakers of each language have different implicit notions of which sound qualities are most important to set down in writing.

Trent Fox, a native speaker of Stoney Nakoda who is an advocate of developing literacy in the language, wanted to know whether it was better to write it one way or the other. In response, Darin summarized how nasal vowels have a different mental status for native speakers of English versus Stoney Nakoda. As for whether one or the other was better, he lobbed the question right back at Trent: What is the main job of the alphabet? Is it to reflect the implicit knowledge that native Stoney Nakoda speakers have about their spoken language? Is it to help English-speaking outsiders learn the language? Trent had remarked on the fact that his English-speaking students had trouble figuring out how to pronounce words when they encoded the nasality of vowels but omitted symbols for the transitional nasal consonants. And what to make of the fact that a growing number of Stoney Nakoda people were no longer being raised in their language, and if they did learn it, often came to it only after they were introduced to reading and writing in English? Given the current circumstances of the language community—as well as its possible futures—does it make the most sense to write down what feels natural in English or what feels natural in Stoney Nakoda? The system of writing the English language has taken centuries to settle into a standardized form; given the precariousness of the Stoney Nakoda language, the community is forced to make these and many other decisions about the language in a very short period of time and under conditions of tremendous language flux and instability.

Over and over, I saw how people's efforts to renew their own Indigenous languages were tangled with their relationship to Western language and culture. Defining this relationship was a constant, central concern. Sometimes, the concerns focused on very specific decisions, like the best way to convey the sound of a nasal vowel in writing. At other times, the concerns were broad and foundational. For example,

Trent shared that many people in his own community questioned the value of writing down their language at all, worried that the living traditions of an oral language might be lost or devalued if it became entombed in writing. The prospect of literacy introduced an entirely different way of relating to their language, as alien to them as farming the land on which they used to roam and hunt.

It seemed to me that some communities had chosen to take in big gulps of Western culture and absorb them into their own. One of the languages spoken by the largest number of participants at CILLDI was the Tłįchǫ language (known in the past as the Dogrib language), which has fewer than two thousand speakers. The Tłįchǫ people live in some of Canada's most remote communities, on a vast, sieve-like region of the Canadian Northwest Territories that contains almost as much water as land. One can only drive between all four Tłįchǫ communities in the winter when the waterways freeze solidly enough to serve as roads; in Gamètì, an outlying community that is home to about 300 people, a doctor flies in at most once a month. Despite being so physically separated from the rest of Canada, the Tłįchǫ people appear to have little desire to isolate themselves from the dominant culture. Their official footprint on the internet is impressively wide for a population about the size of my father's tiny village of Moravská Nová Ves, and one can spend many hours reading about the language, history, and current governance of the Tłįchǫ people. At CILLDI, the Tłįchǫ students arrived at their classes equipped with slickly printed English / Tłįchǫ dictionaries and texts translated from English, including a translation, produced in consultation with elders, of chunks of the Christian Bible. When asked to sing a song in their language, a group of women stood up and performed one whose words sounded foreign to me but whose melody I was instantly able to hum along to—it was a hymn I had heard many times as a child at Catholic Mass. The Tłįchǫ have a motto that they frequently invoke: "Strong like two people," a motto attributed to the late Chief Jimmy Bruneau that captures the belief that a bicultural way of life involving full participation in two cultures is a source of strength rather than a source of confusion.

Despite our different histories and cultural practices, I found myself quite at home among the CILLDI students. The questions that preoccupied them were intensely familiar to me: How can we remain bound to the traditions and values that have shaped us while still reaping a share of the rewards that the dominant culture reserves for those who meet its expectations? What aspects of the majority culture are worth emulating, and what is best left aside? What will we gain if we change? What will we lose?

The aspiration to harvest the best of two cultures and blend them together into a new identity is a heroic one, but in daily practice, it is a brutally difficult discipline that requires the two to be in constant dialogue and negotiation, with systems in place to check the balance of power between them. In August of 2020, I watched the Tłı̨chǫ annual gathering which, due to the COVID-19 pandemic, was streamed online rather than celebrated by people who used the occasion as a reason to crowd together in the town of Behchokǫ̀ to drum, dance, and play hand games (an elaborate sleight-of-hand team sport). Bilingualism was on full display. On the first day of the gathering, various reports were given in English (several of them by non-Tłı̨chǫ employees), summarizing the economic investments and social programs of the community, with remarks in the Tłı̨chǫ language at times serving as a preface to the reports. On the second day, citizens had the opportunity to voice their questions and concerns over videoconference. Most of these were delivered in Tłı̨chǫ, but often bracketed by greetings and closing comments spoken in a perfectly fluent English. Tłı̨chǫ speakers mixed English in to varying degrees, sometimes reserving English for numerals, dates, and phrases such as *strategic plan, federal government,* or *small business,* and sometimes moving back and forth between the two languages as the spirit moved them—which would have posed some challenges, I imagine, to the people who were providing real-time interpretation between the two languages. But beneath the harmonious dance between languages, some of the citizens alluded to tensions and clashes of values. One young woman took the Tłı̨chǫ government to task for placing too much emphasis on the local mine as a source of economic activity and not investing enough in programs that sustained the local language and culture, especially among the youth. Two of the people who delivered their remarks in English expressed their dismay: although they aspired to be "strong like two people," they felt their communities did not offer enough support for them to succeed at being either. Their frustrations echoed the familiar refrain of people I've met throughout my life who feel the pain of being caught between two cultures, slipping into the crevasses between them, sure-footed in neither.

The dominant culture is often suspicious of people whose identities can't be entirely contained within its own borders, leery that their loyalty will run shallow. But I find myself more and more convinced that tending to one's heritage can strengthen a sense of belonging to the majority culture—it is far easier to participate wholeheartedly in a society if you feel you are allowed to show up as your entire self. As challenging as it is to live it, I admit to having bought into the motto coined by Chief Jimmy Bruneau. In the few years since I first began to reclaim my Czech language and culture, I've become more curious—not less—about the history and customs of my adopted home. I find myself wanting to better understand the forces that have shaped the culture in which my life is now embedded. That desire has sparked an odyssey of discovery, including an exploration of the many languages and cultures belonging to the first inhabitants of this place. And it has stoked a wish to explore the blessings and terrors of fitting all of our heritages together into a greater whole with a shared sense of purpose.

As I said goodbye to the CILLDI participants, my Tłı̨chǫ friends pressed me to come visit them in the North. I assured them I would. One of them promised to take time off work, introduce me around to family and friends, and take me along the winter road to the outlying communities. "Don't forget your promise," she said. "We won't forget ours." Though I've had to postpone my visit, first due to illness in the family and then to the COVID-19 pandemic, I have not forgotten. My writing it here is a way of renewing my promise of connection and shared home-making. After all, we are together in this business of trying to be more than one person.

In hearing or reading about the revitalization of Indigenous languages, I often come across mention of "land-based learning." At its core, this phrase refers to a simple concept: that children should not be learning *about* their own languages and cultures in a classroom, as if they were learning about the events leading up to the Second World War in Europe or about the baroque case system of Latin, but that they should learn, as much as possible, to inhabit their languages from the inside. And for peoples whose survival depended on understanding the ways of plants, animals, geography, and climate—who were not estranged from the natural world by thick layers of technology—culture and language cannot be separated from land. For these societies, the outdoors has historically provided the classroom, the apprenticeship, the on-the-job training program. It has been the arena for all of life's successes and failures.

This is reflected in the languages. The Tłįchǫ language, for example, reveals a special preoccupation with the geography of water, reflecting a lifestyle in which much travel took place by boat on the many waterways that shred the northern landscape around Great Slave Lake. There are specific words to refer to the confluence of rivers, to a lake off to the side of a major lake, to the waterway between a side-lake and the main body of water, to the segment of a river between rapids, to the segment of a river between rapids and the mouth of a river, to the far end of a lake, to the place where a stream reaches a lake, to a site for setting a fishnet, to a place where water lengthens out, and on and on.[4] Names for specific sites are not used as monuments to humans, as is often the case in European place names, but are rich in useful description: Kʼàdzàetì ("Dry Willow Lake"), Nį̀htʼèhtìa ("Blackened Earth Pond"), and Gotsʼǫkàtìkʼètɬʼàaʔelàetǫdaaʔàa ("Landing of the Sled Trail at the Far End of Cloudberry Lake"). Geography is so central to Tłı̨chǫ life that many traditional travel narratives are simply a concatenation of the names of the places visited, each name having the power within itself to evoke the sights, sounds, and smells of the place in the minds of listeners, triggering a mental multisensory slideshow.

When I first moved to Calgary in 2008, I embarked on my own version of a land-based language program. I joined my new husband on long hikes, scrambles, and climbs in the Rocky Mountains just west of the city, and I learned an entire vocabulary that I had never encountered before, words related to the unfamiliar natural environment: *scree, col, cairn, hanging cirque, tarn, cornice, talus, gendarme, sastrugi, moraine* (both terminal and lateral), *arete, dihedral, headwall, serac, massif, spur, choss, verglas,* and on and on. For me, these words occupy a place in my memory like no other words. They were learned on the land. They are infused with the sound of the wind howling through lodgepole pines and larch trees, of ravens raucously announcing themselves, and of hidden marmots whistling to each other. They recall the strain of muscles striving for the strenuous moves on a rock climb and the thinness of air near a high summit. They are steeped in the healing that took place and the new love that unfolded for me in this gorgeous, demanding landscape after the pain of a harrowing divorce.

Whenever I leave Calgary for any length of time, I don't feel that I've fully come back home until I head out into the mountains again. It was no different after my long visit to the Czech Republic, and on my first weekend back, as soon as I'd recovered from jet lag, I drove west with my husband, with backpacks, hiking shoes, and poles stashed in the trunk of our car. As soon as I stepped up above the tree line and surveyed the panorama that extended toward the jagged horizon, I thought the usual thought: *How I've missed you, mountains.*

But this time, that thought felt like a single note buried within a complex chord. Vibrating right along with it was the feeling of home for a very different landscape, a European one with softer edges and tamer lighting, and of the bonds I had with the people there. And I could also detect a new overtone: a sense of kinship with the nomadic people who have, in the long past and into the present, looked at these mountains in the same way that my European relatives looked at their countryside, and whose knowledge of the land and whose language for it far surpasses my own.

Those people are the Stoney Nakoda, who used to hunt and camp along the eastern slopes and foothills of the Rocky Mountains, down into Montana, and as far east as Saskatchewan, living on buffalo, moose, elk, deer, moose, mountain sheep and goats, rabbit, and the many plants of this vast and varied territory. They are now confined to three small reserves. The largest of these is the Morley Reserve, which is bisected by the Trans-Canada Highway and unknowingly crossed by hordes of tourists who travel between the Calgary Airport and Banff National Park. They are historically rooted in the Great Sioux Nation and are relatives of the Dakota and Lakota peoples now living in the United States.

The Stoney people (or, as they refer to themselves in their language, the Îyethka) number about five thousand, roughly twice the population of my father's village, and an estimated two thousand of them can speak the language. The Îyethka language has survived decades of residential schooling for its children, but the number of young people who speak it now is dropping sharply. Trent Fox, a resident of Morley, told me that in 1972, 95 percent of the children on the reserve entered kindergarten speaking the Îyethka language; recently, he heard from a local teacher that one child among 203 did. And he rightly worries that the school programs are not nearly enough to make up for the lack of exposure at home.

Europeans first laid eyes on some of the most iconic scenery within the Canadian Rocky Mountains in the presence of Stoney Nakoda guides who had led them there, but there are almost no traces of the Îyethka language on official maps. For example, in 1882, Îyethka guide Edwin Hunter brought European settler Tom Wilson to a place called *Horâ Juthin Îmne* ("Lake of the Little Fishes"), a turquoise-colored lake spread out below a stately glacier.[5] Shortly afterward, it became a world-renowned mountain resort, the site of a gargantuan luxury hotel, and eventually a UNESCO World Heritage Site. But no one knows it by its original name—instead, they know it as Lake Louise, a name it bears in honor of Princess Louise Caroline Alberta, the fourth daughter of Queen Victoria. I doubt Princess Louise ever caught small fishes there.

My attachment to the mountains near Calgary made me want to learn the Stoney Nakoda language. Language can be a way of opening up a deeper intimacy with the land. Some time ago, I was hiking with my husband and his mother, and as we walked, we identified the various wildflowers in bloom by name. My mother-in-law remarked that she had once hiked with a man who said that he enjoyed admiring the flowers but felt no need to know their names. "He's missing out on so much!" she declared. My husband agreed, saying he felt that knowing the names of the plants added something important to the experience, but he wasn't sure he could articulate it. I too felt this, and as we walked, I mulled over what this extra something could be. I think it is this: knowing the name of a plant—or an animal or a place or anything else—is like a doorway into human knowledge of it. It tells you that this plant was deemed important enough to capture human attention and curiosity. It hints at the body of knowledge and experiences that people have compiled about it. The name provides a door that you can choose to open at any time by looking up its name in a book of botany or on the internet.

For me, learning the Îyethka names for the plants, animals, and geography of this beloved place is like this. It hints at the knowledge, stories, and lore that are attached to these name-bearing things, a body of knowledge that is very different from the one I can open on the internet. It is a door that may remain closed to me for the time being, but knowing the name lets me know that the door is there, and this on its own enriches the landscape for me.

And so when I learned that there was a course on the Stoney Nakoda language being offered at the University of Calgary, I decided to attend. The course was co-taught by Trent Fox, a Îyethka scholar, and Corey Telfer, a non-Indigenous linguist. I knew what a university course in German or Russian looked like, but I wasn't sure what to expect in this class. I'm used to arriving at a language course with a dual-language dictionary under my arm, along with a grammar book describing the core patterns of the language, complete with useful homework exercises. But although the language has been studied and described by several scholars, and these documents sit in various university and museum archives, there are no mass-produced, student-friendly materials for Îyethka, perhaps reflecting some ambivalence that the community feels about giving outsiders access to their language. Trent shared with me that a number of people on the Morley Reserve did not approve of his teaching the course at the university, where enrollment was open to non-Îyethka students. This reluctance springs from a view that I've encountered a number of times among Indigenous peoples: that the language and culture of a people are the intellectual property of that people and that they alone should determine how it is used. This is an unfamiliar concept to those of us from Western cultures; we are taught to believe that unless an *individual* can be pegged as the creator of some intellectual content, and unless that individual has lived recently enough to hold legal rights to it, then it belongs to no one, and it is free to be used by anyone for whatever purpose they wish. Interestingly, we readily make exceptions for certain collective groups—we acknowledge that corporations who pay for the creation of intellectual works can claim exclusive rights to it, for example, but this notion does not extend to an ethnic group and the language and oral literature it has created. As a result, we readily accept that the Walt Disney Company has exclusive rights to the images of Cinderella and Sleeping Beauty it has created, whereas the folk tales that inspired their creation are entirely up for grabs. This blind spot has led to some egregious violations of Indigenous property rights—for example, situations in which Western scholars have recorded and translated Indigenous stories, and, without the consent of the community, then proceeded to publish the stories under their own names and become the sole holders of the legal rights to them.

The challenge, of course, is that the odds of survival are reduced for small languages that do not have pedagogical tools for teaching their languages, including a body of written materials, so the Îyethka people are walking a thin line between maintaining cultural control over their language and disseminating the tools and opportunities that will foster learning of the language—such as a mobile app launched in 2017 that teaches basic vocabulary and phrases.

The course taught by Trent and Corey offered some fascinating glimpses into the language. Trent made an effort to provide vocabulary lists of words that were especially relevant for his culture—to my delight, a long list of words related to the natural world (*mâkoche*) and to the preparation of food and feasting. I was enchanted to learn the names linked to the Îyethka lunar calendar: *Rhuya Tawe* ("the golden eagle's month"), marking the arrival of golden eagles; *Nowadethkan Tawe* ("the goose's month"), indicating the noisy return of the Canada goose a month later as rivers and lakes begin to break free of ice; *Wodeja Thmun Wahiâba* ("the deer rut month"), when medium-sized game have grown fat and their meat makes for good hunting. I've heard Calgarians joke that the local climate consists of three seasons: seven months of winter, three-and-a-half months of second winter, and six weeks of summer. And though it's true that the snow in my backyard often begins to pile up in early October and doesn't fully recede until late May, this city-slicker classification misses many changes that can be discerned at a latitude where the dramatic shifts in daylight from one month to the next are accompanied by changes in animal activity apparent to any careful observer. I love the Îyethka calendar for its attunement to the true local rhythm of the seasons.

As for the grammar of Stoney Nakoda, I gleaned just enough to have a sense of how much longer I would need to spend with the language to come close to mastering it. As with many Indigenous languages in North America, the main grammatical action is on the verb. No student of languages is a stranger to the concept of verb conjugation, but some verb systems are a bit gentler on the learner than others. For example, here is what verb conjugation looks like in Farsi (Persian):

miravam	*I go*
miravi	*you go*
miravad	*he / she goes*
mikonam	*I live*
mikoni	*you live*
mikonad	*he / she lives*
mixaram	*I buy*
mixari	*you buy*
mixarad	*he / she buys*

It doesn't take a particularly astute student to quickly notice that verb endings identify the subject of the verb: *-am* for first person (I), *-i* for 2nd person (you), and *-ad* for third person (he / she). There's also a prefix (*mi-*) for all these verbs—a smidgeon of further investigation would reveal that this is how you show that the verb is in the present tense. There are some exceptions, but remarkably few compared with most European languages. For the most part, if you throw a verb stem at a novice learner of Farsi, there is a *very* good chance that they will be able to produce the correct form of the verb in a sentence. Its simplicity may be more than a happy accident. Linguist John Mc-Whorter has argued that Persian became shorn of the usual complications that grow within a language over time because it served as the *lingua franca* within a vast empire whose citizens were native speakers of *other* languages and only learned the common language of the empire as adults.[6]

It's a little bit more difficult to pull out the patterns in Îyethka:

wa'û	*I am at*
ya'û	*you are at*
û	*he / she is at*
mâwanî	*I walk*
mâyanî	*you walk*
mânî	*he / she walks*
ma	*I go*
na	*you go*
ya	*he / she goes*
wamata	*I eat*
wanata	*you eat*
wayata	*he / she eats*
pimîchiya	*I work*
pinîchiya	*you work*
pi'îchiya	*he / she works*
epa	*I say*
eha	*you say*
eya	*he / she says*
awahima	*I sing*
ayahina	*you sing*
ahiya	*he / she sings*

Despite years of training in linguistic analysis, I would not have felt confident in trying to summarize the system without the guidance of my instructors, Trent and Corey. Roughly, Îyethka verb conjugation works like this: the third person form (he / she) is unadorned—basically, it corresponds to the verb stem, with nothing added. This gives us a base from which to work out the rest of the system. And there is nothing simple about the rest of the system. For example, sometimes the portion of the verb that corresponds to a first-person subject (I) is the prefix *wa*, as in *wa'û* ("I am at"); sometimes the snippet *wa* appears, but stuck in the middle of the verb, rather than attached as a prefix, as in *mâwanî* ("I walk"). A similar pattern seems to hold for the segment *ya*, which corresponds to the second person (you). But then, sometimes the first person is communicated by replacing the sound *y* or ' (which refers to a throat-gulp) with the consonant *m* (and the second person replaces these sounds with *n*). But then again, sometimes *y* is replaced by *p* (first person) or *h* (second person), as with the verb for "say." And finally, sometimes first person is doubly marked, both by inserting *wa* (*ya* for second person) and by replacing *y* with *m* (*n* for second person), as in the verb "sing."

In other words, the language clearly has patterns, but there are multiple ways of indicating the subject of the verb, and the precise choice depends on the particular verb. When I asked how you can tell which verb goes with which pattern (linguists refer to these patterns as *wa*-class, *m*- class, *p*-class, and mixed *wa*- and *m*-class), or whether, when it belongs to the *wa*-class, it attaches the *wa* marker at the front or in the middle of the verb, I was told, "You just have to know." In other words, you learn the special requirements of each verb by spending an enormous amount of time in the language and eventually remembering how each verb takes its conjugation. This reminded me somewhat of Czech's elaborate system of case markers on nouns, in which the same case could be marked in any one of a number of different ways, and you just had to know. Of course, if you're new to Czech and are attempting to painstakingly build a sentence, you can always consult a grammar book with lists of the various case markers and the nouns that belong to each class, and perhaps someday such lists will be available to students of Stoney Nakoda. In the meantime, learning the language will require that I spend a great deal of time with fluent speakers willing to have painfully bumpy conversations with me in their language. And perhaps that is as it should be.

Toward the end of the term, our instructors planned a "feast" for the class, and invited students to bring food that was relevant to their own heritage. Next to Trent's moose stew and bannock and Corey's haggis, I set down a plate of moon-shaped cookies. It was a highly symbolic contribution for me. I have a very particular and very strong set of feelings about these cookies, which my mother made every year at Christmas and only at Christmas, and which my own children now make at that time, wherever they may be over the holidays. Although many of our traditional cookies are similar to ones found all over Eastern and Central Europe, I have only ever seen these specific moon cookies in my own family. And they come with stories. Every time I make them, I'm reminded of my mother's story of how in Soviet times, they would save up their rations for nuts and sugar throughout the whole year so they could make their Christmas sweets, the one time of the year that offered the illusion of prosperity. Christmas was the only time in my own childhood when I experienced a reckless abundance, so to me, the taste of these cookies is that of plenty. They are utterly delicious, even without the flavoring of these memories, and when I serve them, I'm inevitably asked for the recipe. I refuse to give it. I joke that one has to marry into our family in order to get the recipe and am often met with the rejoinder that it would be worth it. Though our class feast was held in March, far outside of the only time at which it is appropriate to make these cookies, I decided to prepare them for this occasion. It was my small gesture of willingness to share something of value from my own family history and culture and bring it into an unfamiliar context where it didn't quite fit, just as Trent did with his language. And if any Stoney Nakoda person asks me for the recipe, they can have it.

Trent's willingness to share his language with us, without being able to control in any way the uses to which we might put it, felt like an act of trust. I hope I can repay that trust. In recent years it has become common in Canada to read a declaration of land acknowledgment at public gatherings and events. In an attempt to counter the historical tendency to treat this land as unclaimed real estate simply waiting to be settled by Europeans, this formal land acknowledgment is a statement that names the various Indigenous peoples who lived in the area before mass settlement from overseas. When I go into the mountains now, I bring my smattering of knowledge of the Îyethka language with me, and I try to recall the names for mountain sheep, bluebirds, eagles, marmots, trees, and berries as I encounter them on the trails. It's my way of performing my own private land acknowledgment, not in the still air of a lecture hall or a public library, but out on this windy land that I love like a home, a land that has claimed my heart, a land that is mine and not mine.

The land acknowledgment that is typically recited in Calgary lists the following peoples: the Blackfoot Confederacy (Siksika, Kainai, and Piikani Nations), the Tsuut'ina (also known as Sarcee), the Stoney Nakoda (Bearspaw, Chiniki, and Wesley Nations), and the Métis Nation. Though there is much overlap in their traditional territories, each of these four major groups represents an entirely different language family, hinting at a long history of migration and diversity in the area. Stoney Nakoda belongs to the Sioux family, along with the Dakota and Lakota languages. Tsuut'ina is a Dene language, cousin to the northern languages, Tłįchǫ, Tlingit, and Eyak, and, more distantly, to Navajo and Apache. Blackfoot belongs to the large family of Algonquian languages, which stretch from North America's east coast all the way to the Rocky Mountains, and encompass languages such as Cree, Cheyenne, Delaware, and Mi'kmaq. And Michif, the language of the Métis, is its own creation, a remarkable fusion of (mostly) French and Plains Cree.

Among these, the language of the Tsuut'ina people is in the greatest peril. According to the 2016 census, only eighty individuals throughout all of Canada claimed it as a mother tongue, half of them living on the reserve that abuts the city of Calgary, a community of about two thousand people. As with many Indigenous languages, the vast majority of its fluent speakers are elderly—nonetheless, the language is on prominent display in the enormous Costco warehouse store that opened on the reserve in 2020, with signage in Tsuut'ina rubbing elbows with English. The store is a potent symbol of the dramatic recent transformation of Tsuut'ina society, but this is not the first time the community has had to reinvent itself; originating in the subarctic region of Canada, the Tsuut'ina migrated south around the end of the seventeenth century, in response to other groups being pushed west and north by the new settlers and the fur trade's disruption of existing ways of life. The Tsuut'ina eventually allied with the Blackfoot and became fully adapted to a lifestyle on the plains.

The current residents of the three Blackfoot reserves in Alberta are heirs to the powerful Blackfoot Confederacy, which also included the Blackfeet people of Montana, along with several unrelated allies such as the Tsuut'ina. (As a matter of convenience, I will use the Canadian term *Blackfoot* as the more general term referring to those who live in the United States as well as those in Canada.) Traditionally, their livelihood centered on hunting buffalo (or bison, for those who prefer the more scientific term), and because of this, they suffered what was surely one of the most traumatic upheavals among North American peoples: within the span of a couple of decades, they went from being lords of the plains, living in health and prosperity by hunting an animal that numbered in the tens of millions, to the brink of mass starvation as the buffalo population collapsed into virtual extinction by 1880. I try to imagine a comparable implosion of the economy that I depend upon, and the result veers into pure dystopia.

Before it came to an abrupt end just over a hundred years ago, the traditional Blackfoot way of life showcased the persistence of a truly ancient set of skills and customs. About 200 km (120 miles) south of Calgary, visitors can stop at a place I consider to be the cultural equivalent of Egypt's Great Pyramids: a hunting site called Head-Smashed-In Buffalo Jump. Throughout the plains, there are numerous craggy sites called buffalo jumps, where people used to gather to take part in massive, days-long collaborative efforts to manipulate the movements of a herd of bison, funnel the animals into ever-narrowing lanes, and eventually drive them in a thundering panic over a cliff to their deaths. These gatherings also served as temporary factories for the processing of meat and hides. Enough food was prepared to last several months here, along with buffalo products to be traded far and wide. These hunts, involving hundreds of people, brought together many small bands of between fifty and seventy individuals, some of whom had traveled vast distances to meet at the hunting site. An average hunt, according to Jack Brink, who specializes in North American pre-contact archeology, would result in a tangled heap of about a hundred bison cows, a few bulls, and another fifty or so calves; the total biomass would weigh in at about 60,000 kilograms (132,000 pounds), about the weight of one and a half bowhead whales. In the moments when the herd spilled over the cliff like a waterfall of flesh, writes Brink, "in the blink of an eye, [the hunters] obtained more food in a single moment than any other people in human history."[7]

Owing to the happy combination of a number of important geographic properties (such as a bowl behind the cliff into which the herd could be subtly gathered, and a gentle downward slope just before the cliff, which caused the bison to build up an unstoppable running speed once driven into panic), Head-Smashed-In is one of the oldest and most heavily used buffalo jumps in North America. Archeological evidence shows that hunters gathered there as long as nearly six thousand years ago and as recently as the mid-1800s. While Egypt's pyramids may be a testament to brilliant feats of engineering that immortalized a few powerful individuals in death, this buffalo jump bears witness to a very different sort of accomplishment: the honing of a way of life that sustained entire human populations for thousands of years, outliving the rise and fall of dozens of civilizations. Visitors to the site can get a taste of it by immersing themselves in a stunning film that re-enacts the hunt as they begin their tour through the visitor center, built into the cliff wall. From a distance, readers can savor Jack Brink's account of the buffalo-hunting way of life, rendered in gorgeous detail in his book *Imagining Head-Smashed-In*.

In order to mount such massive and complex communal hunts, the Blackfoot clearly had a sophisticated knowledge of the land and of the biology and habits of the buffalo, as well as highly developed organizational skills. The Blackfoot language is no less sophisticated in its design, as I came to discover. Like the buffalo, however, it has been driven to near-annihilation. Among the roughly 35,000 Blackfoot now living in North America, only 13–14 percent are considered speakers of the language.[8] In Canada, which is home to about two-thirds of the Blackfoot population, the 2012 census data showed that it was the mother tongue of about 3,250 people, only 805 of whom spoke it at home as their main language—and, most alarmingly, only twenty-five of those who frequently spoke it at home were under the age of five. But perhaps the persistence of the buffalo is a hopeful metaphor; once within licking distance of extinction, at a desperate count of 116 remaining animals, the North American bison population now numbers between 350,000 and 400,000, thanks to concerted efforts to re-establish herds on farms and ranches, and on a smaller scale in the wild.[9] Similar conservation efforts are under way to revitalize the Blackfoot language. Because the language has been largely dislodged from the family home, its renewal will rely to a large extent on the efforts of adults who are determined to learn the language from scratch—or, if they have been exposed to it at some point in their childhood, to relearn it as heritage speakers of their language.

Fortunately for these older learners, there are some resources to bolster their studies. One can consult the typical tools of second-language learning: a standard dictionary and a good description of the language's grammar, complete with helpful exercises, as well as an online dictionary.[10] In addition, there are recordings of fluent speech widely available in museum archives, for purchase in CD form, on the Blackfoot Language YouTube channel, or as part of the digital resources collected by the University of Lethbridge in southern Alberta. There is a Blackfoot radio program broadcast out of Montana. And, one can enroll in a sequence of Blackfoot language courses at several colleges and universities in Alberta. So I did.

Whenever I try to learn a new language, I like to spend as much time as possible in what I think of as an infantile state with the language. Before they're able to produce their own first words, babies spend countless hours bobbing about in the flow of speech around them. There is very good evidence that they are learning a great deal about the language they hear, even if they don't yet understand what any of it means. They pick up on the language's sound patterns and learn which sound distinctions to pay attention to and which to relegate to the background of their attention. In fact, some of this learning begins even earlier; by the time they are born, babies can tell the difference between the language spoken by their parents and another language that differs from it in its rhythm and cadences. They also prefer listening to the familiar home language over an unfamiliar tongue.[11] I like to try to replicate this experience so that I can balance my focused study of a language with this in-the-body kind of feel for it.

And so, before I dive into the language classes and the grammar thicket that Blackfoot will turn out to be, I avail myself of all the digital resources I can find, and I spend months just listening to it. I drive around to the sounds of a CD of stories told in Blackfoot by elders, purchased at the gift shop of the Head-Smashed-In visitor center. I wash the dishes to the sounds of Blackfoot on my phone. It's not long before the cadences of the language settle into me. Blackfoot is a phonetically compact language, with a small inventory of eleven consonants and three vowels—it seems to judiciously avoid all the hard-to-pronounce consonants like English's *th, sh* or even *r,* as well as any of the fancy umlauted vowels of Norwegian or French. But almost all of its sounds, consonants as well as vowels, appear in long as well as short versions of themselves, which gives the language a very distinctive rhythm, a bit like a melodic Morse code. These months of listening are rewarded by a lovely experience; one day, while watching the 2017 movie *Wonder Woman,* I hear a character known as "Chief" launching into a language that I recognize with utmost certainty as Blackfoot. It's an instant jolt of recognition, like spotting a friend in an unexpected place. *Hey,* I think with a rush of completely unearned pride, *That's one of "my" languages!* (The actor turns out to be Eugene Brave Rock, a member of the Kainai Nation in my home province of Alberta, and the character he plays turns out be Napi, a godlike figure in Blackfoot mythology who fashioned the physical world—perhaps he will return as a superhero in another Hollywood movie?)

The language may feel familiar to me by the time I step into a Blackfoot language class at the University of Calgary, but the study of the grammar demands intense concentration, at least as it is taught in the compressed style of a university language course. Blackfoot is a language that revolves around a grammatical distinction between animate and inanimate elements. Like the marking of masculine and feminine gender in European languages, the distinction is grounded in some real-world differences—for example, the French phrase *un garçon* ("a boy") is, sensibly enough, grammatically marked as masculine, while *une fille* ("a girl") is marked as feminine, and similarly, in Blackfoot, *natáyowa* ("a lynx") and *nínaawa* ("a man") are grammatically marked as animate, while *óóhkotoki* ("a pebble") is inanimate. But then the dichotomy takes on a linguistic life of its own, galloping off from the landscape of physical reality into realms of pure abstractions—so that in French, *un bol* ("a bowl") is masculine but *une idée* ("an idea") is feminine, and in Blackfoot, *si'káana* ("a blanket") is marked as animate but *isskská'takssini* ("a thought") is inanimate.

Unlike gender in European languages, which at most requires speakers to be attuned to how they express the elements that accompany a noun—articles, adjectives, and the like—animacy in Blackfoot is a central hub from which all spokes radiate outward. For example, verbs are restricted in whether they can consort with animate or inanimate nouns. You would use one verb (*innisi'yi*) if you were talking about a squirrel falling, but a different verb (*innisi*) if you wanted to talk about a pebble falling—but if you were describing a boulder falling, you'd need to be aware that *that* noun is considered animate, so the first verb (*innisi'yi*) would be used rather than the one that goes with the pebble (in fact, *óóhkotok* is the noun used for both "pebble" and "boulder," with the choice of the verb clarifying which of the two was intended). Similarly, to talk about eating bison (animate) or turnip (animate!) would involve the verb *ooyi,* but to talk about eating meat in general (inanimate) would require the use of a different verb, *owatoo.* From here on, things only get spectacularly complicated.

Along with a variety of tags on the verb to indicate its tense, you also have to attach markers that are the grammatical echoes of both the subject *and* the object of the verb. But there is a different set of markers for verbs that take animate subjects as opposed to those that take inanimate subjects, and yet another set of markers for verbs that take animate objects, which naturally are different from those that attach to verbs that accompany inanimate objects. As if this weren't enough to keep track of, the well-dressed verb demands yet another calculation: for verbs that take an object, you have to determine whether the object is lower or higher than the subject on a scale that is known as "the animacy hierarchy," by which grammatical subjects or objects can be ranked as follows: first person (I, we) sits at the top of the hierarchy, followed by second person (you), followed by the "proximate" third person, then by "obviative" third person that is inanimate, then by "obviative" third person that is inanimate at the very bottom of the scale. (Here, "proximate" refers to an element in the third person that is more topical than another third-person element, the "obviative"; this makes it easier to keep track of grammatical elements when there is more than one third-person participant in a sentence—such as in a sentence like "He saw him.") If the subject is higher than the object on the scale (as in the Blackfoot translation of "I love my daughter"), you attach one kind of marker on the verb; if the subject is lower on the hierarchy than the subject (as in "My daughter loves me"), you attach a different kind of marker.

I include this hopelessly rough napkin-sketch of a summary only to offer the barest glimpse of the grammatical complexities that are folded into the Blackfoot language, all miraculously conveyed by means of a briskly efficient collection of three vowels and eleven consonants. In our class, which was again collaboratively taught by a native speaker of the language (Ramona Low Horn, or, as she is known in Blackfoot, Akáípiksi) and a non-Indigenous linguist (Joey Windsor, or Áápohkiááyo), we were given diagrams to help us with the assembly process. With that visual aid, the instructors hoped we would be able to piece together verbs like *máákitsikákomimmokihpinnaana,* which in one word conveys the saga: "You don't love us." Much of the time we were able to do so, but it was a painstaking process that in no way resembled fluent speech. One day, to help us learn to build verbs, our instructor Joey brought in a large board with laminated fragments of Blackfoot that could be attached to the board with the help of Velcro strips, like pieces of magnetic poetry onto a refrigerator. He set up the display so that each fragment was grouped together with similar ones: animate nouns in one section, verbs that take inanimate subjects in another, tense markers in yet another, and so on. Our challenge was to translate simple sentences of English into Blackfoot, a process that involved selecting the right nouns and verbs, and then proceeding to attach all the correct pieces to them. Students took turns at the board, taking an average of two to three minutes to velcro together each simple sentence, and sometimes considerably longer when corrections from the floor were offered and debated.

All the diagrams and grammatical analyses and graphic representations of the animacy hierarchy and charts of verbal conjugations were tremendously helpful in giving me a sense of the language from

30,000 feet. Taking the course was like getting a map of the linguistic layout of Blackfoot, allowing me to then go off and fill in more details myself by drawing on some of the resources that are available elsewhere. But I'm trained as a linguist—and so were roughly half of the students who took the course, as far as I could tell. We brought into the classroom a habit of dismantling language like a clock, eager to see how it worked. And being the language nerds we were, we found the dismantling deeply pleasurable. The longer I sat in the class, however, the more I found myself thinking about the participants I had met earlier at CILLDI, for whom this way of approaching their languages was profoundly alien. I began to wonder what might be lost in the process of pressing language into this mold of language teaching. It was a method that had been developed for efficiency, allowing students to quickly spot patterns that would have taken them thousands of hours of immersion in the language to absorb. But in bypassing those hours of immersion, the course also contributed to stripping the language from its social and cultural context.

Diagrams and Velcro boards were undoubtedly efficient tools for conveying the grammatical structure of the language, but they did not impart the many other aspects of language that also get packed into the hours of practice in the language they are intended to replace: they told us nothing about the bodily gestures or facial expressions that identify true Blackfoot speakers, about the connotations or special contexts in which some words or phrases are used, about whether the style of language should change depending on whether you're speaking to an elder or a child, about the shadings of language that signal intimacy or aloofness, about how long you should pause between conversational turns, or about what Blackfoot speakers think is uproariously funny. It occurred to me that it was a model of teaching that had been developed mainly for languages—most of them European—in which students had a *practical* interest. Many students who sign up for courses in French, German, or Mandarin do so because they want to be able to function in the language, to wield it as a useful instrument. Acquiring the basic frame of a language, into which one can slot any suitable content, can accelerate its usefulness. But as I sat in the Blackfoot class, I often found myself imagining what a language class might look like if it were designed to nurture an emotional attachment to the language or to offer some insights into the social norms of its speakers.

I don't mean to disparage the class in any way—the instructors were excellent, and I very quickly gained an awestruck appreciation for the beautiful and intricate latticework of the language, which only served to stoke my curiosity about what the living language is like when it sparks between one native speaker and another. But as always in the attempt to weld the traditions of a minority culture to the traditions of a majority culture, there is the question of what must be compromised in exchange for survival, the ubiquitous tally of gains and losses.

Many of the participants I met at CILLDI shared the goal of trying to create a home at the juncture of two very different traditions. In the Michif language, these efforts have crystallized into something truly unique. Given my own lifelong struggles to merge multiple identities into some coherent whole, I admit to being completely seduced by Michif. Unlike many Indigenous languages that stretch into the distant past, Michif is a very young language, a magnificent blend of mostly French and Cree that was probably born sometime early in the nineteenth century. It is the language that was spoken by many Métis people whose roots can be traced back to the Red River Settlement at the junction of the Red and Assiniboine Rivers, where the city of Winnipeg now spreads out. Michif (Métis) language and culture is a literal marriage, a union between a male ancestry of French-Canadian *voyageurs,* men who headed West and served as independent fur traders at the height of the North American fur trade in the 1700s, and a female ancestry of Indigenous descent, primarily from the Cree and Ojibwe peoples.

Many of the early Métis would have been fluent in multiple languages, particularly French and Plains Cree, the latter of which served as a sort of *lingua franca* among various Indigenous peoples. Nothing is more natural than for multilingual people to mix their languages together when speaking among themselves. It's a common way to wring the most expressive power from each language and to broadcast allegiance to more than one identity, as is found among the bilingual youth of Montreal and their much-maligned *franglais*. But Michif represents something very different from *franglais* or any other garden-variety example of code-switching—and something far more extraordinary. Most contemporary speakers of Michif speak neither Cree nor French. Somehow, speakers of Michif have done something with French and Cree that language purists fret will happen with *franglais* or other practices of language mixing by bilingual people—something that in fact almost never does happen. Rather than maintain a tradition of bilingualism in French and Cree, Michif speakers have created an entirely new language that lives in its own space between languages and is neither one nor the other. They do not move back and forth between two free-standing languages, but speak the blended version as their mother tongue.

For me, listening to Michif is an enchanting experience, a combination of the tantalizingly familiar and the utterly foreign. I can catch snippets of French, which reel me into comprehension, intertwined with other words that fling me right back out again. It is a remarkable language that has captured the attention of Dutch linguist Peter Bakker, who has written a detailed account of its history and structure, describing it as a sort of linguistic platypus. A short passage of Michif storytelling may convey the flavor of the language; the story below was recorded and transcribed by Bakker and told by Modeste Gosselin, a resident of the Fort Qu'Appelle Valley in Saskatchewan and a speaker of both Michif and English. The French portions of each sentence are set off in bold, and there is the odd English word sneaking in here and there:

Un vieux ê-opahikêt ê-nôcihcikêt, you see, êkwa **un matin**
ê-waniskât âhkosiw, but kêyâpit ana wî-nitawi-wâpahtam **ses
pièges**. Sipwêhtêw. Mêkwât êkotê ê-itasihkêt, **une tempête**.
Maci-kîsikâw. **Pas moyen** si-miskahk **son shack**. Wanisin.
Pas moyen son shack si-miskahk. Pimohtêw, pimohtêw.
Êy-âhkosit êkwa **le-vieux**-iw-it nôhtêsin. **D'un gros arbre**
pimi-cipatapiw. "Ôta nipiyâni," itêyihtam êsa, "**Une bonne
place** ôma si-nipi-yân." Ê-wâpamât ôhi **le loup de bois** ê-pâ-
pahtâ-yi-t. Ha, ha. Pêhêw, ka-kanawâpamêw. **Le loup** awa
pê-isipahtâw êkota itê api-yit. Êkwa pâstinam **sa bouche** ôhi **le
loup** ê-wî-otinât. Pastinên, **son bras** yahkinam, right through
anihi **le loup**. The wolf **dans la queue** ohci-otinêw, **par la
queue** âpoci-pitêw! Kîhtwâm **le loup** asê-kîwê-pahtâw![12]

As Bakker notes, the intertwining of the two languages is far from
haphazard—in fact, it reveals a division of labor that is breathtaking
in its structure. Nouns and parts of speech that support the noun (adjectives, numerals, articles, and so on) are almost always pulled from
French, whereas verbs are almost without exception taken from Cree,
which means that they strut into the sentence with an elaborate re-
galia of prefixes and suffixes. It's clear that the language originated
from speakers who were fluent in both languages rather than people
who had an incomplete command of either, because the French and
Cree portions of the language each preserve almost all of the grammatical integrity of the parent language. As a matter of fact, Michif
can be seen as a fusion of the most complex aspects of Cree and the
most complex aspects of French, rather than settling for a simplified
compromise. When people learn French as a foreign language, they
usually struggle with the arbitrary marking of nouns as either masculine or feminine, so much so that the occasional gender-assignment
error may be one of the few grammatical missteps of an otherwise
very fluent second-language speaker of French. Yet Michif has folded
into itself this tricky bit of grammar, despite the fact that such a

feature is alien to Cree and other North American Indigenous languages. From the Cree side of the family tree, Michif has inherited the complicated system of verbs, one of the most daunting elements to learners of Cree. The verb can compress into itself as much meaning as an English sentence, amalgamating as many as twenty separate grammatical elements.

The sound system of Michif has also remained faithful to the sound structures of French and Cree respectively; words that are drawn from French are generally pronounced in a French manner and words from Cree sound Cree-like. In fact, the two languages are quite distinct in this regard: French has a larger collection of distinct sounds, with fourteen vowels stacked against seven in Cree and twenty-three distinct French consonants against Cree's ten. The sounds *y, l, r,* and *f,* for example, occur in French but not in Cree. Some combinations of sounds are permitted in only one of the two languages, such as the sequence *ht* and *hk,* which turns up only in Cree. These differences are reflected in the French and Cree components of Michif. Michif also seems to apply different rules to the sounds of the language depending on whether they belong to the French side or the Cree side. The French words exhibit a tendency that linguists poetically call *vowel harmony,* in which two different vowels that appear in the same word become more similar to each other; for example, the French word *fusil* ("gun") is pronounced as *fizi* in Michif. On the other bank of the Michif language, adjacent vowels are merged into a single vowel, a process that does not occur on the French side. The independence of the two systems is striking, and adds to the evidence that the earliest speakers of Michif must have been fluently bilingual, probably from childhood; people who pronounce words from a language unknown to them have a strong tendency to reshape foreign words to fit in with the sound patterns of their native language, so that French words would have become assimilated to Cree pronunciation for speakers who did not speak French well, and the reverse would have been true for halting speakers of Cree. The grammars of the two components of Michif are similarly distinct from each other, again hinting at a high level of competence in both.

If Michif's early speakers could speak both French and Cree, why did a new, blended language emerge, when it is infinitely more common for bilingual people to simply swing between both languages, or to eventually neglect one in favor of the other? Bakker argues that an intertwined language like Michif only crystallizes if there are urgent social reasons for it to set itself apart from either of the parent languages. And the history of the Métis people reveals precisely such pressures. It likely wasn't until the early 1800s that the Métis identified themselves as a distinct ethnic group—before this, there were many people of mixed European-Indigenous ancestry across North America, but the children of these mixed marriages typically became absorbed into either the mother's Indigenous community or the father's European one. The present-day Métis Nation is adamant that Métis identity is cultural and not biological, springing from a very specific shared culture and history.[13] As groups of people of mixed French-Indigenous heritage began to move to the Red River Settlement in large numbers, becoming its single most populous and organized group, they no longer had to rein in either of their ancestral cultures. They came together to form a unique community of buffalo-hunting, fiddle-playing, pemmican-eating, drinking-song-singing people. By refusing to assimilate to either culture, they tended to be rebuffed by both, being considered too loud and unruly for the dignified Indigenous peoples, and too impious and free-roaming for the Europeans. And they became embroiled in a critical historical drama at the dawn of Canadian confederation in 1867, when they attempted to set up a local government, resisting efforts to dislodge them from their lands in a series of struggles that ultimately led to the execution of their passionate and articulate leader, Louis Riel. Their efforts at self-government were crushed, and the Métis eventually dispersed throughout the Canadian prairie provinces and into North Dakota. The Michif language is a product of the social bonds that were forged among the Métis during that tumultuous period of history, an orphan language created by children disowned by their parental cultures. Barely two centuries old, this most unusual of languages is now endangered, as English flexes its power. If it is ultimately extinguished, this extraordinary language will have been but a brief flare among the linguistic constellations of North America.

Despite the tragic undertones of the story of Michif, I can't help but fantasize about a language that would be the manifestation of my own medley of allegiances and about a community of similarly blended souls with whom I could speak such a home language. What would it sound like? Perhaps it would preserve the dastardly ř sound of Czech and the lisp-inducing *th* of English. I would want it to keep both the vertiginous case endings of Czech nouns and the mongrel vocabulary of English—and the swearing would all be in joyous Québécois French.

In recent years, it's become fashionable to distinguish between the "Somewheres" and the "Anywheres," terms coined by British author David Goodhart.[14] "Somewheres" are people like my uncle in Moravská Nová Ves, who are profoundly attached to a particular place, deeply loyal to a local community and way of life, generally quite traditional, and whose identities are heavily tied to the home in which their entire lives, and the lives of their ancestors, have unfolded. Rooted. "Anywheres" are supposedly people like me: mobile, aspirational, fluid in identity and social bonds, international in outlook, willing to live anywhere if the circumstances are right. Rootless. Implicit in this partition is the notion that a person whose life has been scattered over multiple places does not have strong feelings about any of these places. It's a notion I've encountered time and time again—in the arguments of a newspaper columnist who claims that dual citizens necessarily have a weakened sense of responsibility to the nations whose passports they carry, in the attitude that immigrants are not "real" Americans or Canadians, and even in a talk given by a well-known author who asserts that one cannot write convincingly unless the writing is grounded in the particular place that made the writer. *The* place. I've heard it so often I've almost allowed myself to become convinced of it.

But it's simply not true. Even the term "Anywhere" conveys an indifference that I do not feel toward any of the places that have shaped me. I may have only a few stories about each of these places, but my stories are not bleached of feeling or devoid of attachment. Nor have I been any less susceptible to the influence of my various homes simply because there are several of them.

Perhaps this is why I feel such kinship with the Michif language. It is a language that does not allow anyone to say *You are not sufficiently this* or *You are not enough of that.* It is a language that defies being categorized as "Anywhere"; it stubbornly retains the complexities of two languages, thereby asserting its claim to both heritages. It is a statement of dual attachment, a refusal to be cut loose from either lineage.

Michif is a language that gives me the courage to say, *These are my stories. They are stories of displacement and loss, of discovery and renewal, of love and of home. They do not reach back into time immemorial, and they are constantly doing battle with each other. But they are mine, and they were lived here, and here, and here.*

Notes

1. Death

1. M. Polinsky, "Incomplete Acquisition: American Russian," *Journal of Slavic Linguistics* 14, no. 2 (2006): 191–262.

2. E. Bylund, N. Abrahamsson, and K. Hyltenstam, "The Role of Language Aptitude in First Language Attrition: The Case of Pre-pubescent Attriters," *Applied Linguistics* 31 (2009): 443–464.

3. B. Köpke, "Language Attrition at the Crossroads of Brain, Mind, and Society," in *Language Attrition: Theoretical Perspectives,* ed. B. Köpke, M.S. Schmid, M. Keijzer, and S. Dostert (Amsterdam: John Benjamins, 2007).

4. J. L. Montag and M. C. MacDonald, "Text Exposure Predicts Spoken Production of Complex Sentences in 8- and 12-year-old Children and Adults," *Journal of Experimental Psychology: General* 144, no. 2 (2015): 447–468.

5. M. S. Schmid, *Language Attrition* (Cambridge: Cambridge University Press, 2011), 105.

6. R. R. Agudo, "The 'English-Only' Nativist Movement Comes with a Cost," *Los Angeles Times,* August 27, 2018.

7. T. Laqueur, "Prelude," in *The Genius of Language: Fifteen Writers Reflect on Their Mother Tongues,* ed. W. Lesser, 85–101 (New York: Anchor Books, 2004), 87–88.

8. D. Hallett, M. J. Chandler, and C. E. Lalonde, "Aboriginal Language Knowledge and Youth Suicide," *Cognitive Development* 22 (2007): 392–399.

9. T. D. LaFromboise, D. R. Hoyt, L. Oliver, and L. B. Whitbeck, "Family, Community and School Influences on Resilience among American Indian Adolescents in the Upper Midwest," *Journal of Community Psychology* 34 (2006): 193–209.

10. M. E. Krauss, "The World's Languages in Crisis," *Language* 68, no. 1 (1992): 4–10. A more recent report, released in 2019 by the Intergovernmental Science-Policy Platform on Biodiversity and Ecosystem Services (IPBES), warns that species extinction and habitat destruction are accelerating, and that of an 8 million estimated species of animals and plants, about 1 million are threatened with extinction over the next few decades.

11. The precise number of remaining languages is open to debate, largely because it is not clear where the borders between languages lie. As different varieties or dialects become more distant from each other over time, they eventually become clearly distinct languages. The rule of thumb is that different dialects have become separate languages once their speakers can no longer understand each other. But this rule is applied inconsistently; Czech and Slovak, for example, are considered different languages even though their speakers can easily understand each other, as is the case with Swedish and Norwegian. Moreover, mutual intelligibility is itself a squishy concept—whether a person can understand a dialect distant from their own depends in part on the body of linguistic experiences they bring to the task, which is one reason why subtitles are often used to help some viewers understand movie dialogue that takes place in a different dialect of their own language. The general consensus is that there are somewhere between 6,000 and 7,000 languages in the world.

12. Krauss, "The World's Languages in Crisis," 8.

13. M. E. Krauss, "A History of Eyak Language Documentation and Study: Fredericae de Laguna in Memoriam," *Arctic Anthropology* 43, no. 2 (2006): 172–217.

14. A. N. Harry, "Lament for Eyak," translated by M. E. Krauss, in *In Honor of Eyak: The Art of Anna Nelson Harry,* edited by M. E. Krauss (Fairbanks: Alaska Native Language Center, 1982).

15. M. Pagel, "The History, Rate and Pattern of World Linguistic Evolution," in *The Evolutionary Emergence of Language,* ed. C. Knight, M. Studdert-Kennedy, and J. Hurtford (Cambridge: Cambridge University Press, 2000), 391–416.

16. L. A. Grenoble, "Language Ecology and Endangerment," in *The Cambridge Handbook of Endangered Languages,* ed. P. K. Austin and J. Sallabank (Cambridge: Cambridge University Press, 2011), 27–44.

17. Krauss, "The World's Languages in Crisis."

18. N. wa Thiong'o, "Recovering the Original," in *The Genius of Language: Fifteen Writers Reflect on Their Mother Tongues,* ed. W. Lesser, 102–110 (New York: Anchor Books, 2005), 105.

19. S. S. Mufwene, *Language Evolution: Contact, Competition and Change* (Cambridge: Cambridge University Press, 2008).

20. B. Hart and T. R. Risley, *Meaningful Differences in the Everyday Experience of Young American Children* (Baltimore: Paul H. Brookes, 1995).

21. Organisation Internationale de la Francophonie, "La langue française dans le monde 2018: synthèse" (Paris, 2018).

22. K. Matsumoto, *Recent Language Change in Shoshone: Structural Consequences of Language Loss*. PhD diss., University of Utah, 2015.

23. W. Dressler and R. Wodak-Leodolter, "Language Preservation and Language Death in Brittany," *International Journal of Bilingual Education and Bilingualism* 9, no. 5 (1977): 557–577.

24. A. Schmidt, *Young People's Dyirbal: An Example of Language Death from Australia* (Cambridge: Cambridge University Press, 1985).

25. For Sutherland Gaelic, see N. C. Dorian, "Grammatical Change in a Dying Dialect," *Language* 49, no. 2 (1973): 413–438; for Central Pomo, see M. Mithun, "Language Obsolescence and Grammatical Description," *International Journal of American Linguistics* 56, no. 1 (1990): 1–26; and for Mani, see G. T. Childs, "What Happens to Class When a Language Dies? Language Change vs. Language Death," *Studies in African Linguistics* 38, no. 2 (2009): 235–255.

26. I. Maddieson, *Patterns of Sounds* (Cambridge: Cambridge University Press, 1984).

27. J. McWhorter, *What Language Is (and What It Isn't and What It Could Be)* (New York: Gotham Books, 2011), 58.

28. D. Everett, "Cultural Constraints on Grammar and Cognition in Pirahã," *Current Anthropology* 46, no. 4 (2005): 621–646.

29. F. Karlsson, "Constraints on Multiple Center-Embedding of Clauses," *Journal of Linguistics* 43, no. 2 (2007): 365–392; D. Biber and M. Hared, "Dimensions of Register Variation in Somali," *Language Variation and Change* 4 (1992): 41–75.

30. G. Lupyan and R. Dale, "Language Structure Is Partly Determined by Social Structure," *PLoS one* 5, no. 1 (2010): e8559.

31. D. Deutsch, K. Dooley, T. Henthorn, and B. Head, "Absolute Pitch among Students in an American Music Conservatory: Association with Tone Language Fluency," *Journal of the Acoustical Society of America* 125, no. 4 (2009): 2398–2403.

32. T. F. Jaeger and E. J. Norcliffe, "The Crosslinguistic Study of Sentence Production," *Language and Linguistics Compass* 3 / 4 (2009): 866–887.

33. Eyak Preservation Council, *The Eyak Language Project,* 2020; http://eyakpreservationcouncil.org/culture/eyak-revitalization-project/

34. E. K. Acton, "Pragmatics and the Social Life of the English Definite Article," *Language* 95, no. 1 (2019): 37–65, 37.

35. R. B. Woodward, "'The Americans' Revisited," *Wall Street Journal,* November 18, 2009.

36. Statement by US Representative Dana Rohrabacher (R-CA), October 27, 2009, quoted in Acton, "Pragmatics and the Social Life of the English Definite Article," 44.

37. D. Nettle and S. Romaine, *Vanishing Voices: The Extinction of the World's Languages* (Oxford: Oxford University Press, 2000).

38. M. Abley, *Spoken Here: Travels among Threatened Languages* (Boston: Houghton Mifflin, 2005).

39. Nettle and Romaine, *Vanishing Voices.*

40. Krauss, "A History of Eyak Language Documentation and Study."

41. Abley, *Spoken Here.*

42. C. Dowrick, *Beyond Depression: A New Approach to Understanding and Management* (Oxford: Oxford University Press, 2004), 23.

43. M. Lock, "Local Biologies," in *Ideas on the Nature of Science,* ed. D. Cayley (Fredericton: Goose Lane Editions, 2009), 60.

44. D. Katz, *Grammar of the Yiddish Language* (London: Duckworth & Co., 1987), 96.

45. E. Kolbert, "Last Words," *New Yorker,* June 6, 2005, 46–59, 46.

46. Nettle and Romaine, *Vanishing Voices.*

2. Dreams

1. S. P. Huntington, *Who Are We? The Challenges to America's National Identity* (New York: Simon & Schuster, 2004), 256.

2. R. Rodriguez, *Hunger of Memory: The Education of Richard Rodriguez* (New York: Bantam Dell, 1982), 15.

3. Rodriguez, *Hunger of Memory,* 16.

4. Rodriguez, *Hunger of Memory,* 18.

5. Rodriguez, *Hunger of Memory,* 21.

6. Rodriguez, *Hunger of Memory,* 24.

7. L. Wong Fillmore, "When Learning a Second Language Means Losing the First," *Early Childhood Research Quarterly* 6, no. 3 (1991): 323–346.

8. Wong Fillmore, "When Learning a Second Language," 344.

9. J. Ford, *Hotel on the Corner of Bitter and Sweet* (New York: Ballantine Books, 2009), 12–13.

10. B. Franklin, *The Papers of Benjamin Franklin,* ed. Leonard W. Labarre (New Haven, CT: Yale University Press, 1959), 234.

11. Pew Research Center, *Modern Immigration Wave Brings 59 Million to U.S., Driving Population Growth and Change through 2065,* September 2015, https://www.pewresearch.org/hispanic/2015/09/28/modern-immigration

-wave-brings-59-million-to-u-s-driving-population-growth-and-change -through-2065/.

12. *Comprehensive Immigration Reform: Becoming Americans, Hearing before the Subcommittee on Immigration of the Committee on the Judiciary, House of Representatives,* 110th Congress, serial no. 110-27 (prepared statement of R. G. Rumbaut) (Washington, DC: US Government Printing Office, 2007).

13. C. Ryan, "Language Use in the United States: 2011," *American Community Survey Reports* 22 (Washington, DC: US Census Bureau, 2013), https://www2.census.gov/library/publications/2013/acs/acs-22/acs-22 .pdf

14. See, for example, Associated Press, "In Miami, Spanish Becoming Primary Language," *NBC News,* May 29, 2008, https://www.nbcnews .com/id/wbna24871558.

15. T. B. Morgan, "The Latinization of America," *Esquire,* May 1, 1983, 47–56.

16. *Comprehensive Immigration Reform,* pp. 22–23.

17. R. Akresh and I. R. Akresh, "Using Achievement Tests to Measure Language Assimilation and Language Bias among the Children of Immigrants," *Journal of Human Resources* 46, no. 3 (2011): 647–667.

18. J. Paradis and R. Jia, "Bilingual Children's Long-Term Outcomes in English as a Second Language: Language Environment Factors Shape Individual Differences in Catching Up with Monolinguals," *Developmental Science* 20, no. 1 (2017): e12433.

19. J. Paradis, "Individual Differences in Child English Second Language Acquisition: Comparing Child-Internal and Child-External Factors," *Linguistic Approaches to Bilingualism* 1, no. 3 (2011): 213–237; H. Goldberg, J. Paradis, and M. Crago, "Lexical Acquisition over Time in Minority First Language Children Learning English as a Second Language," *Applied Psycholinguistics* 29, no. 1 (2008): 41–65.

20. A. A. MacLeod, L. Fabiano-Smith, S. Boegner-Pagé, and S. Fontolliet, "Simultaneous Bilingual Language Acquisition: The Role of Parental Input on Receptive Vocabulary Development," *Child Language Teaching and Therapy* 29, no. 1 (2013): 131–142.

21. T. Soehl, "But Do They Speak It? The Intergenerational Transmission of Home-Country Language in Migrant Families in France," *Journal of Ethnic and Migration Studies* 42, no. 9 (2016): 1513–1535.

22. P. Sabourin, A. Bélanger, and P. Reeve, "The Dynamics of Language Shift in Canada," *Population* 70, no. 4 (2015): 727–757.

23. B. R. Chiswick and P. W. Miller, "International Migration and the Economics of Language," IZA Discussion Papers, no. 7880 (Bonn: Institute for the Study of Labor [IZA], 2014), 76–77.

24. H. Bleakley and A. Chin, "Language Skills and Earnings: Evidence from Childhood Immigrants," *Review of Economics and Statistics* 86, no. 2 (2004): 481–496.

25. Rodriguez, *Hunger of Memory,* 27.

26. N. C. Dorian, "A Response to Ladefoged's Other View of Endangered Languages," *Language* 69, no. 3 (1993): 575–579, 577.

27. M. Zhou and C. L. Bankston III, *The Rise of the New Second Generation* (Malden, MA: Polity Press, 2016).

28. R. L. Bubbico and L. Freytag, *Inequality in Europe* (Kirchberg, Luxembourg: European Investment Bank, 2018), https://www.eib.org /attachments/efs/econ_inequality_in_europe_en.pdf

29. Zhou and Bankston III, *The Rise of the New Second Generation.*

30. E. Telles and V. Ortiz, *Generations of Exclusion: Mexicans, Assimilation, and Race* (New York: Russell Sage Foundation, 2009); see also C. G. E. Coll and A. K. E. Marks, *The Immigrant Paradox in Children and Adolescents: Is Becoming American a Developmental Risk?* (Washington, DC: APA Books, 2012).

31. M. Crul, "Super-diversity vs. Assimilation: How Complex Diversity in Majority–Minority Cities Challenges the Assumptions of Assimilation," *Journal of Ethnic and Migration Studies* 42, no. 1 (2016): 54–68. Crul notes that some of the differences between the Swedish and German groups of immigrants could be attributed to differences in the parents' education level upon arrival, but that the groups were clearly different even when this factor was controlled for.

32. Y. Bar-Haim, T. Ziv, D. Lamy, and R. M. Hodes, "Nature and Nurture in Own-Race Face Processing," *Psychological Science* 17, no. 2 (2006): 159–163.

33. S. Sangrigoli and S. De Schonen, "Recognition of Own-Race and Other-Race Faces by Three-Month-Old Infants," *Journal of Child Psychology and Psychiatry and Allied Disciplines* 45, no. 7 (2004): 1219–1227.

34. P. A. Katz, "Racists or Tolerant Multiculturalists? How Do They Begin?" *American Psychologist* 58, no. 11 (2003): 897–909.

35. A. Doyle and F. Aboud, "A Longitudinal Study of White Children's Racial Prejudice as a Social Cognitive Development," *Merrill-Palmer Quarterly* 41 (1995): 213–223.

36. K. D. Kinzler, E. Dupoux, and E. S. Spelke, "The Native Language of Social Cognition," *Proceedings of the National Academy of Sciences* 104, no. 30 (2007): 12577–12580.

37. K. D. Kinzler, K. Shutts, J. DeJesus, and E. S. Spelke, "Accent Trumps Race in Guiding Children's Social Preferences," *Social Cognition* 27, no. 4 (2009): 623–634.

38. L. A. Hirschfeld and S. A. Gelman, "What Young Children Think about the Relationship between Language Variation and Social Difference," *Cognitive Development* 12, no. 2 (1997): 213–238.

39. K. D. Kinzler and J. B. Dautel, "Children's Essentialist Reasoning about Language and Race," *Developmental Science* 15, no. 1 (2012): 131–138.

40. J. B. Dautel and K. D. Kinzler, "Once a French Speaker, Always a French Speaker? Bilingual Children's Thinking about the Stability of Language," *Cognitive Science* 42 (2018): 287–302.

41. Judg. 12:5–6, *New American Standard Bible.*

42. K. Byers-Heinlein, D. A. Behrend, L. M. Said, H. Girgis, and D. Poulin-Dubois, "Monolingual and Bilingual Children's Social Preferences for Monolingual and Bilingual Speakers," *Developmental Science* 20, no. 4 (2017): e12392.

43. J. M. DeJesus, H. G. Hwang, J. B. Dautel, and K. D. Kinzler, "Bilingual Children's Social Preferences Hinge on Accent," *Journal of Experimental Child Psychology* 164 (2017): 178–191.

44. P. Bourdieu, *Language and Symbolic Power* (Cambridge, MA: Harvard University Press, 1991).

45. J. A. Fishman, *Reversing Language Shift: Theoretical and Empirical Foundations of Assistance to Threatened Languages,* no. 76 (Bristol, UK: Multilingual Matters, 1991).

46. P. Malone, "'Good Sisters' and 'Darling Sisters': Translating and Transplanting the Joual in Michel Tremblay's *Les Belles-Soeurs,*" *Theatre Research in Canada / Recherches théâtrales au Canada* 24, no. 1 (2003), https://journals.lib.unb.ca/index.php/TRIC/article/download/7065/8124?inline=1.

47. W. E. Lambert, R. C. Hodgson, R. C. Gardner, and S. Fillenbaum, "Evaluational Reactions to Spoken Languages," *Journal of Abnormal and Social Psychology* 60, no. 1 (1960): 44–51.

48. J. N. Fuertes, W. H. Gottdiener, H. Martin, T. C. Gilbert, and H. Giles, "A Meta-analysis of the Effects of Speakers' Accents on Interpersonal Evaluations," *European Journal of Social Psychology* 42, no. 1 (2012): 120–133.

49. M. Dragojevic, D. Mastro, H. Giles, and A. Sink, "Silencing Non-standard Speakers: A Content Analysis of Accent Portrayals on American Primetime Television," *Language in Society* 45, no. 1 (2016): 59–85.

50. R. Lippi-Green, *English with an Accent: Language, Ideology, and Discrimination in the United States* (London: Routledge, 2012).

51. Rodriguez, *Hunger of Memory,* 19.

52. W. Zeydanlioglu, "Repression or Reform? An Analysis of the AKP's Kurdish Language Policy," in *The Kurdish Question in Turkey: New Perspectives on Violence, Representation and Reconciliation,* ed. W. Zeydanlioglu and C. Gunes, 162–185 (London: Routledge, 2013), 163.

53. Hawaii State Data Center, Research and Economic Analysis Division, *Detailed Languages Spoken at Home in the State of Hawaii* (2016), http://files .hawaii.gov/dbedt/census/acs/Report/Detailed_Language_March2016.pdf.

54. Lippi-Green, *English with an Accent.*

55. R. R. Day, "The Development of Linguistic Attitudes and Preferences," *TESOL Quarterly* 14, no. 1 (1980): 27–37. Although Day's research was conducted decades ago, there is still relatively little research to trace exactly how and when children absorb negative attitudes toward nonstandard languages, and how these attitudes differ across languages and contexts. However, several studies conducted in various cultural contexts suggest that as early as age five (and perhaps earlier), children learn to stigmatize nonstandard varieties that they themselves speak. See, in particular, the following: K. Fehér, "Status-based Preference of Varieties in Bidialectal Kindergarteners: An Experimental Study," *Argumentum* 16 (2020): 147–172; S. K. Shah and F. Anwar, "Attitudes of Parents and Children towards Multilingualism in Pakistan," *Journal of Literature, Languages and Linguistics* 8 (2015): 22–27; K. D. Kinzler, K. Shutts, and E. S. Spelke, "Language-based Social Preferences among Children in South Africa," *Language Learning and Development* 8, no. 3 (2012): 215–232; M. S. Rosenthal, *The Magic Boxes: Children and Black English* (Urbana, IL: University of Illinois, ERIC Clearinghouse on Early Childhood Education and ERIC Clearinghouse on Languages and Linguistics, 1977).

There is also evidence that school attendance can heighten negative attitudes toward a nonstandard dialect. See C. Cremona and E. Bates, "The Development of Attitudes toward Dialect in Italian Children," *Journal of Psycholinguistic Research* 6, no. 3 (1977): 223–232; B. Bangeni and R. Kapp, "Shifting Language Attitudes in a Linguistically Diverse Learning Environment in South Africa," *Journal of Multilingual and Multicultural Development* 28, no. 4 (2007): 253–269.

56. WHRO Documentaries, *Code-Switching,* aired January 3, 2011, https://www.pbs.org/video/whro-documentaries-code-switching/.

57. Royal Commission on Bilingualism and Biculturalism *A Preliminary Report of the Royal Commission on Bilingualism and Biculturalism* (Ottawa: Queen's Printer, 1965).

58. R. Landry and R. Y. Bourhis, "Linguistic Landscape and Ethnolinguistic Vitality: An Empirical Study," *Journal of Language and Social Psychology* 16, no. 1 (1997): 23–49.

59. R. M. Dailey, H. Giles, and L. L. Jansma, "Language Attitudes in an Anglo-Hispanic Context: The Role of the Linguistic Landscape," *Language & Communication* 25, no. 1 (2005): 2738.

60. R. Y. Bourhis and R. Sioufi, "Assessing Forty Years of Language Planning on the Vitality of the Francophone and Anglophone Communities of Quebec," *Multilingua* 36, no. 5 (2017): 627–661.

61. R. Kircher, "Thirty Years after Bill 101: A Contemporary Perspective on Attitudes towards English and French in Montreal," *Canadian Journal of Applied Linguistics / Revue canadienne de linguistique appliquée* 17, no. 1 (2014): 20–50.

62. A. Mizuta, "Memories of Language Lost and Learned: Parents and the Shaping of Chinese as a Heritage Language in Canada" (PhD diss., University of British Columbia, 2017), 47.

63. Mizuta, "Memories of Language Lost and Learned," 236.

64. R. E. Eilers, B. Z. Pearson, and A. B. Cobo-Lewis, "Social Factors in Bilingual Development: The Miami Experience," in *Childhood Bilingualism: Research on Infancy through School Age,* no. 7, ed. P. McCardle and E. Hoff, 68–90 (Bristol, UK: Multilingual Matters, 2006).

65. J. Didion, *Miami* (New York: Simon & Schuster, 1987), 63.

66. P. Carter and A. Lynch, "Multilingual Miami: Current Trends in Sociolinguistic Research," *Language and Linguistics Compass* 9, no. 9 (2015): 369–385.

67. M. Valencia and A. Lynch, "The Mass Mediation of Spanish in Miami," in *The Routledge Handbook of Spanish in the Global City,* ed. A. Lynch, 73–100 (London: Routledge, 2019).

68. Eilers and Pearson, "Social Factors in Bilingual Development."

3. Duality

1. V. T. Nguyen, *The Sympathizer* (New York: Grove Press, 2015), 1.

2. E. Hoffman, *Lost in Translation* (New York: Penguin, 1990), 199.

3. Hoffman, *Lost in Translation,* 199–200.

4. A. Pavlenko, "Bilingual Selves," in *Bilingual Minds: Emotional Experience, Expression, and Representation,* ed. A. Pavlenko, 1–33 (Clevedon: Multilingual Matters, 2006).

5. S. Ervin-Tripp, *Language Acquisition and Communicative Choice: Essays by Susan M. Ervin-Tripp* (Palo Alto, CA: Stanford University Press, 1973).

6. N. Ramírez-Esparza, S. D. Gosling, V. Benet-Martínez, J. P. Potter, and J. W. Pennebaker, "Do Bilinguals Have Two Personalities? A Special Case of Cultural Frame Switching," *Journal of Research in Personality* 40, no. 2 (2006): 99–120.

7. N. Ramírez-Esparza, S. D. Gosling, and J. W. Pennebaker, "Paradox Lost: Unraveling the Puzzle of Simpatía," *Journal of Cross-Cultural Psychology* 39, no. 6 (2008): 703–715.

8. D. Akkermans, A. W. Harzing, and A. Van Witteloostuijn, "Cultural Accommodation and Language Priming," *Management International Review* 50, no. 5 (2010): 559–583.

9. K. Y. Wong, "The System of Honorifics in the Korean Language." Outstanding Academic Papers by Students (OAPS). Retrieved from City University of Hong Kong, CityU Institutional Repository, 2011.

10. B. V. Lal, "Three Worlds: Inheritance and Experience," in *Translating Lives: Living with Two Languages and Cultures,* ed. M. Besemeres and A. Wierzbicka, 26–44 (St. Lucia, Australia: University of Queensland Press, 2007), 39–40.

11. R. Donadio, "Surreal: A Soap Opera Starring Berlusconi," *New York Times,* January 22, 2011.

12. F. Sautet, "Is Language a Determinant of Reform Success?" https://austrianeconomists.typepad.com/weblog/2006/12/is_language_a_d.html.

13. A. Tan, "Yes and No," in *The Genius of Language: Fifteen Writers Reflect on Their Mother Tongues,* ed. W. Lesser, 25–34 (New York: Anchor Books, 2005), 27.

14. Tan, "Yes and No," 33.

15. A. H. Bloom, *The Linguistic Shaping of Thought: A Study in the Impact of Language on Thinking in China and the West* (Hillsdale, NJ: Lawrence Erlbaum, 1981).

16. For an interesting discussion of studies investigating the link between hypotheticals in language and thought, see: J. H. McWhorter, *The Language Hoax: Why the World Looks the Same in Any Language* (Oxford: Oxford University Press, 2014).

17. K. Chen, *The Effect of Language on Economic Behavior: Evidence from Savings Rates, Health Behaviors, and Retirement Assets,* Cowles Foundation Discussion Papers, no. 1820 (New Haven: Yale University, 2012).

18. B. Berlin and P. Kay, *Basic Color Terms: Their Universality and Evolution* (Oakland, CA: University of California Press, 1991).

19. J. Winawer, N. Witthoft, M. C. Frank, L. Wu, A. R. Wade, and L. Boroditsky, "Russian Blues Reveal Effects of Language on Color Discrimination," *Proceedings of the National Academy of Sciences* 104, no. 19 (2007): 7780–7785.

20. G. Thierry, P. Athanasopoulos, A. Wiggett, B. Dering, and J. R. Kuipers, "Unconscious Effects of Language-Specific Terminology on Preattentive Color Perception," *Proceedings of the National Academy of Sciences* 106, no. 11 (2009): 4567–4570.

21. J. Trueswell and A. Papafragou, "Perceiving and Remembering Events Cross-linguistically: Evidence from Dual Task Paradigms," *Journal of Memory and Language* 63, no. 1 (2010): 64–82.

22. McWhorter, *The Language Hoax,* 21.

23. M. J. Fitzgerald, "Limpid, Blue, Poppy," in *The Genius of Language: Fifteen Writers Reflect on Their Mother Tongues,* ed. W. Lesser, 127–144 (New York: Anchor Books, 2004), 130.

24. Hoffman, *Lost in Translation,* 106.

25. P. A. Kolers, "Interlingual Word Associations," *Journal of Verbal Learning and Verbal Behavior* 2, no. 4 (1963): 291–300.

26. R. A. Javier, F. Barroso, and M. A. Muñoz, "Autobiographical Memory in Bilinguals," *Journal of Psycholinguistic Research* 22, no. 3 (1993): 319–338; V. Marian and M. Kaushanskaya, "Self-Construal and Emotion in Bicultural Bilinguals," *Journal of Memory and Language* 51, no. 2 (2004): 190–201.

27. V. Marian and U. Neisser, "Language-Dependent Recall of Autobiographical Memories," *Journal of Experimental Psychology: General* 129, no. 3 (2000): 361–368.

28. Pavlenko, *The Bilingual Mind.*

29. Hoffman, *Lost in Translation,* 245.

30. T. Laqueur, "Prelude," in *The Genius of Language: Fifteen Writers Reflect on Their Mother Tongue,* ed. W. Lesser, 85–101 (New York: Anchor Books, 2005), 92.

31. Hoffman, *Lost in Translation,* 107.

32. A. Pavlenko, *Emotions and Multilingualism* (Cambridge: Cambridge University Press, 2005).

33. T. Teicholz, ed., *Conversations with Jerzy Kosinski* (Jackson: University Press of Mississippi, 1993), 125.

34. J. M. Dewaele, "The Emotional Force of Swearwords and Taboo Words in the Speech of Multilinguals," *Journal of Multilingual and Multicultural Development* 25, no. 2 / 3 (2004): 204–222.

35. C. L. Harris, A. Ayçíçeğí, and J. B. Gleason, "Taboo Words and Reprimands Elicit Greater Autonomic Reactivity in a First Language than in a Second Language," *Applied Psycholinguistics* 24, no. 4 (2003): 561–579.

36. C. L. Harris, "Bilingual Speakers in the Lab: Psychophysiological Measures of Emotional Reactivity," *Journal of Multilingual and Multicultural Development* 25, no. 2 / 3 (2004): 223–247.

37. W. Toivo and C. Scheepers, "Pupillary Responses to Affective Words in Bilinguals' First versus Second Language," *PLoS one* 14, no. 4 (2019): e0210450.

38. A. Costa, A. Foucart, S. Hayakawa, M. Aparici, J. Apesteguia, J. Heafner, and B. Keysar, "Your Morals Depend on Language," *PLoS one* 9, no. 4 (2014): e94842.

39. J. Geipel, C. Hadjichristidis, and L. Surian, "How Foreign Language Shapes Moral Judgment," *Journal of Experimental Social Psychology* 59 (2015): 8–17.

40. For a review, see S. Hayakawa, A. Costa, A. Foucart, and B. Keysar, "Using a Foreign Language Changes Our Choices," *Trends in Cognitive Sciences* 20, no. 11 (2016): 791–793.

41. I. Ulman, "Playground and Battlegrounds: A Child's Experience of Migration," in *Translating Lives: Living with Two Languages and Cultures,* ed. M. Besemeres and A. Wierzbicka, 45–55 (St. Lucia, Australia: University of Queensland Press, 2008).

42. Akkermans et al., "Cultural Accommodation and Language Priming."

43. Hoffman, *Lost in Translation,* 186.

44. E. Buxbaum, "The Role of the Second Language in the Formation of Ego and Superego," *Psychoanalytic Quarterly* 18 (1949): 279–289.

45. R. R. Greenson, "The Mother Tongue and the Mother," *International Journal of Psychoanalysis* 31 (1950): 18–23; 19.

46. R. Pérez Foster, "Psychoanalysis and the Bilingual Patient: Some Observations on the Influence of Language Choice on the Transference," *Psychoanalytic Psychology* 9, no. 1 (1992): 61–76.

47. J. M. Dewaele and B. Costa, "Multilingual Clients' Experience of Psychotherapy," *Language and Psychoanalysis* 2, no. 2 (2013): 31–50.

48. J. S. Schwanberg, "Does Language of Retrieval Affect the Remembering of Trauma?" *Journal of Trauma & Dissociation* 11, no. 1 (2010): 44–56; 52.

49. Pérez Foster, "Psychoanalysis and the Bilingual Patient," 68–69.

50. Dewaele and Costa, "Multilingual Clients' Experience of Psychotherapy."

51. W. James, *The Principles of Psychology* (New York: Henry Holt and Company, 1890), 1: 294.

52. Hoffman, *Lost in Translation,* 164.

4. Conflict

1. K. Matsumoto, "Recent Language Change in Shoshone: Structural Consequences of Language Loss" (PhD diss., University of Utah, 2015).

2. R. Bringhurst, *The Tree of Meaning* (Berkeley, CA: Counterpoint, 2006), 288–289.

3. D. M. Abrams and S. H. Strogatz, "Modelling the Dynamics of Language Death," *Nature* 424, no. 6951 (2003): 900.

4. M. J. Spivey and V. Marian, "Cross Talk between Native and Second Languages: Partial Activation of an Irrelevant Lexicon," *Psychological Science* 10, no. 3 (1999): 281–284.

5. T. H. Gollan, R. I. Montoya, C. Fennema-Notestine, and S. K. Morris, "Bilingualism Affects Picture Naming but Not Picture Classification," *Memory and Cognition* 33, no. 7 (2005): 1220–1234.

6. C. Baus, A. Costa, and M. Carreiras, "On the Effects of Second Language Immersion on First Language Production," *Acta Psychologica* 142, no. 3 (2013): 402–409.

7. C. Frenck-Mestre, "Use of Orthographic Redundancies and Word Identification Speed in Bilinguals," *Journal of Psycholinguistic Research* 22, no. 4 (1993): 397–410.

8. T. H. Gollan and N. B. Silverberg, "Tip-of-the-Tongue States in Hebrew–English Bilinguals," *Bilingualism: Language and Cognition* 4, no. 1 (2001): 63–83.

9. N. Huston, *Losing North: Musings on Land, Tongue, and Self* (Toronto: McArthur & Company, 2002), 46.

10. C. B. Chang, "Rapid and Multifaceted Effects of Second-Language Learning on First-Language Speech Production," *Journal of Phonetics* 40, no. 2 (2012): 249–268.

11. M. L. Sancier and C. A. Fowler, "Gestural Drift in a Bilingual Speaker of Brazilian Portuguese and English," *Journal of Phonetics,* 25, no. 4 (1997): 421–436.

12. P. Athanasopoulos, B. Dering, A. Wiggett, J. R. Kuipers, and G. Thierry, "Perceptual Shift in Bilingualism: Brain Potentials Reveal Plasticity in Pre-attentive Colour Perception," *Cognition* 116, no. 3 (2010): 437–443.

13. B. C. Malt, R. L. Jobe, P. Li, A. Pavlenko, and E. Ameel, "What Constrains Simultaneous Mastery of First and Second Language Word Use?" *International Journal of Bilingualism* 20, no. 6 (2016): 684–699.

14. A. Pavlenko and B. C. Malt, "Kitchen Russian: Cross-linguistic Differences and First-Language Object Naming by Russian–English Bilinguals," *Bilingualism: Language and Cognition* 14, no. 1 (2011): 19–45.

15. M. S. Schmid and B. Köpke, "The Relevance of First Language Attrition to Theories of Bilingual Development," *Linguistic Approaches to Bilingualism* 7, no. 6 (2017): 637–667; 641.

16. T. Kupisch, F. Bayram, J. Rothman, "Terminology Matters II!: Early Bilinguals Show Cross-linguistic Influence but They Are Not Attriters," *Linguistic Approaches to Bilingualism* 7, no. 6 (2017): 719–724; H. Gyllstad and L. V. Suhonen, "Is Attrition a Type of Learning?" *Linguistic Approaches to Bilingualism* 7, no. 6 (2017): 700–703; A. Gürel, "Is Every Bilingual an L1 Attriter? The Unbearable Complexity of Defining L1 Attrition," *Linguistic Approaches to Bilingualism* 7, no. 6 (2017): 696–699; C. Flores, "Problematizing the Scope of Language Attrition from the Perspective of Bilingual Returnees," *Linguistic Approaches to Bilingualism* 7, no. 6 (2017): 691–695; I. M. Tsimpli, "Crosslinguistic Influence Is Not Necessarily Attrition," *Linguistic Approaches to Bilingualism* 7, no. 6 (2017): 759–762.

17. D. J. Saer, "The Effect of Bilingualism on Intelligence," *British Journal of Psychology* 14 (1923): 25–38; 38.

18. F. L. Goodenough, "Racial Differences in the Intelligence of School Children," *Journal of Experimental Psychology* 9 (1926): 388–397; 393.

19. M. K. Adler, *Collective and Individual Bilingualism: A Sociolinguistic Study* (Hamburg: Helmut Buske Verlag, 1977), 40.

20. E. Peal and W. E. Lambert, "The Relation of Bilingualism to Intelligence," *Psychological Monographs: General and Applied* 76, no. 27 (1962): 1–23.

21. B. Hart and T. R. Risley, *Meaningful Differences in the Everyday Experience of Young American Children* (Baltimore: Brookes Publishing, 1995).

22. The Annie E. Casey Foundation, *Early Reading Research Confirmed: A Research Update on the Importance of Third-Grade Reading* (Baltimore: The Annie E. Casey Foundation, 2013).

23. C. S. Hammer, E. Hoff, Y. Uchikoshi, C. Gillanders, D. C. Castro, and L. E. Sandilos, "The Language and Literacy Development of Young

Dual Language Learners: A Critical Review," *Early Childhood Research Quarterly* 29, no. 4 (2014): 715–733.

24. E. Bialystok, "Bilingual Education for Young Children: Review of the Effects and Consequences," *International Journal of Bilingual Education and Bilingualism* 21, no. 6 (2018): 666–679.

25. Y. S. G. Kim and B. Piper, "Cross-language Transfer of Reading Skills: An Empirical Investigation of Bidirectionality and the Influence of Instructional Environments," *Reading and Writing* 32, no. 4 (2019): 839–871.

26. M. Kaushanskaya and V. Marian, "The Bilingual Advantage in Novel Word Learning," *Psychonomic Bulletin & Review* 16, no. 4 (2009): 705–710; H. Yoshida, D. N. Tran, V. Benitez, and M. Kuwabara, "Inhibition and Adjective Learning in Bilingual and Monolingual Children," *Frontiers in Psychology* 2, no. 210 (2011), doi: 10.3389/fpsyg.2011.00210; P. Escudero, K. E. Mulak, C. S. Fu, and L. Singh, "More Limitations to Monolingualism: Bilinguals Outperform Monolinguals in Implicit Word Learning," *Frontiers in Psychology* 7, no. 1218 (2016), doi: 10.3389/fpsyg.2016.01218.

27. C. B. Chang, "Bilingual Perceptual Benefits of Experience with a Heritage Language," *Bilingualism: Language and Cognition* 19, no. 4 (2016): 791–809.

28. L. Singh, "Bilingual Infants Demonstrate Advantages in Learning Words in a Third Language," *Child Development* 89, no. 4 (2018): e397–e413.

29. J. Cummins, "Bilingualism and the Development of Metalinguistic Awareness," *Journal of Cross-Cultural Psychology* 9 (1978): 131–149; E. Bialystok, K. F. Peets, and S. Moreno, "Producing Bilinguals through Immersion Education: Development of Metalinguistic Awareness," *Applied Psycholinguistics* 35, no. 1 (2014): 177–191.

30. E. Bialystok, G. Luk, K. F. Peets, and S. Yang, "Receptive Vocabulary Differences in Monolingual and Bilingual Children," *Bilingualism: Language and Cognition* 13, no. 4 (2010): 525–531.

31. E. Hoffman, *Lost in Translation* (New York: Penguin, 1990), 272.

32. E. Dąbrowska, "Different Speakers, Different Grammars: Individual Differences in Native Language Attainment," *Linguistic Approaches to Bilingualism* 2, no. 3 (2012): 219–253.

33. S. Poplack, "Contrasting Patterns of Code-Switching in Two Communities," *Codeswitching: Anthropological and Sociolinguistic Perspectives* 48 (1988): 215–244.

34. E. Bialystok, F. I. Craik, R. Klein, M. Viswanathan, "Bilingualism, Aging, and Cognitive Control: Evidence from the Simon Task," *Psychology and Aging* 19, no. 2 (2004): 290–303.

35. These studies are reviewed in E. Bialystok, "The Bilingual Adaptation: How Minds Accommodate Experience," *Psychological Bulletin* 143, no. 3 (2017): 233–262.

36. E. Bialystok, F. I. Craik, and M. Freedman, "Bilingualism as a Protection against the Onset of Symptoms of Dementia," *Neuropsychologia* 45, no. 2 (2007): 459–464.

37. M. Antoniou, "The Advantages of Bilingualism Debate," *Annual Review of Linguistics* 5 (2019): 395–415.

38. S. Laporte, "Pourquoi parler français?" *La Presse,* January 1, 2012. The original French text reads as follows:

> Pour de plus en plus de gens, une langue n'est qu'un code. Un outil interchangeable. Si c'est plus pratique parler anglais, parlons anglais. Si c'est plus pratique parler chinois, parlons chinois.
>
> Une langue, ce n'est pas seulement un ensemble de sons et de symboles qui permettent de parler au cellulaire et d'envoyer des textos. Une langue, c'est l'empreinte du coeur de ceux qui la parlent. C'est le répertoire des réflexions, des émotions, des expériences et des rêves partagés par une communauté. Notre langue n'est pas meilleure que celle des autres, mais c'est la nôtre. C'est notre vécu. C'est à nous qu'elle parle. Bien au-delà des mots. Nos rires, nos pleurs, nos soupirs sonnent français. Et si on est fier de ce qu'on est, on est fier de la langue qui nous a permis de devenir ce que nous sommes. Notre réalité, c'est en français que nous l'avons nommée. Que nous la sommes appropriée.

39. A. Mizuta, "Memories of Language Lost and Language Learned: Parents and the Shaping of Chinese as a Heritage Language in Canada" (PhD diss., University of British Columbia, 2017).

40. C. Charalambous, "Language Education and 'Conflicted Heritage': Implications for Teaching and Learning," *Modern Language Journal* 103, no. 4 (2019): 874–891.

41. S. S. Mufwene, "The Ecology of Gullah's Survival," *American Speech* 72, no. 1 (1997): 69–83.

42. R. Castro, "Shifting the Burden of Bilingualism: The Case for Monolingual Communities," *Bilingual Review / La Revista Bilingüe* 3 (1976): 3–28.

43. Castro, "Shifting the Burden of Bilingualism," 15.

44. Castro, "Shifting the Burden of Bilingualism," 20.

45. A. Alesina and B. Reich, "Nation-Building," NBER Working Paper 18839, National Bureau of Economic Research, 2013.

46. With regard to regions with violent conflict, see P. Collier and A. Hoeffler, "Greed and Grievance in Civil War," *Oxford Economic Papers* 56, no. 4 (2004): 563–595; H. Hegre and N. Sambanis, "Sensitivity Analysis of Empirical Results on Civil War Onset," *Journal of Conflict Resolution,* 50, no. 4 (2006): 508–535; for regions with sluggish economies, see A. Alesina and E. La Ferrara, "Ethnic Diversity and Economic Performance," *Journal of Economic Literature* 43, no. 3 (2005): 762–800.

47. R. D. Putnam, "*E pluribus unum:* Diversity and Community in the Twenty-First Century," The 2006 Johan Skytte Prize Lecture, *Scandinavian Political Studies* 30, no. 2 (2007): 137–174.

48. P. T. Dinesen and K. M. Sønderskov, "Ethnic Diversity and Social Trust: A Critical Review of the Literature and Suggestions for a Research Agenda," in *The Oxford Handbook on Social and Political Trust,* ed. E. Uslaner (Oxford: Oxford University Press, 2018).

49. For a detailed meta-analysis of eighty-seven studies spanning many countries and using a variety of different measures of ethnic diversity and social trust, see P. T. Dineson, M. Schaeffer, and K. M. Sønderskov, "Ethnic Diversity and Social Trust: A Narrative and Meta-analytical Review," *Annual Review of Political Science* 23 (2020): 441–465.

50. R. D. Enos, "Causal Effect of Intergroup Contact on Exclusionary Attitudes," *Proceedings of the National Academy of Sciences* 111, no. 10 (2014): 3699–3704.

51. J. D. Fearon and D. D. Laitin, "Explaining Interethnic Cooperation," *American Political Science Review* 90, no. 4 (1996): 715–735.

52. S. Bazzi, A. Gaduh, A. D. Rothenberg, and M. Wong, "Unity in Diversity? How Intergroup Contact Can Foster Nation Building," *American Economic Review* 109, no. 11 (2019): 3978–4025.

53. K. Desmet, J. F. Gomes, and I. Ortuño-Ortín, "The Geography of Linguistic Diversity and the Provision of Public Goods," *Journal of Development Economics* 143 (2020): 102384.

54. D. Stolle, S. Soroka, and R. Johnston, "When Does Diversity Erode Trust? Neighborhood Diversity, Interpersonal Trust and the Mediating Effect of Social Interactions," *Political Studies* 56 (2008): 57–75.

55. See, for example, G. Hodson, K. Costello, and C. C. McInnis, "Is Intergroup Contact Beneficial among Intolerant People? Exploring Individual Differences in the Benefits of Contact on Attitudes," in *Advances in*

Intergroup Contact, ed. G. Hodson and M. Hewstone (London: Psychology Press, 2012), 49–80; G. Hodson, "Interracial Prison Contact: The Pros for (Socially Dominant) Cons," *British Journal of Social Psychology* 47 (2008): 325–351; K. Dhont and A. Van Hiel, "We Must Not Be Enemies: Interracial Contact and the Reduction of Prejudice among Authoritarians," *Personality and Individual Differences,* 46, no. 2 (2009): 172–177; E. P. Visintin, J. Berent, E. G. T. Green, and J. M. Falomir-Pichastor, "The Interplay between Social Dominance Orientation and Intergroup Contact in Explaining Support for Multiculturalism," *Journal of Applied Social Psychology* 49 (2019): 319–327.

56. Putnam, *"E pluribus unum."*

57. In current times, segregated digital spaces may take on some of the functions of separate physical spaces. See, for example, S. M. Croucher and D. Rahmani, "A Longitudinal Test of the Effects of Facebook on Cultural Adaptation," *Journal of International and Intercultural Communication* 8 (2015): 330–345.

58. W. Labov, "Unendangered Dialects, Endangered People," in *Sustaining Linguistic Diversity,* ed. K. A. King, N. Schilling-Estes, L. Fogle, J. J. Lou, and B. Soukup, 219–238 (Washington, DC: Georgetown University Press, 2008).

59. *"Su proprio idioma"* translates into English as "his own language." R. Rodriguez, *Hunger of Memory: The Education of Richard Rodriguez* (New York: Bantam Dell, 1982), 28–29.

60. M. Schmid, *Language Attrition* (Cambridge: Cambridge University Press, 2011), 83–84.

61. A-M. D. Nguyen and V. Benet-Martínez, "Biculturalism and Adjustment: A Meta-analysis," *Journal of Cross-Cultural Psychology* 44, no. 1 (2013): 122–159.

62. M. A. Yampolsky, C. E. Amiot, and R. de la Sablonnière, "Multicultural Identity Integration and Well-Being: A Qualitative Exploration of Variations in Narrative Coherence and Multicultural Identification," *Frontiers in Psychology* 4 (2013): Article 126.

63. A. K-y. Leung, S. Liou, E. Miron-Spektor, B. Koh, D. Chan, R. Eisenberg, and I. Schneider, "Middle Ground Approach to Paradox: Within- and Between-Culture Examination of the Creative Benefits of Paradoxical Frames," *Journal of Personality and Social Psychology* 114, no. 3 (2018): 443; M. A. Gocłowska and R. J. Crisp, "How Dual-Identity Processes Foster Creativity," *Review of General Psychology* 18, no. 3 (2014): 216–236.

64. Putnam, *"E pluribus unum."*

65. A. Levy, E. Halperin, M. van Zomeren, and T. Saguy, "Inter-racial Gateways: The Potential of Biracials to Reduce Threat and Prejudice in Inter-racial Dynamics," *Race and Social Problems* 11 (2019): 119–132.

66. A. Levy, T. Saguy, M. van Zomeran, and E. Halperin, "Ingroups, Outgroups, and the Gateway Groups Between: The Potential of Dual Identities to Improve Intergroup Relations," *Journal of Experimental Social Psychology* 70 (2017): 260–271.

67. The term *translanguaging* was first used by Welsh educators who advocated for the blending of Welsh and English in bilingual education. See, for example, C. Williams, *"Arfarniad o ddulliau dysgu ac addysgu yng nghyd-destun addysg uwchradd ddwyieithog* [An Evaluation of Teaching and Learning Methods in the Context of Bilingual Secondary Education]" (PhD diss., University of Wales, Bangor, UK, 1994). The term was picked up and popularized by influential educational experts, among them O. García, *Bilingual Education in the 21st Century: A Global Perspective* (Oxford: Wiley-Blackwell, 2009).

68. A. Ticheloven, E. Blom, P. Leseman, and S. McMonagle, "Translanguaging Challenges in Multilingual Classrooms: Scholar, Teacher and Student Perspectives," *International Journal of Multilingualism* (2016), 3; doi: 10.1080/14790718.2019.1686002.

69. Ticheloven, Blom, Leseman, and McMonagle, "Translanguaging Challenges in Multilingual Classrooms."

70. Dead Obies. Do 2 Get. *Gesamtkunstwerk,* 2016.

71. C. Rioux, "J'rape un suicide," *Le Devoir,* July 18, 2014, https://www.ledevoir.com/opinion/chroniques/413795/j-rape-un-suicide.

72. S. Poplack, L. Zentz, and N. Dion, "Phrase-Final Prepositions in Quebec French: An Empirical Study of Contact, Code-Switching and Resistance to Convergence," *Bilingualism: Language and Cognition* 15, no. 2 (2011): 203–225.

73. Bringhurst, *The Tree of Meaning,* 289.

5. Revival

1. E. Fromm, "Age Regression with Unexpected Appearance of a Repressed Childhood Language," *International Journal of Clinical and Experimental Hypnosis* 18, no. 2 (1970): 79–88.

2. R. Footnick, "A Hidden Language: Recovery of a 'Lost' Language Is Triggered by Hypnosis," in *Language Attrition: Theoretical Perspectives,* ed. B. Köpke, M. Schmid, M. Keijzer, and S. Dostert, 169–187 (Amsterdam: John Benjamins, 2007), 169–189.

3. C. Pallier, S. Dehaene, J. B. Poline, D. LeBihan, A. M. Argenti, E. Dupoux, and J. Mehler, "Brain Imaging of Language Plasticity in Adopted Adults: Can a Second Language Replace the First?," *Cerebral Cortex* 13, no. 2 (2003): 155–161.

4. H. Ebbinghaus, *Memory: A Contribution to Experimental Psychology,* trans. H. A. Ruger and C. E. Bussenius (New York: Columbia University, 1885); T. Nelson, "Detecting Small Amounts of Information in Memory: Savings for Non-recognized Items," *Journal of Experimental Psychology: Human Learning and Memory* 4 (1978): 453–468.

5. L. Isurin and C. Seidel, "Traces of Memory for a Lost Childhood Language: The Savings Paradigm Expanded," *Language Learning* 65, no. 4 (2015): 761–790.

6. T. K. F. Au, J. S. Oh, L. M. Knightly, S. A. Jun, and L. F. Romo, "Salvaging a Childhood Language," *Journal of Memory and Language* 58, no. 4 (2008): 998–1011.

7. P. K. Kuhl, "Early Language Acquisition: Cracking the Speech Code," *Nature Reviews Neuroscience* 5 (2004): 831–843.

8. Emily Dickinson, *The Poems of Emily Dickinson: Reading Edition,* edited by Ralph W. Franklin (Cambridge, MA: The Belknap Press of Harvard University Press, 1998). Copyright © 1998, 1999 by the President and Fellows of Harvard College.

9. L. Singh, J. Liederman, R. Mierzejewski, and J. Barnes, "Rapid Reacquisition of Native Phoneme Contrasts after Disuse: You Do Not Always Lose What You Do Not Use," *Developmental Science* 14, no. 5 (2011): 949–959.

10. J. Choi, A. Cutler, and M. Broersma, "Early Development of Abstract Knowledge: Evidence from Perception–Production Transfer of Birth-Language Memory," *Royal Society Open Science* 4 (2017): 160660.

11. L. J. Pierce, D. Klein, J. K. Chen, A. Delcenserie, and F. Genesee, "Mapping the Unconscious Maintenance of a Lost First Language," *Proceedings of the National Academy of Sciences* 111, no. 48 (2014): 17314–17319.

12. L. Hansen, Y. Umeda, and M. McKinney, "Savings in the Relearning of Second Language Vocabulary: The Effects of Time and Proficiency," *Language Learning,* 52, no. 4 (2002): 653–678.

13. J. D. Greene, J. R. Hodges, and A. D. Baddeley, "Autobiographical Memory and Executive Function in Early Dementia of Alzheimer Type," *Neuropsychologia* 12 (1995): 1647–1670. However, some neurogenerative diseases show the opposite pattern to Alzheimer's: that is, recent memories are

easier to access than more distant ones. See, for example, P. Piolino, B. Desgranges, S. Belliard, V. Matuszewski, C. Lalevée, V. De La Sayette, and F. Eustache, "Autobiographical Memory and Autonoetic Consciousness: Triple Dissociation in Neurodegenerative Diseases," *Brain* 126, no. 10 (2003): 2203–2219.

14. M. S. Schmid and M. Keijzer, "First Language Attrition and Reversion among Older Migrants," *International Journal of the Sociology of Language* 200 (2009): 83–101.

15. C. M. Morrison and A. W. Ellis, "Roles of Word Frequency and Age of Acquisition in Word Naming and Lexical Decision," *Journal of Experimental Psychology: Learning, Memory, and Cognition* 21, no. 1 (1995): 116.

16. C. J. Fiebach, A. D. Friederici, K. Müller, D. Y. Von Cramon, and A. E. Hernandez, "Distinct Brain Representations for Early and Late Learned Words," *NeuroImage* 19, no. 4 (2003): 1627–1637.

17. J. K. Hartshorne, J. B. Tenenbaum, and S. Pinker, "A Critical Period for Second Language Acquisition: Evidence from 2 / 3 Million English Speakers," *Cognition* 177 (2018): 263–277.

18. A. S. Finn, T. Lee, A. Kraus, and C. L. H. Kam, "When It Hurts (and Helps) to Try: The Role of Effort in Language Learning," *PloS one* 9, no. 7 (2014): e101806.

19. B. Chandrasekaran, H. G. Yi, and W. T. Maddox, "Dual-Learning Systems during Speech Category Learning," *Psychonomic Bulletin & Review* 21, no. 2 (2014): 488–495.

20. B. Vermaercke, E. Cop, S. Willems, R. D'Hooge, and H. P. O. de Beeck, "More Complex Brains Are Not Always Better: Rats Outperform Humans in Implicit Category-Based Generalization by Implementing a Similarity-based Strategy," *Psychonomic Bulletin & Review* 21, no. 4 (2014): 1080–1086.

21. E. H. Smalle, M. P. Page, W. Duyck, M. Edwards, and A. Szmalec, "Children Retain Implicitly Learned Phonological Sequences Better than Adults: A Longitudinal Study," *Developmental Science* 21, no. 5 (2017): e12634.

22. R. M. DeKeyser, "The Robustness of Critical Periods Effects in Second Language Acquisition," *Studies in Second Language Acquisition* 22, no. 4 (2000): 499–533.

23. B. H. Huang, "A Synthesis of Empirical Research on the Linguistic Outcomes of Early Foreign Language Instruction," *International Journal of Multilingualism* 13, no. 3 (2016): 257–273.

24. See, for example, S. Beaudrie, and C. Ducar, "Beginning Level University Heritage Programs: Creating a Space for All Heritage Language Learners," *Heritage Language Journal* 3 (2005): 1–26; M. A. Bowles and S. A. Montrul, "Heritage Spanish Speakers in University Language Courses: A Decade of Difference," *ADFL Bulletin* 43, no. 1 (2014): 112–122.

25. M. M. Baese-Berk, A. R. Bradlow, and B. A. Wright, "Accent-Independent Adaptation to Foreign Accented Speech," *Journal of the Acoustical Society of America* 133, no. 3 (2013): EL174–EL180.

26. Statistics Canada, 2016 Census of Population, Statistics Canada Catalogue no. 98-400-X2016159, https://www12.statcan.gc.ca/census-recensement/2016/dp-pd/dt-td/Rp-eng.cfm

27. N. H. Lee and J. Van Way, "Assessing Levels of Endangerment in the Catalogue of Endangered Languages (ELCat) using the Language Endangerment Index (LEI)," *Language in Society* 45, no. 2 (2016): 271.

28. W. O'Grady and R. Hattori, "Language Acquisition and Language Revitalization," *Language Documentation and Conservation* 10 (2016): 46–58.

29. R. K. Hill, "Bilingual Education in Aotearoa / New Zealand," in *Bilingual and Multilingual Education,* 3rd ed., ed. O. García, A. Lin, and S. May, 329–345 (Cham, Switzerland: Springer, 2017).

30. C. Gallegos, W. E. Murray, and M. Evans, "Research Note: Comparing Indigenous Language Revitalisation: Te reo Māori in Aotearoa New Zealand and Mapudungun in Chile," *Asia Pacific Viewpoint* 51, no. 1 (2010): 91–104.

31. N. A. Chambers, "'They All Talk Okanagan and I Know What They Are Saying.' Language Nests in the Early Years: Insights, Challenges, and Promising Practices" (PhD diss., University of British Columbia (Okanagan), 2014).

32. Chambers, "They All Talk Okanagan and I Know What They Are Saying."

33. E. K. Okura, "Language Nests and Language Acquisition: An Empirical Analysis" (PhD diss., University of Hawai'i at Mānoa, 2017).

34. D. Stiles, "Four Successful Indigenous Language Programs," *Teaching Indigenous Languages,* 1997, https://files.eric.ed.gov/fulltext/ED415079.pdf.

35. O'Grady and Hattori, "Language Acquisition and Language Revitalization."

36. R. Berman, "The Re-emergence of a Bilingual: A Case Study of a Hebrew-English Speaking Child," *Working Papers on Bilingualism* 19 (1979): 158–179.

37. T. H. Gollan, J. Starr, and V. S. Ferreira, "More than Use It or Lose It: The Number of Speakers Effect on Heritage Language Proficiency," *Psychonomics Bulletin Review* 22, no. 1 (2015): 147–155.

38. M-L. Olthuis, S. Kivelä, and T. Skutnabb-Kangas, "Revitalising Indigenous Languages: How to Recreate a Lost Generation," *Multilingual Matters* (2013): 10.

39. Olthuis, Kivelä, and Skutnabb-Kangas, "Revitalising Indigenous Languages," 138.

40. N. Lakritz, "More Money Won't Save Aboriginal Languages," *Calgary Herald,* July 11, 2015.

41. Chambers, "They All Talk Okanagan and I Know What They Are Saying."

42. H. Bliss and M. Creed, *Costing Models for Language Maintenance, Revitalization, and Reclamation in Canada,* Report for the First Peoples' Cultural Council, 2018, https://fpcc.ca/wp-content/uploads/2020/07/Bliss_and _Creed_Costing_Models_-_FINAL_FORMATTED.pdf.

43. J. McWhorter, *Language Interrupted: Signs of Non-native Acquisition in Standard Language Grammars* (Oxford: Oxford University Press, 2007).

44. McWhorter, *Language Interrupted,* 15.

45. G. Lupyan and R. Dale, "Language Structure Is Partly Determined by Social Structure," *PloS one* 5, no. 1 (2010): e8559; P. Trudgill, "Social Structure, Language Contact and Language Change," in *The Sage Handbook of Sociolinguistics,* ed. R. Wodak, B. Johnstone, and P. Kerswill (Los Angeles: Sage, 2011), 236–248; A. Wray and G. W. Grace, "The Consequences of Talking to Strangers: Evolutionary Corollaries of Socio-cultural Influences on Linguistic Form," *Lingua* 117, no. 3 (2007): 543–578.

46. W. Labov, *Principles of Language Change: Cognitive and Cultural Factors,* vol. 3 (Chichester, UK: Wiley-Blackwell, 2010).

47. J. Fellman, "Concerning the 'Revival' of the Hebrew Language," *Anthropological Linguistics* 15, no. 5 (1973): 250–257.

48. G. Zuckermann, "Hebrew Revivalists' Goals vis-à-vis the Emerging Israeli Language," in *The Handbook of Language and Ethnic Identity: The Success and Failure Continuum,* ed. J. A. Fishman and O. García (Oxford: Oxford University Press, 2011), 2:70.

49. W. James, *The Principles of Psychology,* vol. 1 (New York: Henry Holt and Company, 1890).

50. Olthuis, Kivelä, and Skutnabb-Kangas, "Revitalising Indigenous Languages," 19.

6. Home

1. J. E. Chamberlin, *If This Is Your Land, Where Are Your Stories? Finding Common Ground* (Toronto: Vintage Canada, 2003).

2. Translation by Julie Sedivy.

3. B. Hrabal, *Too Loud a Solitude,* translated by M. H. Heim (San Diego: Harcourt, 1990), 1.

4. L. Saxon, S. A. Zoe, G. Chocolate, and A. Legat, *Dogrib Knowledge on Placenames, Caribou, and Habitat.* Report submitted by the Dogrib Treaty 11 Council to the West Kitikmeot Slave Study Society, 2002, https://www.enr.gov.nt.ca/sites/enr/files/wkss_dogrib_knowledge_2002.pdf.

5. J. Dulewich, "Stoney Ceremony Commemorates Untold Lake Louise History," *Rocky Mountain Outlook,* August 30, 2020.

6. J. McWhorter, *What Language Is (and What It Isn't and What It Could Be)* (New York: Gotham Books, 2011).

7. J. W. Brink, *Imagining Head-Smashed-In: Aboriginal Buffalo Hunting on the Northern Plains* (Edmonton: Athabasca University Press, 2008), xiii.

8. I. Genee and M.-O. Junker, "The Blackfoot Language Resources and Digital Dictionary Project: Creating Integrated Web Resources for Language Documentation and Revitalization," *Language Documentation and Conservation* 12 (2018): 274–314.

9. W. Olson, "Bison," *The Canadian Encyclopedia,* 2013, https://www.thecanadianencyclopedia.ca/en/article/bison

10. For a standard Blackfoot dictionary, see D. G. Frantz and N. J. Russell, *The Blackfoot Dictionary of Stems, Roots, and Affixes,* 3rd ed. (Toronto: University of Toronto Press, 2017); for a grammar, see D. G. Frantz, *Blackfoot Grammar,* 3rd ed. (Toronto: University of Toronto Press, 2017). An online resource, *Blackfoot Dictionary,* from Blackfoot Language Resources, is available at https://dictionary.blackfoot.atlas-ling.ca/#/help.

11. J. Mehler, P. Jusczyk, G. Lambertz, N. Halsted, J. Bertoncini, and C. Amiel-Tison, "A Precursor of Language Acquisition in Young Infants," *Cognition* 29, no. 2 (1988): 143–178.

12. Adapted from P. Bakker, *A Language of Our Own: The Genesis of Michif, the Mixed Cree-French Language of the Canadian Métis* (Oxford: Oxford University Press, 1997), 5.

13. J. Teillet, *The North-West Is Our Mother: The Story of Louis Riel's People* (Toronto: HarperCollins, 2019).

14. D. Goodhart, *The Road to Somewhere: The Populist Revolt and the Future of Politics* (Oxford: Oxford University Press, 2017).

Acknowledgments

This book was written during a very difficult period, and my deep appreciation for the central relationships that have sustained me is pressed between every page. To my mother, Vera, and all of my siblings, Silvester, Marie, Vaclav, Jana, and Patrick: It has been a great privilege to have traveled with you through the events described in this book and many others, both painful and joyous. My memories are immeasurably enriched by your presence in them. In particular, I treasure the memory of my brother Vaclav, who died during the writing of this book, but whose love and influence continue to transform me. To my children, Kate and Ben, for being the greatest source of joy and hope. To my uncle František, for helping me to get to know my father, and to all the members of the diasporic Sedivy and Vychytil clans, who continue to serve as steadfast anchors to my native culture. To my in-laws, Jim and Ann Murphy, for their very cheerful, very Anglo (in the best way possible) brand of encouragement. To Weyman Chan, for being my sturdy raft on stormy seas. To Florian Jaeger and Chigusa Kurumada, who know all about crisis. And to my beloved husband, Ian Graham, for always being the home I need; thank you for continuing to live and continuing to love me.

I owe a great debt of gratitude to the many academic colleagues whose work, feedback, and conversations helped propel this book forward, but especially to Darin Flynn, Betsy Ritter, Olga Mladenova, Jordan Lachler, and Inge Genee, whose knowledge and insights left a special imprint.

Many, many thanks to all the participants at the 2017 session of the Canadian Indigenous Languages and Literacy Development Institute (CILLDI) for sharing their experiences and stories with me. I am especially grateful to Trent Fox, Marie Rose Blackduck, and Helena Welsh.

It has been a great gift to learn from my Stoney Nakoda teachers, Trent Fox and Corey Telfer, and from my Blackfoot teachers, Akáípiksi and Joey Windsor.

This book benefited greatly from the feedback of three anonymous readers solicited by Harvard University Press, who generously read a complete draft of the manuscript and provided detailed and insightful commentary. I also thank the editorial board of Harvard University Press for their helpful suggestions, my editor Janice Audet for her steady, clear-headed guidance and support, and Kate Brick, my copy editor, for her astute sensitivity to language and her devotional attention to the manuscript. I truly have only myself to blame for any remaining shortcomings.

I am grateful to the Alberta Foundation for the Arts, whose financial support provided the precious gift of unencumbered time to research and write this book.

Chapter 1 includes text first published in and Chapter 3 builds on ideas first discussed in "The Strange Persistence of First Languages," *Nautilus,* no. 30, November 5, 2015. Many thanks to its editors Amos Zeeberg and Michael Segal for helping me to explore and shape these ideas.

Index